ROMAN SOLDIER

Simon Forty has asserted his moral right to be identified as the author of this work.

First published in August 2019

A catalogue record for this book is available from the British Library.

ISBN 978 1 78521 565 0

Library of Congress control no. 2019934669

Published by Haynes Publishing,
Sparkford, Yeovil, Somerset
BA22 7JJ, UK.
Tel: 01963 440635
Int. tel: +44 1963 440635
Website: www.haynes.com

Haynes North America Inc.,
859 Lawrence Drive, Newbury Park,
California 91320, USA.

Printed in Malaysia.

Dates

All AD/BC dates are identified as such (AD41/41BC). The Romans, of course, did not do this. If they used anything similar it would have been *ab urbe condita* (AUC) – from the founding of the city, which was determined as being 21 April 753BC. In fact, most of their dating referred to regnal dates during the monarchy or the consuls of the year during the Republic.

Acknowledgements

This book is a team effort and would not have been possible without the material written contributions of Jonathan Forty, Sandra Forty and Patrick Hook, and the photographs and artwork of Graham Sumner who was more than generous with his material. Thanks also to other kind contributors: the Ermine Street Guard and the indefatigable Chris Haines, James Lancaster, Carole Raddato and Jona Lendering. Thanks, too, to all those at Haynes, especially James Robertson and Joanne Rippin.

Photo credits

Air Sea Media: 27T; *Alamy:* 32B dpa picture alliance, 45 imageBROKER, 74 Science History Images, 75B Prisma Archivo, 76B Detail Heritage, 77 Cultural Archive; Anness: 106B; *Author:* 17, 58, 60B, 71T, 76T, 81, 92B, 99B, 101T, 105, 109B, 110B, 114 (both), 125L; *Conrad Cichorius, from* Die Reliefs der Traianssäule*, 1900:* 41T, 80, 143B, 145T; *Jo Forty:* 7T&B, 122B; *Elly Forty:* 50, 60T, 62B, 65B, 122T; *Ermine Street Guard:* 94, 100L, 109R, 123, 137, 139TR; *Getty Images:* 9, 70, 85, 151 DeAgostini, 34 Fine Art Images/ Heritage Images, 42T, 43T, 75T, 78, 107R DEA/A. Dagli Orti/ De Agostini, 42B DEA Picture Library/De Agostini, 44R Markus Matzel/ullstein bild, 46 DEA/G. Dagli Orti/De Agostini, 49 DEA/G. Nimatallah/De Agostini, 51 Werner Forman/ Universal Images Group, 57 PHAS/UIG, 68 English Heritage/ Heritage Images, 73 Artist Philip Corke, English Heritage/ Heritage Images, 82B Hulton Archive, 83T Andrea Andreani, Universal History Archive/UIG, 83B Patrick Aventurier, 84 Florilegius/SSPL, 89T Birgit Gierth/ullstein bild, 91L Museum of London/Heritage Images, 95T CM Dixon/Print Collector, 104B DEA/M. Carrieri/De Agostini; *James Lancaster/ CastlesFortsBattles.co.uk* 59T; *Carole Raddato:* 28, 35, 121, 126B, 141R, 142 (all); *Shutterstock:* 4 Katoosha, 18–9 Travellight, 29T Yury Shkrebiy, 30–1 roibu, 36 View Apart, 37 Steve Estvanik, 39 Juriaan Wossink, 41C HildaWeges Photography, 41B, 61T Rainer Lesniewski, 43B Ale Argentieri, 55B Gail Johnson, 64T, 124 Peter Lorimer, 66 Aleoks, 67 Glevalex, 69B BlackMac, 72 mgallar, 86–7 meunierd, 88R Maljalen, 107C Juan Aunion, 108T Aron M, 112T Barry Paterson, 112B Maren Winter, 115L, C & B B-1972, 115B ChiccoDodiFC, 118–9 Seth Aronstam, 125R Ruth Swan, 127 meunierd, 128 GChristo, 129B verityjohnson, 140T Anze Mulec, 140B photosounds, 143T Conde, 143CB Zoltan Tarlacz; *Graham Sumner:* 12, 40, 52–3, 56, 59 (all), 61B, 62T, 63R (all three), 64B, 65T, 69T, 88L, 89B, 90, 91R, 92T, 93T, 93BL and BR, 95C, 96–7, 98 (both), 100R, 101B, 102B, 103, 104T, 109L, 111 (both), 116R, 117, 135, 138, 139TL; *Nick Thompson/Flickr*: 108BL; *Wikimedia Commons:* 6–7 Greg O'Beirne (CC BY 2.5), 8 Arnaud Fafournoux (CC BY-SA 3.0), 14 © Ad Meskens, 20 Med, 21 Sb2s3 (CC BY-SA 4.0), 27B Andrei nacu at English Wikipedia, 29B Lalupa, 38 O.Mustafin, 44L, 110T Photograph by Rama, Wikimedia Commons, Cc-by-sa-2.0-fr, 47 MiguelHermoso, 55T Ji-Elle, 79 By Barosaurus Lentus, 81T, 106TR, 107B, 126T MatthiasKabel, 95L, 99T, 136, 139B, 143CT, 144 CristianChirita, 102T Wolfgang Sauber, 107L Michel wal, 108BR, 113 Medium69, 116L NotFromUtrecht, 132 based on Public Domain, https:// en.wikipedia.org/w/index.php?curid=7792838, 133 Codrin B, 141L Juan Francisco Adame Lorite; *Richard Wood:* 63TL and BL; *https://westpoint.edu:* 22 and 23; *(c) Livius.org/Jona lendering:* 24, 25, 71B, 129T, 130; © VARUSSCHLACHT in the Osnabrücker Land GmbH 32T; CMA Cummins 1732, scene 61, Classics, accessed May 16, 2019, https://omeka1. grinnell.edu/Classics/items/show/60, 145B

ROMAN SOLDIER

OPERATIONS MANUAL

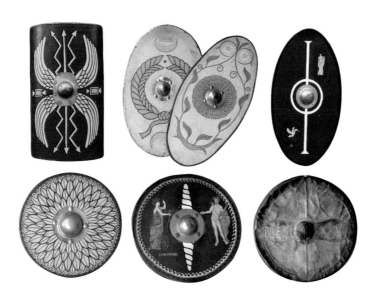

DAILY LIFE • FIGHTING TACTICS • RELIGION • ART • WEAPONS

SIMON FORTY

CONTENTS

INTRODUCTION

The ancient world has left us pyramids, Neolithic henges, Minoan temples and Greek cities, but nothing can compare to the permanence of Roman remains. Roads, aqueducts, walls, cities, villas and forts: hardly a country in western Europe or around the Mediterranean is without a permanent feature that announces the presence of Rome, and many of the feats of civil engineering or scars on the landscape were placed there by the Roman Army. Even more important than that, the Romans were literate and left written evidence of their lives, politics and deaths in the form of books, letters, inscriptions and other epigraphy. On the edges of Empire, the limes border systems are still very obvious: there was a lot of fighting there so there are legionary fortresses, fortified borders such as the Antonine Wall or Hadrian's Wall and other military aspects of occupation (gravestones, altars, equipment finds) are readily visible.

Indeed, it's at these far-flung boundaries of the Roman Republic and Empire that it becomes apparent just how much of the building was done by the army. This was useful for many reasons – particularly physical. Vegetius opined: 'It is advisable that [soldiers] should very frequently be felling trees, carrying burdens, jumping ditches, swimming in the sea or rivers, marching at full step or even running in their arms, with their packs on. The habit of daily labour in peace may not then seem arduous in war. Whether they be legion or *auxilia*, let them be training constantly. As a well-drilled soldier looks forward to battle, so an untrained one fears it.' Building kept the army busy and a busy army doesn't have time for politics; there was a nasty tendency – particularly during the Imperial period – for the army and the Praetorian Guard to raise emperors or pretenders.

The provinces were built on the hard physical labour of the Roman soldiers – and as Vegetius suggests, that included both legionaries and auxiliaries. It's an important distinction. Until around AD206 when Emperor Caracalla promulgated the Antonine Edict, making everyone in the Empire a citizen, the legionaries were Roman citizens – raised by levy (*legio* = levy) – and the auxiliaries weren't. Citizenship was important, particularly in the days of the Republic, and was something that people wanted. It conferred privileges and protections … and the right to vote.

SOCIAL STATUS AND THE BALANCE OF POWER

Not many people could vote in Ancient Rome and its surrounding areas. Women couldn't. Slaves couldn't (but their children, if free, could, and could hold office). The *socii* – Roman allies, initially in Italy and then in some provinces – couldn't.

The Latin War of 340–338BC created a patchwork of different rules for different people: those who were seen as Roman and those who were seen as allies. The allies provided more than half of the Roman Army but had no say over where they went or what they did – that was controlled by the wealthy senators of Rome. This state of affairs meant that the *socii* felt like second-class citizens and took the opportunity to rebel whenever they could (such as when a foreign power – Pyrrhus or Hannibal are good examples – entered Italy). This simmering discontent was stirred up more by the attempts of the Gracchi (133BC and 123–121BC) to redistribute the lands of the wealthy among the poor and improve Latin rights. The big bang took place in the Social War of 91–88BC, which started after the assassination of Marcus Livius Drusus, a tribune who proposed that all Italians

would have citizenship. The war scared the Romans sufficiently to ensure that all Italians received the vote. The problem was that less than 60 years later, the appearance of an Imperial system of government from 30BC onwards meant that most people lost the opportunity to vote on most subjects.

During this Republican period, from 340 to 30BC, Rome's possessions expanded considerably thanks to the army of the Republic. It had started out as a levy, based on a five-yearly census of Roman citizens, that raised troops for fighting: the rich as cavalry and the poor as infantry, everyone paying for his own arms and equipment and being prepared to serve, nominally, for up to six years. Latterly, the *socii* were obliged to provide a similar number of men. However, the expansion of the army necessitated by the growth of the Republic's territories – especially during the Second Punic War – meant that other means were necessary to raise the manpower. Conscription – especially of the richest men in the community – was not going to work when troops were needed for long campaigns far from home. So, the volunteer element of the army grew and property – the yardstick of wealth that had determined in which body of men a soldier in the Republican army served – no longer became a credential for recruitment. From the reforms of the statesman Gaius Marius around 107BC, the volunteer army provided an excellent career for those without the property qualifications most Roman positions required. If they survived, these soldiers could look forward to financial rewards and land at the end of their service.

It wasn't just the poor who benefited from a military career, however; the *cursus honorum* (the succession of offices that was followed by aspiring Roman politicians) meant that the army was still an essential route to power by the elite.

▲ *Evidence of Roman army building: this is Hadrian's Wall near Gilsland. A farmhouse nearby has reused a stone with an inscription identifying the cohort who built in this area.*

▼ *The heart of Rome: the building right is the Curia Julia, one of the locations where the Senate sat. Construction was started by Julius Caesar and finished by Augustus, by which time much of the Senate's power had been eroded.*

THE LANGUAGE OF POWER

▶ *This inscription maps out the cursus of Caius Furius Sabinus Aquila Timesitheus (190–243), who rose from commanding an infantry cohort to become Praetorian prefect and, after Emperor Gordian III married his daughter, de facto ruler of the empire.*

Cursus honorum This was the path to power for a Roman, the age and years of service increasing until, at the tip of the iceberg, ultimate power sat with the consuls (or a dictator). To start, a man must spend 10 years in military service, either in the cavalry or on the staff, or as a military tribune.

Tribune of the Plebs Started with two but was increased to 10 by 449BC and stayed at that number. Elected by the *Concilium Plebis Tributa* (Plebeian Council), this was a significant plebeian position that kept the Senate (and, therefore, the patricians) in check. It was illegal to harm a tribune, who could veto magistrates, the Senate and other assemblies. Since the tribune was not a magistrate, he could not be vetoed by one.

Quaestor Their number increased from four in 421BC to six in 267BC, to eight in 227BC, to 20 in 81BC. The position was held for a year, and they were elected by *Comitia Populi Tributa* (Assembly of the Tribes). The candidate had to be 30 years old if a pleb and 28 if a patrician, and they served in financial administration in Rome or with a governor of a province.

Aedile There were two pairs, one plebeian, one curule. This wasn't a necessary part of the cursus but showed a commitment to public service and also meant that if the holder spent well (at the festivals and games the *aediles* organised) it would buy votes in later elections. The plebian *aediles* were created in 494BC, the curule *aediles* in 367BC when an extra day was added to the games and the plebian *aediles* refused to pay for it. Initially open to patricians alone, the role of curule *aediles* was expanded to include both plebs (from age 36) and patricians (from age 34).

Censor Two elected every five years to oversee a census that identified property ownership for tax and service requirements.

Praetor Either an army commander or a judge in the law courts, holding position for a year, they were elected by the *Comitia Centuriata* (Assembly of the Centuries). Initially two, their number increased to four in 227BC, to six in 197BC and to eight in 81BC. Caesar increased the number to 10 and again to 14 and later 16. Under the Principate their numbers reduced to 12 (Augustus) and then increased to 16 under Tiberius. They were aged over 39 (or 37 if a patrician) and were accompanied by lictors (who carried *fasces* – a ceremonial bundle of rods – with axes when outside Rome's *pomerium* – the boundary that surrounded Roman cities). They took over control if the consuls were absent and often moved on to rule a province as a *propraetor* (provincial governor).

Consul The highest magistrate in Rome. The minimum age was 42 for plebs; 40 for patricians. Two were elected annually by the *Comitia Centuriata* (Assembly of the Centuries), one being senior on alternate months. They were accompanied by 12 lictors. They presided over the Senate, served as commanders-in-chief of armies, and often moved on to rule a province as a proconsul (governor).

Dictator An emergency position used when the state was threatened. Usually for six months, he would choose a *magister equitum* (Master of the Horse).

Magistrate = *magistratus* = elected official with *maior potestas* (major powers).

Curule Higher-level magistrates whose badges of office were a special stool, the *stella curule*, and a *toga praetexta* (white toga bordered with a wide purple strip).

Imperium Authority to fulfil duties of state, military or judicial.

THE COST OF WAR

The hidden problem in all of this was the cost to the Roman economy. War is expensive. Civil wars are even more expensive because of the damage they do to infrastructure, crops and trade and because there are no slaves and booty being brought in: Roman captives can't be sold as slaves. The armies of the 1st century BC were sizeable. After Actium, Octavian had some 60 legions, although not all full-strength, including those of Mark Anthony. Just paying an estimated 300,000 legionaries their 900 sesterces a year – without allowing for higher payments to centurions, *immunes,* etc – produces a cost of 270 million sesterces. Add to that the cost of fleets, equipment, etc and it's unsurprising that Augustus had to cut the number of legions back to between 25 and 28.

Augustus' legions also conquered territory, which yielded slaves and booty that helped the exchequer. His successors continued to expand the Empire that reached its peak around AD117 during the reign of Trajan. These included Hadrian, who retrenched and secured the borders and – apart from the occasional upset – that's the way things stayed until the 3rd century AD. During that period, the main problems the Empire faced were internal crises as rival emperors contested succession and their armies fought for power – AD69 has gone down in history as the Year of the Four Emperors; AD193 went one better with five emperors involved; and between AD235 and AD285 there were 22 emperors and 26 claimants, almost all of them generals who used their legions to carve out their own empires.

THE RISE OF THE DOMINATE

The winner in AD284 was Diocletian. He took control and did away with the Principate – the collegiate form of government that Augustus had set up. Over the next few years, the Dominate was created: a form of administration that spread the load of government between more leaders – the Tetrarchy consisted of two senior co-emperors and two junior co-caesars. It had the downside of adding to the number of people with power – and, therefore, the number of positions to be fought over – but it helped prolong the life of the Western Roman Empire through to the 5th century AD, although its capital moved to Mediolanum (Milan) in AD286 and Ravenna in AD402, and Constantine moved the capital of the Empire to Constantinople in AD330. The Eastern Roman Empire, in one form or another, remained until Byzantium fell to the Turks in 1453, lasting a further 1,000 years.

THE FIELD OF STUDY

This book examines the Roman soldier from the founding of the city of Rome to the end of the Principate: 1,000 years of history. It covers the development from what was, essentially, a Greek hoplite army to the all-conquering army of the Principate and the developments of the 2nd and 3rd centuries AD, stopping at the accession of Diocletian and the formation of the Tetrarchy. This is not to say that the soldiers of the 4th and 5th century AD were not Roman soldiers; they and the armies that fought on into the years of the Byzantine Empire

▲ *Augustus had created an imperial government that, after 200 years, was creaking badly. Diocletian's reforms increased the bureaucracy, decentralised government and created the Tetrarchy, which saw control of the Empire split between co-emperors (Augusti) and their junior partners (Caesar).*

were certainly based in the armies of the past, but there's only so much room in one book. I accept that I am guilty of finding the Principate more interesting than the Dominate. Part of the reason for this is that until Diocletian, the story of the Roman Empire is centred on Rome. After Diocletian, and particularly after Constantine, the story has no centre.

ESTABLISHING SOME BASICS

Italy Today's country is named after the Italic people who migrated into the peninsula in the 2nd millennium BC.

Latin The language of Rome and the Roman Empire is named after Latium, the area of central western Italy in which Rome was sited. The 'Latin' tribes colonised the area and formed the Latin League to withstand external forces such as the Etruscans. Rome became the leader of the league and, eventually, some of the cities became part of 'Rome' and were treated as Roman citizens. Others were termed Latini and were granted the rights of the *ius latinum* ('Latin law').

Romans Originally a term applied only to the people of Rome, this privilege was extended out to those communities that were subsumed into the Republic. After an edict by Caracalla in AD211, all citizens of the Empire became Romans.

TIMELINE 753BC TO AD285

Although some dates can be cross-checked from written sources and epigraphic record, many are debatable; most of the early information was written long after the event, and errors are compounded by multiple copying in medieval times. So, while every effort has been made to provide the current view, many dates are unconfirmable.

THE REGAL PERIOD (753–509BC)

753BC Foundation of Rome.

616–579BC Reign of Lucius Tarquinius Priscus, the first of the Etruscan kings.

578–535BC Servius Tullius, the penultimate king of Rome, reforms the army.

REPUBLICAN ROME (509–30BC)

509BC The creation of the Roman Republic when the last Etruscan king, Lucius Tarquinius Superbus, having been deposed, was defeated at the Battle of Silva Arsia.

508BC Horatius holds the bridge and Lars Porsena's army is kept out. The Republic is safe!

503–495BC Conflict with various Latin towns and cities, probably linked to continued Etruscan attempts to regain Rome, ends at the Battle of Lake Regillus. A treaty, the Foedus Cassianum, cements a league that helps protect them against incursions from the Aequi and the Volsci.

483–476BC The Fabian War with the Veii, a rich city in the Etruscan League. Undertaking the war themselves, the Fabii family are almost completely wiped out at the Battle of the Cremera in 477BC. The war ends with a Roman victory.

406–396BC Another war breaks out with the Veii, and ends when dictator Marcus Furius Camillus subjugates the city. However, internal politics saw him exiled in 394BC.

c.396BC Livy records that the Senate decrees that Roman soldiers should be paid from the public treasury.

c.390BC The Gallic chieftain Brennus of the Senones beats the Romans at the Battle of Allia River, and then sacks most of Rome. The embarrassment ends when Marcus Furius Camillus – 'Second Founder of Rome' – returns from exile.

343–341BC First Samnite War: Rome reacts to the Samnite invasion of Campania and wins a number of victories, including the Battle of Mons Gaurus (343BC).

340–338BC Latin War: Rome and its erstwhile enemies, the Samnites, pitted against the Latin League – as the latter made a bid to shake off Roman control. The Romans are victorious, annex a number of states and expand its territories.

326–304BC Second Samnite War: the power struggle for central Italy exploded again in a protracted war that saw periods of truce interspersed with battles, with defeats at the Caudine Forks (321BC) and Lautulae (315BC) before final Roman victory at Bovanium (310BC).

298–290BC Third Samnite War: this last instalment saw Rome finally take control of the bulk of central Italy, in spite of the return of the Senones on the side of the Samnites. The crucial battle took place at Sentinum (295BC). Livy suggests 25,000 enemy dead and 8,200 Romans.

285–282BC After a major defeat by the Gauls at Arretium (284BC), Rome advances into Gallic territory, defeating the Senones in 283BC, a combined army of Gauls and Etruscans in 283BC and Etruscans in 282BC.

280–275BC Pyrrhic War: Pyrrhus of Epirus lands at Taranto and threatens Roman territory, defeating the Republic at the attritional battles of Heraclea (280BC) and Asculum (279BC). However, at Beneventum (275BC), Manius Curius Dentatus defeated Pyrrhus, captured eight elephants and forced the Epirotes back across the Adriatic.

264–241BC First Punic War: independent from Phoenicia from 650BC, Carthage had amicable relations with Rome until they clashed in Sicily. Rome won big victories at sea such as Ecnomus (256BC) and gained its first overseas possessions as the treaty at the end of the war ceded Central and Western Sicily. This was a massive war, with huge casualty figures mainly caused by the loss of fleets to bad weather. Sicily becomes a province and the breadbasket of Rome.

238BC While Carthage is dealing with a revolt by unpaid mercenaries, Rome annexes Sardinia and Corsica, which become provinces in 237BC and 238BC respectively.

229–228BC First Illyrian War: Rome intervenes across the Adriatic to subdue Ardiaei pirates. Their Queen regent, Teuta, pays tribute to Rome.

225BC Another Gallic tribe, the Boii, attacked Rome from the north. They were destroyed first at the Battle of Telamon and then at Clastidium in 222BC. Rome had expanded into Cisalpine Gaul – today's Provence.

220–219BC Second Illyrian War: after which the Romans' erstwhile client, Demetrius of Pharos, flees to Macedon.

218–201BC Second Punic War. Three years of Carthaginian success as Hannibal marched over the Alps and won great victories at Trebia (218BC) and Lake Trasimene (217BC) were nullified by the attritional strategy of Quintus Fabius Maximus Verrucosus. But the policy was disliked in Rome. Fabius was displaced and a huge Roman army engaged Hannibal at Cannae (216BC). The Carthaginian victory saw Roman losses – casualties and captured – of 65,000–70,000. Many Roman allies changed sides, but in the end, an expedition by Scipio Africanus, in Spain, captured Cartago Novo in 209BC. The Carthaginian army of Hasdrubal (Hannibal's brother) was destroyed at the Metaurus River (207BC) on his way to reinforce Hannibal. And, finally, Scipio's invasion of Africa forced the recall of Hannibal, who was bested at Zama in 202BC. The peace that followed saw Rome take Carthaginian territories in Spain: in 197BC they became the provinces Hispania Citerior (Nearer Spain) and Hispania Ulterior (Further Spain). There were regular rebellions against the Romans.

214–205BC First Macedonian War: while there were no great victories, Rome won the strategic battle – keeping Philip V of Macedon out of Italy and away from being an ally of Hannibal.

200–196BC Second Macedonian War: paved the way into the east for later Roman incursions. Philip V's attempt to take Greece ended with complete defeat and allowed the Romans to declare 'the freedom of the Greeks'. The key battle was at Cynoscephalae in 197BC.

194BC The Romans advanced into Boii territory in Cisalpine Gaul and defeated them in 194BC at Placentia and 193BC at Mutina. The Boii then moved towards the Danube around 191BC (Bohemia is named after them).

192–188BC The War of Antiochus pitted Rome and its allies against Antiochus III, the Seleucid emperor. Beaten at Thermopylae in 191BC, Antiochus III was heavily defeated by the Scipio brothers at Magnesia in Asia Minor in 190BC. The Romans continued the campaign against the Galatians.

181–179BC A major rebellion in Hispania is put down by Tiberius Sempronius Gracchus.

172–168BC Third Macedonian War: Philip V's son Perseus fomented rebellion against Rome and was crushed at Pydna in 168BC by Lucius Aemilius Paullus, who granted a payout of 400 denarii to cavalrymen and 200 to foot soldiers.

169–167BC Third Illyrian War: Lucius Anicius Gallus and a large force crush the Ardiaean king, Gentius, at Scodra. Gallus is awarded a triumph.

156–155BC Dalmatian Wars: after Illyria fell, the northern tribes – who would go on to provide many Roman auxiliaries in the future – came into conflict with their southern neighbours. The Senate sent an army and after initial setbacks, Consul Publius Cornelius Scipio ended the war by sacking the capital, Delminium.

150–148BC Fourth Macedonian War: an uprising is crushed and the Roman Province of Macedonia is established. This leads to a short war against the Achaean League of Greek states which become the Senatorial Province of Achaea.

149–146BC Third Punic War: the final act as an army of 80,000 infantry and 4,000 cavalry attacks Carthage, leading to the destruction of the city and enslavement of the people.

135–132BC First Servile War: extreme conditions led to a slave revolt. After a number of defeats, the revolt was put down with more than 20,000 crucifixions.

135BC Piratical raids by the Ardiaei on Illyria sees a punitive force of 10,000 men and 600 cavalry sent over the Adriatic under Servius Fulvius Flaccus.

118BC Dalmatian Wars: Lucius Caecilius Metellus is given the title 'Delmaticus' after fighting in the area.

113–105BC Cimbrian War, part 1: probably the most serious threat to Rome since Hannibal, the arrival of the migrating tribes of the Cimbri on the Danube was a significant threat. In 112BC, they defeated the army of Consul Gnaeus Papirius Carbo. Heading into Gaul, victories against Rome culminated at Arausio (105BC). A catalogue of errors led to catastrophe for the legions. Over 80,000 men are said to have died.

112–106BC Jugurthine War: Numidia had been an ally of Rome against Carthage, but succession issues led to Rome's involvement when Jugurtha executed his last rival. Jugurtha was able to bribe his way out of trouble and when fighting did take place, he escaped from his opponents. In the end, Gaius Marius, assisted by a certain Lucius Cornelius Sulla, beat him.

104–101BC Cimbrian War, part 2: Marius returns from Numidia, becomes consul and reforms the army. The Cimbri, joined by another Germanic tribe, the Teutones, and others along its path, headed for Italy. Marius defeated the Teutones at Aquae Sextiae (Aix-en-Provence) in 102BC and the Cimbri at Vercellae in 101BC. Marius then flouted Roman law by granting citizenship to all his Italian allies.

104–100BC Second Servile War: another rebellion by slaves on Sicily was eventually put down by Marius.

91–88BC Italian War: a rebellion against Rome by their allies in Italy, sparked by the assassination of Marcus Livius Drusus, who wanted the Senate to grant the allies citizenship. Some 120,000 men, most of whom were veterans, rebelled. The revolt did well initially, but Consul Lucius Julius Caesar proposed a law granting Roman citizenship to all Italians uninvolved in the revolt and, probably, to those who were ready to lay down their arms. This helped assuage many of the Italians, and the Roman armies under Gnaeus Pompeius Strabo in the north and Lucius Cornelius Sulla in the south ended the rebellion.

89–85BC First Mithridatic War: the complex internal politics of the start of the 1st century BC continued with two rivals – Marius and Sulla – fighting each other for power while at the same time confronting external enemies. Mithridates came to the throne of Pontus and began to expand his domain. In 88BC he massacred the Romans and Italians in Asia. In the same year, in Rome, the consul, Sulla, made ready to attack Mithridates, while Marius schemed against him. Sulla responded by marching his legions into Rome, taking power and declaring Marius and his men enemies of the state. He then sailed for Greece, besieged and sacked Athens and Piraeus, and won the Battle of Chaeronea (86BC). In Rome, Marius and his son had regained power and voided Sulla's laws, but Gaius Marius died shortly after becoming consul for the seventh time. A mission sent to Asia to deal with both Mithridates and Sulla got nowhere and Sulla made peace with Mithridates in 85BC before returning to Rome.

83–81BC Second Mithridatic War: Roman general Lucius Licinius Murena causes the second war with Mithridates although the latter hadn't broken the treaty he had made with Sulla. Inconclusive fighting ended in stalemate. While this was going on, Sulla landed in Italy with three legions and was joined by many supporters, including Gnaeus Pompey. Sulla then marched on Rome. The armies of the two sides were veterans, Sulla's on one side; younger Marius' on the other. Sulla's won and while Marius got away, his Marian supporters murdered Sullan followers in Rome and attempted to defend the city. Finally, Sulla defeated the Marian forces at the Colline Gate (82BC), the younger Marius killed himself and some 50,000 Romans and Italians died. More deaths were to follow as Sulla became dictator and 'filled the city with deaths

▼ *Caesar turns the tide during the Battle of the Sabis. He grabbed a shield, advanced to the front of the line and bolstered his men's flagging spirits sufficiently to win the day.*

without number or limit.' (Plutarch) Altogether, the death toll reached nearly 10,000. Sulla was not interested in keeping his position for long and resigned the dictatorship in 81BC.

80–72BC Sertorian War: the brilliant Quintus Sertorius fought Rome first in Hispania (83BC), then Africa before being called back to Lusitania – Portugal – in 80BC to aid the Lusitani against the Sullan regime. Sertorius was a clever general who knew his forces were best equipped for a guerrilla war. He kept Rome at bay for nearly eight years before being assassinated by Marcus Perperna Vento, who was then beaten and executed by Gnaeus Pompeius Magnus.

78–76BC Dalmatian Wars: the Delmatae had moved into the area around Salona (today's Solin, Croatia). C. Cosconius captured the city and defeated the Delmatae.

77BC After Sulla's death in 78BC, Marcus Aemilius Lepidus rebels against the Sullan Senate. His supporter Marcus Junius Brutus the Elder is besieged by Pompey. Lepidus heads an army from Etruria that is defeated by Catullus and Pompey, although sources differ.

73–63BC Third Mithridatic War: when Nicodemes IV of Bithynia died, Mithridates' attack on Bithynia took place at the same time as his ally, Sertorius, was fighting in Lusitania. It

ended the same way, with Gnaeus Pompeius Magnus hunting down Mithridates at Lycus (66BC).

73BC Third Servile War: another slave revolt, this one was the war of Spartacus. It took eight legions under Marcus Licinius Crassus to defeat the gladiators and crucify 6,000 of them.

64–63BC At the end of the Mithridatic War, Pompey moved south to Syria. In 64BC, he dethroned Antiochus XIII and Syria became a Roman province. In 63BC, he went to Jerusalem, besieged the temple and made Judea a satellite of Syria. He heard about the death of Mithridates and headed north, leaving Marcus Aemilius Scaurus in charge of Syria.

63–62BC The Catiline Conspiracy – to overthrow the Republic – is exposed by Cicero. Catiline dies bravely at the head of his men during the Battle of Pistoria (62BC).

61BC Pompey returns to Rome and celebrated triumphs for victories in Asia, Africa and Hispania. In Rome, he sided with Crassus and Caesar to form the first Triumvirate, a political alliance against the Optimates – the traditionalists in the Senate. The result was that Caesar was elected consul, pushed Pompey's settlements in the east and married his daughter Julia to Pompey. He then left for Gaul as governor.

58–51BC Caesar's conquest of Gaul: over a period of years, Caesar conquers Gaul, leads expeditions to Britain in 55BC and 54BC, besieges the great Gaul leader Vercingetorix at Alesia, and begins to overshadow Pompey. Key battles included the Arar (58BC) against the Helvetii; Bibracte (58BC) against the Helvetii; Vosges (58BC) against the Suebi; the Sabis (57BC) against the Belgian tribes (in this battle Caesar himself had to pick up a shield and join in); and finally Alesia (52BC) against Vercingetorix's Gauls.

53BC Parthian War: Triumvir Marcus Licinius Crassus invaded Mesopotamia and his seven legions are destroyed with very few escaping. Crassus and his son are killed.

50–42BC Dalmatian Wars: Roman settlers appealed to Julius Caesar, who was proconsul of Illyricum, when attacked by the Dalmatae. Caesar's forces under A. Gabinius were badly beaten, five cohort standards taken, and Gabinius died. Further fighting in 45–44BC saw the Delmatae retake Salona.

49–45BC Civil war: Caesar was ordered to relinquish his army by the Senate, controlled by Pompey. Instead, he crossed the Rubicon at the head of Legio XIII Gemina and headed for Rome. Pompey and his supporters fled and five years of civil war followed. Caesar first neutralised Spain, which was on Pompey's side, then followed Pompey to Greece, besieging him at Dyrrhachium (48BC). Here, Pompey attacked and beat Caesar, although not decisively, and both sides moved into Thessaly. The decisive moment was at Pharsalus when the outnumbered Caesarian legions defeated Pompey the Great. Pompey escaped the field but was assassinated by Ptolemy XIII, who sent Caesar his head. Caesar went to Egypt, killed the assassins, and having defeated Ptolemy XIII at the Battle of the Nile (47BC), he placed Cleopatra on the throne. After fighting in Pontus (the Battle of Zela in 47BC after which Caesar's immortal '*veni, vidi, vici*' is supposed to have been uttered) and at Thapsus in Egypt (46BC), the last battle of the civil war, against Pompey's sons, was in Spain at Munda

(45BC). Caesar returned to Rome and was declared *dictator perpetuo* by the Senate. He was assassinated while planning a campaign in Parthia. Gaius Octavius Thurinus (later Augustus) is Julius Caesar's adopted son and heir.

43–42BC Civil war: The Second Triumvirate (Mark Antony, Marcus Aemilius Lepidus, and Gaius Julius Caesar Octavianus) chased down Julius Caesar's assassins and at two battles at Philippi in 42BC, around 200,000 men fought – 19 legions on the side of the Second Triumvirate and 17 legions under Brutus and Cassius.

41–40BC Civil war: Mark Antony's wife Fulvia and his brother, Lucius, raised eight legions in Italy and took Rome to push Mark Antony's position. Octavian forced them to retreat to Perusia (today's Perugia), besieged the city and took it. Mark Antony's family was spared but it wouldn't be long before Octavian and Antony went head to head.

40–33BC Caesar had been planning a Parthian war but was assassinated before he could undertake it. During the civil war, Parthia occupied Roman Syria and even advanced into Anatolia, where they were defeated by Publius Ventidius Bassus, a career soldier and one of Julius Caesar's favourites. In 37BC, Herod took back Jerusalem. Antony attacked Parthia through Atropene (Azerbaijan) but the campaign was an expensive failure. After this, Antony marched into Armenia.

35–33BC Dalmatian Wars: Illyricum had sided with Pompey and the Dalmatian coastline across from Italy hid pirates. Octavian reconquered the area and won back the standards taken in 48BC. The province of Illyricum was formed in 27BC. The Delmatae would revolt again in 12BC and again in AD6.

32–30BC Civil war: the final battles of the Republic as Octavian and Antony, the latter now in Egypt with his lover, Cleopatra (he was actually married to Octavian's sister, Octavia) and her son with Julius Caesar, Caesarion. Octavian gained control of the Senate, which declared war on Cleopatra. Antony and Cleopatra's fleet – and 19 legions – is beaten by that of Augustus, commanded by Agrippa, in the Battle of Actium (31BC). Mark Antony and Cleopatra died by suicide; Caesarion was murdered. Egypt becomes an Imperial province and Augustus its pharaoh: the civil war and the Republic were over.

THE PRINCIPATE (30BC–284AD)

29BC Octavian returns to Rome where – over a period of 30 years – he consolidates his hold over the constitution and the territories of Rome.

27BC Octavian becomes Augustus, the Senate having entitled him Augustus and Princeps.

27–19BC Cantabrian Wars: the conquest of north-western Spain required eight legions and numerous auxiliaries, and led to the complete subjugation of the Iberian peninsula.

27BC Augustus creates the Praetorian Guard.

27BC Augustus reorganises the Roman provinces, separating Achaia from Macedonia, and reorganising the elements of Hispania and Gaul.

24–22BC Gaius Petronius campaigns in Nubia following an attack of Syrene. The Nubians eventually make peace.

14–10BC Pannonian War: rebellions in southern Pannonia and northern Dalmatia. Marcus Vipsanius Agrippa is sent to sort it out but his unexpected death in 12BC saw fighting flare up again and the campaign was continued by Tiberius.

12BC Germanic Wars: Roman forces under Drusus cross the Rhine into Germania, retaliating for persistent raids.

9BC Pannonia annexed and incorporated into Illyricum.

AD4 Augustus adopts Tiberius.

AD5 Tiberius conquers Germania Inferior.

AD6–9 Batonian War: another rebellion on the Dalmatian coast leads to a protracted and bloody war involving at least five legions, but possibly more.

AD9 Augustus creates the *aerarium militare*, a treasury drawn from taxes in order to fund the pensions for the professional army. These took the place of land grants, which had stirred up discontent with the aristocracy. In AD14 that was 12,000 sesterces. Caracalla increased it to 20,000.

AD9 Judea becomes a province.

AD9 Defeat of the Roman Army, three legions (Legio XVII, XVIII and XIX) and six cohorts of cavalry under the command of Publius Quinctilius Varus, at the Battle of the Teutoburg Forest. The enemy was an alliance of German tribes. In the wake of the battle, the German troops were held up on the Rhine long enough for Tiberius to bring an army and hold the frontier. Augustus' response was '*Quintili Vare, legions redde!*' ('Quinctilius Varus, give me back my legions!')

AD14 The death of Augustus leads to mutinies of legions on the Rhine and the Danube. They want more pay, shorter service, and retirement benefits. Tiberius' two sons, Drusus and Germanicus, are instrumental in putting the rebellions down, Germanicus in Germania and Drusus in Pannonia.

AD14–16 Germanicus attacks the tribes over the Rhine and retrieves two of the lost eagles.

AD23 The Castra Praetoria, permanent camp of the Praetorian Guard, is built in Rome by Sejanus.

AD41 Caligula is assassinated by the Praetorian Guard. Claudius is chosen as his replacement.

AD43 Emperor Claudius organises the invasion of Britain by four legions commanded by Aulus Plautius. Lycia is annexed by Emperor Claudius.

AD44 Mauretania, a vassal state, becomes two provinces – Mauretania Tingitana and Mauretania Caesariensis.

AD44 Herod Agrippa, King of the Jews, dies and Judea reverts to direct Roman control.

AD46 Thrace becomes a Roman province.

AD50 Publius Pomponius Secundus, governor of Germania Superior, attacks the Chatti and regains Varus' final lost eagle.

AD58–63 Parthian War: caused by problems in buffer state Armenia, the deciding battle was a Parthian victory in AD62 at Rhandeia. Gnaeus Domitius Corbulo invaded Parthia and a peace treaty saw the Parthian King Tiridates accept the crown of Armenia from Rome.

AD60–61 While Suetonius Paulinus is attacking the druids on Anglesey, the Iceni revolt under Boudicca. The revolt is extinguished as Suetonius Paulinus rushes back.

AD66–73 First Jewish War: Vespasian sent to Judea with four legions to quell the 'Great Revolt'. In AD69, Vespasian

SOLDIER OF ROME:
GNAEUS JULIUS AGRICOLA (AD40–93)
General of the Empire and Governor of Britain

Coming from a Gallo-Roman political family of senatorial rank in Gallia Narbonensis, Agricola was a formidable general and an able administrator, much of whose life was spent in the conquest and consolidation of Britain, where he served three times: first, as military tribune, when he took part in the defeat of Boudicca's AD61 rebellion; second, in AD70 as the commander of Legio XX Valeria Victrix; and finally as general and governor from AD77–85, when he defeated the Ordovices and completed the conquest of Wales and of the Caledonians at Mons Graupius (AD83), then set about building up the infrastructure of the province with the construction of roads, forts and towns. Recalled by (jealous?) Emperor Domitian in AD85, in spite of his experience he never served again (declining the governorship of the province of Africa) and died on his family estates in AD93, aged just 53.

becomes emperor. He leaves Titus in charge. In AD70, Titus captures Jerusalem. In AD73, Masada fell after a long siege.

AD68 Nero's suicide ends a period of disruption and sees Servius Sulpicius Galba proclaimed emperor.

AD69–70 Julius Civilis – like Arminius, a Roman officer – leads a significant Batavian rebellion in Germania Inferior. The revolt was defeated by Quintus Petillius Cerialis, but not before Legio I Germanica and XVI Gallica had sided with Civilis.

AD69–70 Julius Sabinus, a Roman officer, sets up an independent Gaulish state, but was easily defeated by a local tribe – the Sequani – who remained loyal to Rome.

AD72–74 Quintus Petillius Cerialis becomes the new governor of Britain and arrives with Legio II Adiutrix. Ably assisted by Agricola (commanding Legio XX Valeria Victrix) Petillius Cerialis conquers the Brigantes, defeating Venutius, and advancing as far north as Carlisle, where a fort is constructed.

AD75–84 Gnaeus Julius Agricola defeats the last of the Northern tribes at the Battle of Mons Graupius in AD83.

AD76 Parthian invasion of Syria is repulsed.

AD83 Domitian campaigns against the Chatti in Germania.

AD85–88 Dacian War: Dacia invades Moesia and the units there are destroyed. Domitian and his Praetorian prefect, Cornelius Fuscus, reorganise the province and build up the forces by bringing in three legions. Having cleared the province of invaders, Cornelius Fuscus invades Dacia but loses the battle and his life. Events are clouded by a post-regnal damnatiae memoriae on Domitian, but it appears that peace was made and Dacia became a client kingdom.

AD87 Inchtuthil (a legionary fort on the Tay) is evacuated before completion; the legions have left all forts north of Newstead by AD90. Legio II Adiutrix leaves Britain for Dacia.

AD101–106 Dacian Wars: Trajan conquers Dacia in two wars, after which it becomes a province.

AD106 Trajan captures the city of Petra.

AD113–117 Trajan starts aggressive action in the east against the Parthians, first taking Armenia and then Mesopotamia before advancing to the Parthian capital, Ctesiphon, creating the provinces of Babylon and Assyria. The Roman Empire reached its greatest size, 3.5 million sq miles (9 million sq km), and an estimated 60 million people.

AD113 Trajan's Column is completed in Rome.

AD114–118 Jewish revolts in Cyrenaica, Egypt and Cyprus.

AD116–117 At Hatra Trajan fails in a siege attempt, retires from the eastern campaign and dies travelling back to Rome.

AD118 New emperor Hadrian retrenches, withdrawing from Trajan's eastern conquests and parts of Dacia.

AD119–122 Fighting in Britain. The *expeditio Britannica* is sent from the continent with 3,000 legionaries. Legio IX Hispana leaves Britain and Legio VI Victrix arrives.

AD121–126 On Hadrian's first voyage, he visits Britain with new governor Aulus Platorius Nepos. The wall is probably planned and started during this visit. Nepos oversees much of the construction work.

AD128–132 Hadrian's second voyage sees him travel through Africa and the Eastern Empire.

AD132–135 Second Jewish War: a rebellion led by Simon bar Kokhba. Initial success sees an independent state created. Hadrian reacts with the full force of empire: six legions – including three from Britain under the general who commanded the army, Sextus Julius Severus – with a total force of around 100,000 men. This army arrived in AD133–134 and by the end of AD135 the fighting was over. The retribution had been close to genocide: Cassius Dio says 580,000 Jews were killed. Roman losses were also great: one, possibly two, legions were disbanded: XXII Deiotariana and, possibly, IX Hispana, although the case for the latter's demise in Britain in AD108 is also strong.

AD139 The British Brigantes tribe is defeated by Quintus Lollius Urbicus.

AD140–143 The Romans move north to the Forth-Clyde line, roughly the southern Caledonian boundary, reoccupying Lowland Scotland on a permanent basis and beginning construction of the turf-and-timber Antonine Wall.

AD150/163 Rebellions in Scotland. The Antonine Wall is abandoned and reoccupied several times.

AD152 Revolts in the province of Egypt.

AD154 Revolt of the Brigantes.

AD161–166 Parthian War: in AD162, the Parthians invaded the Roman province of Armenia; AD162–166 Lucius Verus successfully campaigns against the Parthian Empire; AD165–166 Avidius Cassius invades Parthia.

AD162–165 The Chatti and Chauci invade Raetia and Germania Superior but are repulsed.

AD166–180 The Antonine Plague – perhaps a smallpox or measles pandemic – decimates Rome and the Roman Army, reducing capabilities on the Rhine. Probably introduced by soldiers returning from the Parthian wars.

AD167–180 Marcomannic Wars: hardly had the Parthian wars ended than Rome was threatened by invasions of Pannonia (by the Lombards) and Dacia (by the Vandals). The bitter Marcomannic Wars and Quadi Wars were fought under Marcus Aurelius: one of his key generals was Tiberius Claudius Pompeianus, who married Marcus Aurelius' daughter Lucilla. The fighting expanded to Thrace. In AD174, the Quadi were defeated; in AD175, the Iazyges – but Cassius' rebellion forces the emperor to pull out. This led to a peace treaty that saw 5,000 surrendered Sarmatian cavalry sent to Britain and assigned to Legio VI Victrix.

AD170–175 A large rebellion in Egypt – the Bucolic War – is supressed by Gaius Avidius Cassius, who was given the title *Rector Orientis* – Supreme Commander in the East. Cassius declared himself emperor but before the rebellion could gain traction, one of his centurions killed him.

AD177 Second Marcomannic War: starts with a rebellion by the Quadi followed by the Marcomanni. Commodus becomes joint emperor with his father, Marcus Aurelius, who dies in AD180. Commodus negotiates a peace treaty, although Tiberius Claudius Pompeianus wants to continue.

AD182 Third Marcomannic War: further Roman victories don't hide the fact that the Germanic frontier will require a permanent military presence and as many as 16 legions will be garrisoned there.

AD184–185 Commodus sends Ulpius Marcellus (governor AD176–180) back to Britain when northern tribes – the Caledonii – take advantage of the death of Marcus Aurelius and cross the wall. Ulpius Marcellus possibly advances to the Antonine Wall to chastise the enemy and his victories allow Commodus to take the title *Britannicus*.

AD192–195 Civil war follows the murder of the erratic Commodus at the end of AD192 (a plot that may well have involved Septimius Severus). Publius Helvius Pertinax – son of a freed slave – is heralded as emperor. He is murdered by the Guard and Didius Julianus gains the purple by promising more money to the army than his rivals. Septimius Severus marched on Rome, scaring the Senate enough to outlaw Julianus and the Praetorians to kill him. Almost Severus' first act is to discharge the Praetorian Guard for the murder of Pertinax (Severus identifies Pertinax as a legitimate emperor) and replace it from his Danubian legions.

AD195–196 Parthian War: Severus attacks the Parthians. He annexes the kingdom of Osrhoene, but has to move west to deal with Albinus, who has invaded Gaul.

AD196–197 Civil war: when Clodius Albinus hears that Severus has made his son Caracalla caesar (and changed his named to Marcus Aurelius Antoninus) he rebels. Proclaimed emperor at Eboracum (York) he moves his army into Gaul but loses the Battle of Lugdunum (Lyon) in February AD197, leaving Severus as undisputed emperor. As at the Battle of Issus, Severus' cavalry have played a crucial role in the battle. Severus increases army pay and legalises their marriages. In Britain, the Maeatae, Brigantes and Caledonii attack and cross Hadrian's Wall to cause major problems. They are too strong for the weakened Romans and the new governor, Virius Lupus, has to buy peace.

AD198 Raising three new legions (Legio I, II and III Parthica), Septimius Severus invades Parthia. He is able to capture the capital Ctesiphon and to rebuild the province of Mesopotamia (leaving the new legions as a garrison).

AD202–203 Severus returns to Africa, advancing the frontier to the Sahara.

AD208 Severus brings a large number of troops – 40,000 – to Britain. The army marches north, re-establishes the Antonine Wall and defeats the tribes ranged against him, although his losses against the guerrilla tactics of the Caledonii are substantial. The new position doesn't hold for long after Severus' death in AD211. His son, Caracalla, succeeds him.

AD212 Emperor Caracalla granted Roman citizenship to most of the freeborn inhabitants of the Empire. This was a significant change for the Roman Army; until then, there had been a citizenship distinction between the legions and the *auxilia*. This change had a clear fiscal reason, as it immediately increased the numbers of taxable citizens, helping Caracalla to augment the revenues flowing into the *aerarium militare* – military treasury.

AD216–217 Parthian War: Caracalla's first year of war against Parthia was unsuccessful and he was assassinated by a member of the Imperial bodyguard as campaigning was about to start in AD217. Macrinus, the Praetorian prefect, who probably put the soldier up to it, is nominated by the troops as the new emperor. The first emperor to be drawn out of the Roman equestrian order, he made peace with the Parthians.

AD220 The first Saxon raids start in south-east Britain.

AD222 Elagabalus replaces Jupiter with the sun god Elagabalus and after four years of religious controversy and sexual excess is killed by members of the Praetorian Guard. He is succeeded by Severus Alexander.

AD224 Rome will have a new, more vibrant enemy in the east after the Battle of Hormozdgan sees Ardashir the Unifier of the Sassanian Empire defeat the Parthians.

AD230–232 The Sassanid dynasty of Persia launches a war to reconquer lost lands in the Roman east.

AD234 Germanic and Sarmatian tribes invaded over the Rhine and Danube. Alexander Severus takes an army north.

AD235 Severus is killed by his troops near the town of Mogontiacum (Mainz) because he tries to buy off the enemy. Maximinus Thrax, commander of Legio IV Italica, becomes emperor and continues the campaign against the Alemanni successfully and then launches a punitive raid, defeating another Germanic army at the Battle of the Harzhorn.

AD235–236 Maximinus then moves to Pannonia where he campaigns against the Dacians and Sarmatians.

AD237 Persians invade the Roman province of Mesopotamia.

AD238 Maximinus was heading for Rome when the city of Aquileia refused to open its gates for him and his army. He, his son and their advisers are assassinated. Praetorian prefect Timesitheus marries his daughter to Gordian III and effectively becomes ruler.

AD239 Gothic invasion of Lower Moesia is repelled.

AD240 Sabinianus, Governor of Africa, rebels but this is squashed near Carthage.

AD242 Gordian III marches against the Persian invasion by Shapur I and relieves besieged Antioch. Timesitheus defeats the Persians in a number of battles.

AD244 After invading southern Mesopotamia, Timesitheus and Gordian III are killed at Misiche, after which Praetorian prefect Philip the Arab becomes emperor.

AD245 Philip campaigns against the Carpi, who have crossed into Moesia.

AD247 Rome celebrates its millennium with *Ludi Saeculares* (the Secular Games). Philip makes his son co-emperor.

AD248 Rebellions by the army in Pannonia and Moesia see a Danube commander, Tiberius Claudius Marinus Pacatianus, proclaimed emperor. Many tribes invade the northern provinces. A senator, Decius, who had been governor of Moesia and Germania Inferior, was sent to subdue Pacatianus' rebellion. He does so and is then proclaimed emperor by his men.

AD249 Decius defeats Philip at Verona: both Philip and his son are killed.

AD249–253 Goth Invasion: King Kniva crossed the Rhine into Roman territory in AD249 or 250. He is defeated by the Romans at Nicopolis ad Istrum (in Bulgaria) but then defeats Trajan Decius at Beroe near Ulpia Augusta Traiana (today's Stara Zagora, Bulgaria). In AD251, Decius and his son are beaten and killed at the Battle of Abritus (or Forum Terebronii).

AD251 Trebonianus Gallus becomes emperor with Decius' younger son Hostilian co-emperor, although he dies within a few months and Gallus' son replaces him.

AD252 King Shapur I of Persia attacks again, invading Armenia. He defeats a Roman army at the Battle of Barbalissos and invades the province of Syria.

AD253 Aemilianus, commander in Moesia, defeats the Goths and is proclaimed emperor by his men. He advances on Rome and defeats Gallus at Interamna Nahars. Gallus and his son flee but are killed by their own men. Valerian heads south from his command on the Rhine with an army. Aemilianus' army mutinies and kills him. Valerian is proclaimed emperor with his son Gallienus as caesar.

AD254–260 The new emperors have a hornets' nest to cope with. Valerian goes east; Gallienus west. In the east, Valerian regains Antioch and Syria, but plague at Edessa decimates his men, he is defeated in AD260 and is captured by Shapur I.

AD256–260 The Franks, a Germanic tribe made up of the Cherusci and Chatti, invade Gaul and Spain. The Alemanni invade Italy but are defeated outside Rome by the Praetorian Guard and then at Mediolanum (Milan) by Gallienus. Scared by this encroachment into Italy, Gallienus introduces a mobile cavalry army to stay at Mediolanum to protect Italy.

AD260 In the east, after the Battle of Edessa, a cosmopolitan army of what was available in the east, including Odaenathus of Palmyra, pushed the Persians back and two more pretenders decided to become emperors – Quietus and Macrianus. They headed towards Rome, picking up legions in Pannonia but were defeated by Imperial Horsemaster Aureolus. Odaenathus is left in charge of the east and Gallienus heads west again. Odaenathus attacks the Parthians, retaking all Roman land lost since AD252 and ruling the east only nominally under the aegis of the emperor.

AD260 Britain and Gaul are in revolt and Marcus Cassianus Latinius Postumus, second-in-command on the Rhine, has declared himself emperor. The legions in Britain, Germany and Gaul support him and create the Empire of the Gallic Provinces. He kills Gallienus' son.

AD262 Lucius Mussius Aemilianus proclaims himself emperor in Egypt. Gallienus sends Aurelius Theodotus to Egypt and Aemilianus is defeated and killed.

AD263 Gallienus is badly wounded while besieging Postumus and is forced to retire. The Gallic Empire survives to AD275.

AD267–269 Ship-borne invasions by Goths, who attack the Black Sea coast, Byzantium etc. Defeated by the navy, they attack southern Greece where Gallienus defeats them at Nestos River. Gallienus is assassinated and Claudius II becomes emperor in AD268 and defeats the Alemanni who have invaded Raetia and north Italy at Lake Benacus (AD268 or 269). In AD269, Claudius II (with future emperor Aurelian commanding his cavalry) defeated the Goths at Naissus – and henceforth is known as Gothicus. He then dies of the same epidemic that kills many of the Goths.

AD267 Odaenathus is assassinated by unknown perpetrators for unknown reasons. His wife, Zenobia, acts as regent for his son Vaballathus.

AD269 Postumus is killed. Victorinus is proclaimed emperor in Gaul and Britain.

AD270 The *cohortes urbanae* in Rome is given its own camp, the Castra Urbana.

AD270 The army of Zenobia invades Egypt and enters the city of Alexandria. Zenobia declares herself empress.

AD270 Aurelian succeeds. A Dacian, his five-year reign does much to hold together the Empire at a time when a weaker man could have seen it shatter. Although he had to abandon the province of Dacia, he was able to reunify much of the Empire that had split away from Rome. Aurelian inherited an empire split in three (Rome, Gallic and Palmyrene empires) with external threats mainly along the Rhine and Danube. Aurelian's first action was to expel the Vandals, Juthungi and the Sarmatians from Italy.

AD271 While having to contend with a number of revolts and attempted usurpations, Aurelian continued reunifying the Empire. However, the year started badly with the Battle of Placentia, in which a combined Germanic invasion of the Alemanni, Marcomanni and Juthungi ambushed Aurelian's army. He had been dealing with the Vandals and rushed to the defence of Italy. Having beaten the Romans, the Germanic invasion advanced on a defenceless Rome. However, Aurelian rallied his men and defeated the invaders at Fano. Aurelian subsequently defeated them again at Pavia and chased the remnants down and destroyed them in Raetia. He started the building of the Aurelian Walls around Rome.

In the same year, Emperor Aurelian defeated the Gothic chieftain Cannabas (Cannabaudes) beyond the Danube but abandoned the province of Dacia on the north bank of the river and created a new province, Dacia Aureliana in Moesia.

AD272 Aurelian moved east and defeated Zenobia at the Battle of Immae, outside Antioch, then at Emesa before taking Palmyra. He showed restraint and did not destroy Antioch after its surrender and this allowed a domino effect as other eastern cities surrendered without damage. Zenobia was captured and sent to Rome. Aurelian's general Marcus Aurelius Probus retook the other African provinces.

AD273 Palmyra revolts. The city is destroyed by Aurelian.

AD274 Aurelian returns to Europa and defeats the army of Emperor Tetricus I of the Gallic Empire at the Châlons (also known as the Catalaunian Fields), re-annexing it after 13 years of schism. Aurelian is honoured with the title *Restitutor Orbis* ('Restorer of the World') having revitalised the Empire inside four years.

AD275 On his way towards another campaign in Parthia, Aurelian is murdered by a Praetorian named Mucapor. His wife Ulpia Severina may have ruled the Empire before the Senate elected the next emperor (the last time it would ever do so). The new emperor, Tacitus, lasts long enough to dispose of mercenary tribes who had been gathered by Aurelian for his Parthian campaign and who had been raiding before Tacitus died of fever in AD276. He is succeeded by his maternal half-brother, Florianus, who is overthrown by Aurelian's general, Probus.

AD277 Probus and his generals defeat the Burgundians, Longiones, Alemanni and Franks, clearing the Goths and Germanic tribes from Gaul, following them across the Rhine to ensure they stay put. He exacts tribute from them in the form of manpower, which he settles in border areas to help provide auxiliaries. He rebuilds Hadrian's limes (frontier) between Rhine and Danube.

AD278–280 Probus campaigns against Germanic tribes in Raetia and Vandals in Illyricum, also putting down three usurpers.

▲ *The Tetrarchy personified – this porphyry sculpture of the four emperors dates to around 300. It was looted from Constantinople during the Fourth Crusade.*

AD282 Another successful soldier emperor ends his days assassinated by his own troops. Carus was proclaimed emperor but Probus was killed by his own troops before he could do anything. The new emperor, Praetorian Guard commander Marcus Numerius, named his sons Carinus and Numerian caesars and left the former to look after the west while he went east.

AD282 En route for Persia, Carus defeats the Quadi and Sarmatians on the Danube thrusting deep into Persia, gaining ample revenge for Rome's earlier defeats. The Sassanid Empire is going through a moment of internal weakness so the attack is well timed.

AD283–284 However, before he can go further, Carus dies in Persia, it is said by lightning strike. His son, Numerian, becomes emperor and immediately gives up his father's gains, dying himself in AD284, probably assassinated and Diocletian is proclaimed emperor.

AD285 Diocletian wins the Empire by defeating his nearest rival, Carus' son the emperor Carinus, at the Battle of the Margus in Moesia (today's Serbia) after the defection of Carinus' Praetorian prefect Aristobulus. Carinus, while en route to fight Diocletian, beat another rival for the crown, Julianus, in Pannonia. Diocletian soon co-opted a military strong man, Maximian, as co-emperor.

CHAPTER ONE

THE ROMAN WORLD

Rome was not always a major force in western Europe. Indeed, until the 3rd century BC it wasn't even the major force on the Italian peninsula. The growth of Roman territory, from the legendary founding of the city in 753BC to its dominance of the Western world, took more than 750 years and while it may look inevitable with hindsight, for much of that time Rome was fighting for survival.

◄ *The Romans left their mark on the world. This late Roman fort, Burgh Castle on the Waveney estuary in Norfolk, is part of the British east coast defensive line commanded by the Count of the Saxon Shore. Burgh housed a cavalry unit.*

THE ROMAN REPUBLIC

As with all legends, it's difficult to separate truth from fantasy, and there are plenty of stories covering Rome's rise to control first Latium and then Italy. During this period – roughly 509–272BC – Rome fought against the Aequi, Sabines and Volsci or against its neighbours (to the north the Veii, then to the south the Samnites – three wars between 343BC and 290BC).

There was, however, a stark reminder of relative power around 390BC (as with many Roman dates there is little consensus among the sources) when the Republic bit off more than it could chew by antagonising the Senones, a Gallic tribe that had expanded south over the Alps under the leadership of Brennus. After being roundly defeated at the Battle of the Allia, about 10 miles (16km) from Rome, the Gauls sacked the city and would have taken complete control had not their attempt to infiltrate the Capitoline Hill, to which the Romans had retreated, been stymied when the defenders were aroused by the gaggle of geese sacred to Juno.

▶ *Brennus taught the Romans a lesson in 390BC, when the 'Gauls' (as the Romans called the Celts) defeated the Romans at the Allia. It is likely this defeat led the Romans to change their tactics, ending the dominance of the phalanx.*

After a long siege, the Romans finally agreed to pay off the Gauls, who cheated when their 1,000lb (450kg) of gold was being weighed out. When the Romans remonstrated, Brennus threw his sword on to the scales, uttering the immortal words '*Vae victis!*' ('Woe to the vanquished!')

It's difficult to put flesh on the bones of these accounts. None of the sources agree on numbers – the Roman army at the Allia is variously assessed at 24,000 (Diodorus Siculus), 40,000 (Plutarch) and four legions along with a levy – some 35,000 men (Dionysius of Halicarnassus). The Gauls' numbers were probably nearer 15,000 than 70,000. Because of this, figures are approached cautiously in this book.

As the Roman Republic slowly rose to dominance over Italy – and after the Gaulish sack of the city, Rome took control of the peninsula in less than 200 years – so it came into contact with the Greek states and Carthage, the major maritime power in the Mediterranean. There's much debate about the aims of the Republic, whether it was reactive to threats or actively seeking war to expand its power base. Hindsight also provides – as it did in North America – an element of 'manifest destiny'. Certainly, Romans were always prepared for war, rarely turned down a challenge and individually saw warfare as a way to advance their personal prestige. However, it would be wrong to see Rome's progression to empire as being strategically based – and the wars it fought between 290BC and 146BC show this well.

First off, the war against Pyrrhus. This was triggered by a dispute between Rome and the Greek city of Tarentum, the latter calling in help from the Greek mainland. This came in the form of a man who had aspirations to be a new Alexander the Great, Pyrrhus of Epirus, Alexander's second cousin. The Romans had to divide their strength, creating four armies, three of which had to threaten other states to keep them from joining Pyrrhus. When – at Heraclea in 280BC – one of the Roman armies came into contact for the first time with war elephants and the sarissa-wielding phalanx of the Greek hoplites, they were defeated and sustained many casualties. Critically, so did Pyrrhus and subsequently, in 279BC at Asculum, another 'victory' led to the famous line (John Dryden's translation of Plutarch): 'Pyrrhus replied to one that gave him joy of his victory that one other such would utterly undo him' – the 'Pyrrhic Victory'. In 275BC, a Roman army under Consul Manius Curius Dentatus (aptly named: the *cognomen* Dentatus – 'toothed' – was given as he was born with teeth) defeated Pyrrhus at Beneventum and forced him from Italy. The garrison he left at Tarentum did not survive his death in battle on the Greek mainland in 272BC.

THE ROMAN NAVY

The Punic Wars also had another significant byproduct: a Roman navy. Until its wars with Carthage, the Romans had not needed anything more than coastal vessels for trading. Against the Carthaginians, however, a fleet was essential and the Romans went about creating one in a most Roman way. According to Polybius, they reverse-engineered a captured Carthaginian quinquireme (a heavyweight of the seas, with five rowers on either two or three levels, a complement of around 400 all told including up to 100 marines) and built 100 of these – with 20 triremes thrown in, to boot.

'When they saw that the war was dragging on, they undertook for the first time to build ships, a hundred quinqueremes and twenty triremes. As their shipwrights were absolutely inexperienced in building quinqueremes, such ships never having been in use in Italy, the matter caused them much difficulty, and this fact shows us better than anything else how spirited and daring the Romans are when they are determined to do a thing. It was not that they had fairly good resources for it, but they had none whatever, nor had they ever given a thought to the sea; yet when they once had conceived the project, they took it in hand so boldly, that before gaining any experience in the matter they at once engaged the Carthaginians who had held for generations undisputed command of the sea. Evidence of the truth of what I am saying and of their incredible pluck is this. When they first undertook to send their forces across to Messene not only had they not any decked ships, but no long warships at all, not even a single boat, and borrowing fifty-oared boats and triremes from the Tarentines and Locrians, and also from the people of Elea and Naples they took their troops across in these at great hazard. On this occasion the Carthaginians put to sea to attack them as they were crossing the straits, and one of their decked ships advanced too far in its eagerness to overtake them and running aground fell into the hands of the Romans. This ship they now used as a model, and built their whole fleet on its pattern; so that it is evident that if this had not occurred they would have been entirely prevented from carrying out their design by lack of practical knowledge.'[1]

Next, they made use of a new technique using a *corvus* – essentially a bridge with a hook at the end to attach itself to an enemy ship – to allow troops to board and take an enemy ship. The Romans lost their first naval battle (the Lipari Islands in 260BC) but thereafter more than held their own against the more experienced Carthaginians – although they also lost significant numbers of ships and men in storms.

▲ *Carthage had dominated Mediterranean naval warfare until the Romans built a navy. This ram dates to the 2nd century BC and weighs 465kg. At 2.26m long it would have been attached to a large warship.*

The navy allowed the Romans to transport troops and support expeditions abroad – such as Marcus Atilius Regulus' unsuccessful foray into Africa during the First Punic War and that of Publius Cornelius Scipio in the second – and Roman dominance of the seas forced Hannibal to enter Italy by land over the Alps rather than attempt a ship-borne landing. The navy would go on to be used to help patrol the important route bringing Egyptian grain to Rome and the limes when the border stretched along the major rivers of Europe; to transport and help supply the legions – for example when building Hadrian's Wall; and to keep *Mare Nostrum* free of pirates following their pacification by Pompey the Great.

THE MEDITERRANEAN, AND BEYOND

Masters, now, of Italy, Rome's next battle was for her very existence as she butted up against one of the Mediterranean world's great powers: the Carthaginians. At the same time, for much of the next 125 years, problems in Greece led Rome to intervene regularly, but after each incursion Rome withdrew – not the sign of empire seeking – and the Greek states were left to foment discord.

At times – such as when menaced by Hannibal after his daring crossing of the Alps with his army and his elephants, or when threatened by the Seleucid Empire – Rome seemed on the point of ultimate defeat. But in the end the fighting would leave Rome the dominant force in the Mediterranean as it first took Carthaginian territories in Gaul, Spain and north Africa and then finally moved into Greece with purpose, subjugating the area and creating two provinces, Achaea and Macedonia. In between, Rome defeated the Seleucid Empire that had

CLASSIC 3rd-CENTURY BC BATTLES

Battle: Cannae (216BC)
Sources: Livy; Polybius; Plutarch
Opponents: Roman Republic against the Carthaginians
Location: Apulia, south-east Italy
Romans: 86,400 (40,000 Roman infantry; 40,000 allied infantry; 2,400 Roman cavalry; 4,000 allied cavalry)
Carthaginians: 50,000 (32,000 heavy infantry; 8,000 light infantry; 10,000 cavalry)
Result: Carthaginian victory, massive Roman losses
Progress: Hannibal, Carthage's outstanding and perceptive general, designed the perfect trap for the Romans. By threatening their most important food supply depot at Cannae, he drew a massive Roman response, then comprehensively destroyed it with masterful use of his own multinational force of mercenaries and regular troops from north Africa, Iberia and Cisalpine Gaul. Distributing his crack African troops covertly throughout the army, he initially presented a convex crescent formation whose centre then made a gradual withdrawal in the face of the Roman heavy infantry maniples, while his cavalry on the wings put the Roman and allied cavalry to flight. The Roman infantry, already in tighter formations with greater manipular depth, advanced into the now concave centre of

deliberate retreat and were enveloped on both sides, with catastrophic results.

Battle: Zama (202BC)
Sources: Polybius; Livy; Appian
Opponents: Roman Republic against the Carthaginians
Location: Zama, Carthage, Tunisia
Romans: 35,100 (29,000 infantry and 6,100 cavalry)
Carthaginians: 40,000 (36,000 infantry, 4,000 cavalry plus 80 war elephants)
Result: Decisive Roman victory (Carthaginians 20,000–25,000 killed and 8,500–20,000 captured; Romans and Numidians 4,000–5,000 killed)
Progress: The most critical factor in this battle was the Numidian cavalry, who fought on both sides. Masinissa, who had defected to the Romans and was initially lured away by the Carthaginian cavalry, won the eventual duel between the two and returned to attack Hannibal's rear, breaking the stalemate that had developed. (With the defeat of Carthage he went on to found the kingdom of Numidia and rule it for more than 50 years.) Hannibal's war-elephant opening gambit had been countered by Scipio's hidden skirmisher-infested open lanes, the three

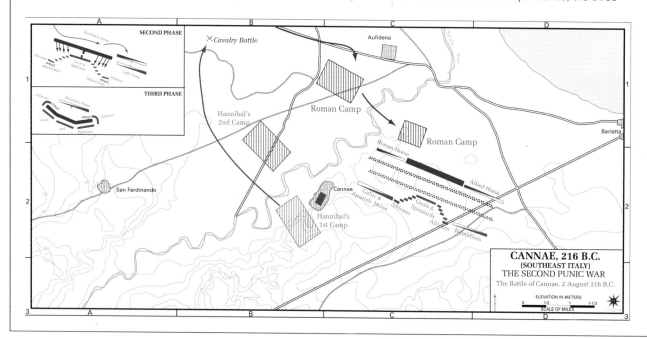

CANNAE, 216 B.C.
(SOUTHEAST ITALY)
THE SECOND PUNIC WAR
The Battle of Cannae, 2 August 216 B.C.

attempted to move into Greece. In doing so, Roman soldiers fought in Asia for the first time – a portent of things to come.

WIN SOME, LOSE SOME

During this period, the Roman Army was not all-powerful and lost many battles, such as those against Hannibal at Trebia (218BC), Lake Trasimene (217BC) and Cannae (216BC), but won the important ones – Agrigentum (262BC), Zama (202BC), Thermopylae (191BC), Pydna (168BC) and Scarpheia (146BC) – to be the only man standing at the end of the period. *'Cartago delenda est'* ('Carthage must be destroyed'), said Cato the Elder, and in 146BC the city was razed and its surviving population was enslaved. That same year, Corinth suffered a similar fate at the hands of Lucius Mummius Achaicus. In a cruel world, Rome rarely had second thoughts when it came to the butcher's bill.

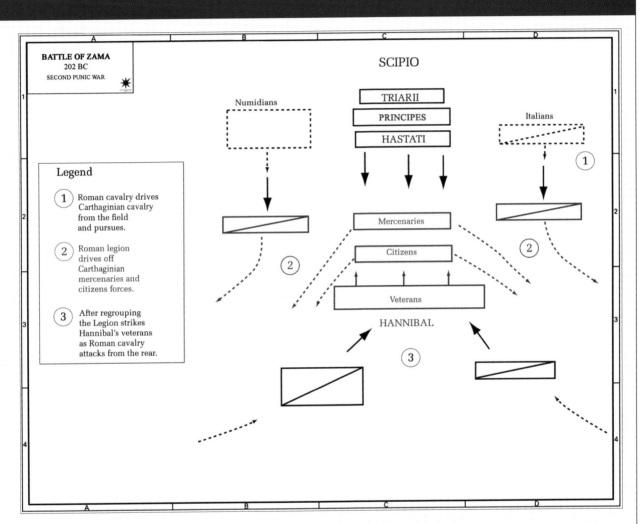

BATTLE OF ZAMA
202 BC
SECOND PUNIC WAR

SCIPIO

Numidians

TRIARII

PRINCIPES

HASTATI

Italians

Legend

1. Roman cavalry drives Carthaginian cavalry from the field and pursues.

2. Roman legion drives off Carthaginian mercenaries and citizens forces.

3. After regrouping the Legion strikes Hannibal's veterans as Roman cavalry attacks from the rear.

Mercenaries

Citizens

Veterans

HANNIBAL

lines of opposing forces then launched their separate attacks and ripostes, finally arriving after a bitter bloody struggle at a single-line stalemate until the return of the Roman cavalry decided the issue.

Battle: Thermopylae (191BC)
Sources: Appian
Opponents: Roman Republic against Seleucid Empire and Aetolian League
Location: Thermopylae, Greece
Romans: 22,000 (20,000 infantry, 2,000 cavalry plus 15 war elephants)

Seleucids and Aetolians: Seleucids – 10,500 (10,000 infantry and 500 cavalry); Aetolians 2,000 infantry
Result: Decisive Roman victory (Seleucids and Aetolians – 10,000 killed or captured; Romans – 200 killed)
Progress: Outnumbered, the Seleucid Antiochus tried to use the narrow coastal pass at Thermopylae in the same way the Spartans had, positioning the Aetolians to guard the no-longer-secret high route around it. Eventually the second of two Roman detachments sent to dislodge the Aetolians succeeded and attacked the Seleucids in their rear.

THE END OF THE REPUBLIC

These wars – particularly the fighting in Italy – had taken their toll, killing many, forcing others to serve for years, devastating the countryside and reducing crop levels. It also built up the power and wealth of the aristocracy, increasing the size of their estates and the number of slaves to run them, and increased the movement of the rural poor to the cities.

These massive social changes resulted in a period of unrest – three Servile (slave) wars and the attempts by the Gracchi brothers to pass legislation that would see some of the land of the rich redistributed to the poor and ex-servicemen. The result of the unrest was to usher in a series of powerful military statesmen who expanded Roman hegemony, but at the same time fostered internal strife leading to civil wars and, ultimately, the fall of the Republic and the creation of the Empire.

The first of these statesmen, Gaius Marius, can be seen as the creator of what became the Imperial Roman Army. The army had changed substantially between the Samnite Wars and the Jugurthine War of 110BC but increasingly it needed allies to help make up the numbers – legions took to the field alongside a similar number of allied infantry (slingers, light infantry, archers) but with significant numbers of allied cavalry, too. Originally composed of rich citizens, the qualification levels had been reduced as manpower was required: Marius needed trained men and a professional army as there was much discord in the Roman world, both internal and external. For instance, Marius had to cope with external threats from the north in the form of the Cimbri and Teutones and from the south in Numidia; internal threats from another Servile war were whipped up by the

ROMAN SLAVE-TAKING

One area of Roman society that is often overlooked – mainly because of our abhorrence of the subject – is the level of slavery. Walter Scheidel assessed the total number of slaves taken during Rome's history as 100 million, with as much as 30–40 per cent of the population of Italy in the 1st century BC being slaves, most of whom had been taken in war by the Roman Army. Indeed, part of the reason for war was not just to take land but also to feed the Roman requirement for slaves. With the army composed of citizens and campaigning every year, slaves were needed to work the fields, in the mines or for domestic duties. And while they were used in senior positions, as scribes and clerks, as well as for hard labour, for the bulk of those taken into slavery life was definitely brutish and short. The majority of *foreigners* taken in war became slaves – note the emphasis: Romans taken in civil wars did not. Scheidel quotes figures for the 130 years between 297 and 167BC as:

Third Samnite War (297–293BC)	58,000–77,000
First Punic War (264–241BC)	107,000–133,000
Gallic War (225–222BC)	32,000
Second Punic War (218–202BC)	172,000–186,000
Various wars (201–168BC)	153,000
Sack of Epirus (167BC)	150,000
Total	672,000–731,000

◀ *One of the pedestals that supported columns in the fortress at Kästrich, a suburb of Mainz (Mogontiacum), depicts bound prisoners. Until the 1st century BC most of Rome's substantial slave requirement was filled by those captured in battle or conquest.*

maltreatment of the slaves; and there was a war with Rome's Italian allies who wanted land and the benefits of citizenship. They rose up and, at the same time so did Mithridates in Greece and Asia Minor. All the time, Marius and another military strong man, Lucius Cornelius Sulla, were vying for power, each killing opposition supporters while the other was away from Rome.

This story was continued for 70 years. Marius, Sulla, Pompey, Julius Caesar: all fought wars to extend the territory of the Roman Republic, and all created legions that were loyal to them. Roman fought Roman in a bloody century that saw Syria, Gaul, Pontus et Bithynia and Africa Nova added to the Roman hegemony but also saw civil wars between the adherents of Marius and Sulla, Pompey and Caesar before the final Armageddon of the Republic, the civil war that followed the assassination of Caesar in 44BC: first, the battles between the Second Triumvirate – Octavian, Antony and Lepidus – and Caesar's assassins, and then between Octavian and Antony. Last man standing was Octavian and it was he, as Caesar Augustus, who ushered in the Imperial era and the Principate.

SOLDIER OF ROME: GAIUS MARIUS (157–86BC)

General and Consul of the Republic

Born at Arpinum in Latium (which only received full citizenship in 18BC), Marius had a lifelong hatred of the Senate's patrician insider club. A tough 'soldier's soldier', in an extraordinary career spanning several decades he held more consulships than any other (seven), commanded victorious armies in the east against Jugurtha and in the west against Germanic tribes, and initiated crucial army reforms that increased its recruiting base and made it a fully professional fighting force. In doing so he (unintentionally?) paved the way for the demise of the Republic, because Roman armies now relied on their generals for their fortune. As a result of his struggles with his rival Marius, Sulla became the first general to march his army on Rome and seize power, establishing a precedent many others would attempt to follow.

These captives would be transported to slave markets in Italy or locally, perhaps even bought by slave traders following the army.

Unsurprisingly, there were slave uprisings, the best-known being the last of the three Servile Wars (*servile* = slave) led by Spartacus. The First (135–132BC) and Second (104–100BC) took place in Sicily, and were caused by the maltreatment of slaves. As with the Nazis in the 1940s, the abundance of slave labour led to the masters working their slaves to death, it being cheaper to do this and buy new ones, rather than feed and house existing slaves properly. The Third War took place on the Italian mainland and had to be put down by significant numbers of Roman legions under Marcus Licinius Crassus, Gnaeus Pompeius Magnus and Marcus Terentius Varro Lucullus.

The period of relative peace that followed the accession of Augustus saw some revision to the slave laws, and improvement in the treatment of slaves, but their use continued. The further increases to the Empire under the Flavian and Nerva–Antonine emperors, for example, would see significant numbers of enemies enslaved during the Jewish Wars (AD66–73 and AD132–135) and the Dacian Wars of AD101–106 (Scheidel quotes 500,000 enslaved by Trajan).

▶ *While Roman soldiers couldn't own slaves, it's apparent that there were servants in the army and many could well have been slaves. This is another of the Mainz pedestal images, a 'looting soldier'.*

THE PRE-EMINENCE OF EMPIRE

The fighting that had started with Caesar's crossing the Rubicon ended with Octavian's victory over Antony and Cleopatra: first at Actium in 31 BC and then ensuring the death of Caesarion, Caesar's son with Cleopatra. Voted joint consul with Agrippa, in 27BC the Senate gave Octavian the title *Princeps* (first citizen), and then *Augustus* (revered one).

THE 'GREAT MIGRATIONS'

- The first movement of what is known as the Migration Period happened in the second part of the 2nd century AD as pressure from the Goths and Vandals pushed German tribes across the Danube in AD160–188, causing the Marcomannic Wars.
- The Alemanni thrust across the Rhine, invading Gaul, but were defeated at Benacus in AD268 or 269. There would be more fighting between this date and AD554.
- The Goths attacked first in AD249 and would fight a series of wars up untill AD554. They had been paid tribute since AD238 and when Rome stopped paying, the Goths attacked. They were responsible for killing two emperors – Decius at the Battle of Abritus in AD251 and Valens at Adrianople in AD378, the latter as they were pushed west by the Huns. A key battle was fought at Naissus in AD269. A heavy defeat saw the Goths pushed back and no further warfare until AD367.
- The Vandals were pushed west into Dacia and Pannonia, and were then forced west by the Huns and moved across Gaul, through Hispania to north Africa. They would later sack Rome from the south in AD455. Belisarius, Justinian I's general, retook Africa and the Vandal kingdom in AD534.
- The Visigoths emerged from the Goths and sacked Rome in AD410, moving then to settle in Gaul and Hispania in the wake of the Vandals. They were pushed out of Gaul in AD507 by the Franks at the Battle of Vouillé.
- The Huns, probably pushed by the Alans, had built a kingdom by AD430 that came into contact with the Romans in both east and west. Spurred on by their leader Attila, in the AD430–440s they were in conflict with the eastern Empire, and they invaded Gaul in AD451, causing much damage and devastation. After the indecisive Battle of Châlons in AD451, the Huns invaded Italy in AD452 and were preparing to attack Constantinople when Attila died. After his death in AD453, they dissipated their strength fighting each other, particularly at Nedao in AD454.

First, Augustus had to cope with the huge numbers of men in arms: his army, that of Mark Antony and all the others forces who had been fighting in the civil war. Second, he then had to walk a tightrope to ensure that he treated those who were leaving and those who were staying in well enough to stop the former from taking up arms again and the latter from finding another leader.

Augustus walked that tightrope with precision. First, as noted in the *Res Gestae Divi Augusti*, he made all units swear an oath of allegiance not to their generals but to him. 'The number of Roman citizens who bound themselves to me by military oath was about 500,000.' Second, he cut back the legions and allocated 170 million sesterces to the retiring veterans. 'Of these I settled in colonies or sent back into their own towns, after their term of service, something more than 300,000, and to all I assigned lands, or gave money as a reward for military service.'

In fact, the 1st century BC, between Gaius Marius and Augustus by way of Sulla, Pompey and Mark Antony, saw so much fighting, with such large armies involved, that the Empire was only sustainable if there were a growth of Roman territory and taxation. To this end, Augustus introduced an inheritance tax of 5 per cent and an auction tax of 1 per cent. After paying off half those in arms after his victory over Mark Antony at Actium in 31BC, Augustus also regulated pay and the *praemia militia*: the amount of cash settled on veterans in lieu of land. Cassius Dio records this figure as 12,000 sesterces for soldiers and 20,000 sesterces for Praetorians.

SHIFTING BOUNDARIES

During the reigns of Augustus through to Trajan, the Roman Empire expanded towards its greatest extent (it would get there under Septimius Severus once Osrhoene [Upper Mesopotamia, now in Turkey] was annexed), and was divided into Senatorial and Imperial provinces – the former, the older ones, had governors appointed by the Senate; the latter came under the emperor. However, as time went on the provinces were altered, particularly as those under threat were subdivided to help the defence. The map shows the position under Trajan. He had expanded the Empire in Arabia, Mesopotamia and Armenia (all annexed), Dacia (conquered), Epirus Nova and Assyria (both created). Hadrian's retrenchment saw Hadrian's Wall and the German limes (frontier) set as a border, and some withdrawal from Trajan's boundaries in Armenia and Mesopotamia: Hadrian restored the king to the throne of Armenia, and gave Mesopotamia back to the Parthians in AD118. Other than Septimius'

▲ *Maiden Castle, near Dorchester, dates back to the Iron Age. It was still occupied at the time of the Roman invasion of Britain although it's unlikely that the battle-scarred warriors found in the cemetery tell the story of a Roman attack.*

SOLDIER OF ROME: GAIUS JULIUS CAESAR (100–44BC)

General and Dictator of the Republic

The premier Roman general, whose name has become synonymous with the ultimate military rank, Caesar was an outstanding military commander and a wily politician. His campaigns in Gaul literally became a textbook for future generations. Caesar had direct experience of what occurred between Marius and Sulla and crossing his famous Rubicon replicated the tussle in his own struggle for supremacy with Pompey. His pursuit and defeat of Pompey, his tryst with Cleopatra and continued military success are the stuff of legend. As a triumphant dictator, he revised the calendar and established a new constitution, but aroused much jealousy. His murder in 44BC precipitated the final crisis of the Roman Republic.

creation of a new province when he annexed Osrhoene, the only significant boundary change before the Dominate was Aurelian's creation of Dacia Aureliana after the withdrawal from Dacia north of the Danube.

The enemies of Rome for this period are identified on the map: the Pictish tribes of north Britain, the German tribes along the Rhine and Danube, the Parthians in the east. Indeed, nearly a third of all *auxilia* units spent most of the 2nd century AD in Britain or Dacia. However, new threats developed, and from the 4th century AD there were numerous conflicts as tribes were pushed eastwards and into the Roman territories by the 'Great Migrations' – possibly caused by the movement of the Huns.

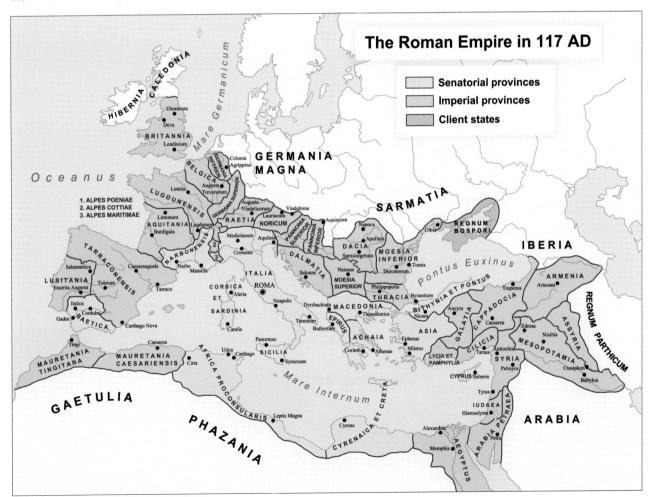

The Roman Empire in 117 AD

- Senatorial provinces
- Imperial provinces
- Client states

POLITICS AND PESTILENCE

After nearly 200 years of the *Pax Romana* – the Roman peace – the death of Marcus Aurelius in AD180 precipitated a period of discord that was further worsened by the Year of the Five Emperors in AD193. The Severan dynasty taped over the cracks, but the assassination of Severus Alexander in AD235 heralded 50 years of turmoil: the 'Crisis of the 3rd century AD'.

On top of the social and political problems, the Empire had to contend with a major pandemic: the Plague of Cyprian. This was possibly smallpox or flu but could also have been measles. It was the second to have afflicted the Empire. The first, the Antonine Plague in AD165–180, was probably smallpox, and had a significant effect on the army. It started in the east and was brought back by soldiers returning from Seleucia. It is said to have decimated the army. The later Plague of Cyprian started in Egypt in AD251 and was still going strong in AD270 when it may well have been the cause of the death of Emperor Claudius Gothicus.

The army was badly affected and it is perhaps unsurprising that as a result this century saw so much upheaval. During the plague years there were incursions into Gaul and the Balkans by the Alemanni and Goths but their advance into Italy was stopped in its tracks at the Battle of Lake Benacus (Lake Garda, Italy) in AD268 or 269. The same year, another significant battle at Naissus (in today's Serbia) saw the Gothic threat eliminated for a century. Again, it is not surprising, with all this upheaval, that emperors Aurelian and Probus built new walls around Rome in AD271–275.

The problems of the 3rd century contributed to the difficulties of the 4th. There was rampant inflation, issues with recruiting men and, therefore, an increased dependency on 'Barbarian' troops – although, as Mary Beard points out, it's difficult to know who is the barbarian when one considers some of the regular aspects of Roman life: infanticide, slavery, genocide, crucifixion. Most of the barbarians were more interested in enjoying some of the advantages of the Roman Empire and getting out of the way of the other barbarians who were pushing them west. Using these warriors in the Roman Army was one way that it could make up the shortfall in numbers. However, the *cursus honorum* broke down, and as the emperors began to build up their personal forces in order to forestall ambitious rivals other border units became smaller and more fixed in location.

PERPETUAL THREAT

The Roman world view at the end of the 3rd century AD was considerably different to that of 753BC. They had evolved from being a city state to a huge empire. As with all empires, there were some areas that were relatively peaceful and others that weren't, often because of outside forces. Those outside forces were a combination of border tribes for whom

▼ *Castra Arutela in Dacia (modern Romania) was erected in AD138 by a unit of Syrian archers.*

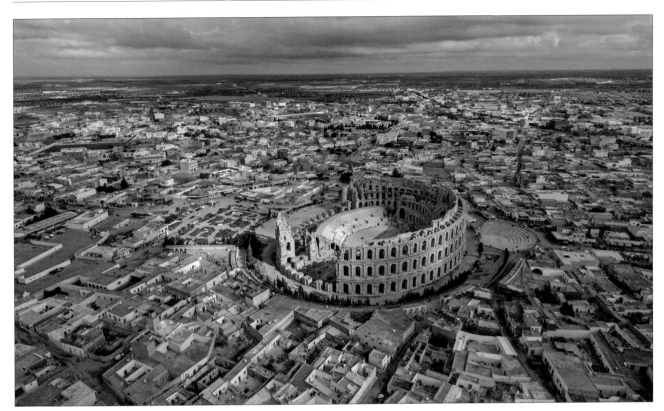

the grass was definitely greener on the wealthy Roman side and who wanted to enjoy the trade and lifestyle privileges of the Empire; those tribes who simply wanted to raid their wealthy neighbours; those who were displaced from their homelands by other migrations and were forced to migrate themselves; and those who wanted to carve out an empire of their own. The most dangerous from the point of view of Rome or the Italian peninsula were definitely those on the Danube border. However, there's no doubt that the Sasanian Empire, which became a threat after it had taken over the empire of the Parthians, was the most threatening for the Empire in Asia Minor, the eastern Mediterranean and Africa.

External menaces would certainly worry Diocletian and the emperors of the Dominate, but what had also become apparent was that the most serious threat to the security of the emperor and the Empire in the 3rd century AD was the Roman Army itself. During that century, the majority of the many people who proposed themselves or were proposed for the Imperial throne were backed by Roman legions. The army in general and the Praetorian Guard in particular had lost any pretence of being apolitical. Future military changes evolved, therefore, not just from the need to counter external threats, but also from the need to be prepared for internal problems. It was a recipe for disaster and it is only surprising that that disaster had been postponed and did not take place in the 3rd century AD.

▶ *The Aurelian Walls of Rome were built AD271–5. Their height was increased in the 4th century and saw improvements over the centuries, staying in use until the 19th. This ensured that they remain in a good state of preservation.*

▲ *Built around AD238 in Thysdrus – today's El Djem – this is one of the best-preserved of all Roman amphitheatres and, understandably, a World Heritage Site since 1979.*

CHAPTER TWO

THE ROMAN ARMY

Before the Republic was founded, the history of Rome is mixed in legend and storytelling. However, there's no doubt that the military tradition was born during Etruscan times. The division of the citizens fighting for Rome into centuries graded by wealth is said to have happened during the reign of King Servius Tullius, an Etruscan. Livy and Dionysius talk of a slightly different division into five classes, the first class wearing bronze armour, helmet, greaves and carrying a round shield with sword and spear, progressing to the fifth class, who were slingers and were one grade above the general public. Servius is also said to have increased the cavalry from six centuries to 12 – but the first 'plausible evidence', to quote Nicholas Sekunda, 'for the establishment of a force of true cavalry at Rome comes in 403BC'.[1] This was during the war with the Veii, which also saw the introduction of military pay. It is unlikely that there were many real cavalry soldiers before this.

◀ *Typical Roman re-enactment equipment – Lorica segmentata, manica (arm guard), scutum (shield, in this case linked to Legio XIV Gemina, which took part in the defeat of Boudicca) and belt (cingulum militare) whose studded baltea (thongs) end in pensilia (pendants).*

THE ARMY OF THE PUNIC WARS

The Punic Wars saw Rome become the Mediterranean superpower. To achieve this, the Romans first had to combat the wealthy Carthaginians at sea. Then, in a second bloody war they had to survive an onslaught on Italy itself by one of history's greatest military leaders, Hannibal Barca, before taking the fight to their enemies in Spain and, ultimately, Africa.

The Roman Army of the 2nd century BC was very different to the Greek-influenced hoplite phalanx that had won the Samnite wars. They fought in legions formed of maniples (see p. 000 for a discussion of the manipular legion's tactics), some 4,200 legionaries with 300 cavalry attached were divided into 60 maniples per legion, each maniple divided into two centuries. The legion lined up against the enemy in four distinct groupings: light skirmishers (*velites*) first, then the heavier infantry in three ranks – *hastati*, *principes* and *triarii* at the rear. The cavalry, organised in turmae of 30 men, protected the flanks.

This was still a militia army, whose order of battle was determined by wealth: the cavalry horse owners, the richest; the lightly armed *velites* the poorest. Most of the levy owned property of 400 denarii, served between the ages of 17 and 46 as *iuniores* (up to 50 in times of emergency) usually to a maximum of six years in one legion at a time and up to 16 years in total (infantry) or 10 (cavalry).

The length of the Punic Wars, however, began to change this. While the common ties of citizenship and obligation were sufficient to ensure that Romans were prepared to serve in the army at the beginning of this period, the lengthy campaigns – some overseas – and the need for troops to garrison the territories conquered changed the length and character of military service. Nic Fields quotes Hopkins's figures that estimate the percentage of the adult male citizens serving as 17 per cent (in 225BC) growing to 29 per cent (in

213BC).[2] When the grave losses of manpower are also taken into account, it is unsurprising that the next century would see changes to the composition of the army.

On top of the Roman citizens who served there was a large number of *socii Latini* – Latin allies – involved: usually in *alae* (wings) of the same size as the companion legion, and with as much as three times the cavalry of the Roman units. The allies mainly supplied light infantry – such as, later, Pompey's cohorts of slingers – and, increasingly, cavalry.

THE FIRST PUNIC WAR

At the time of the First Punic War, Rome controlled the whole Italian peninsula and most of their allies were required to supply troops. The number of soldiers provided by the allies was determined by the treaties that bound them: strong treaties whose durability, Nic Fields identifies, 'is famous, and here we should note the great difficulty that Hannibal had in detaching Rome's allies in Italy.'[3] This meant a substantial increase in the number of men available to fight – in 225BC Polybius says as many as 750,000 were in the pool – and they were needed. The losses sustained in the First Punic War were mainly at sea where legionaries fought as marines. Indeed, two of the greatest losses of life were caused by storms: off Camarina in 255BC, Polybius says that the Romans lost 280 ships and 100,000 men; and in 254BC, a further 150 ships were lost with large numbers of dead.

THE SECOND PUNIC WAR

The *casus belli*, as Polybius recounts, was not just the Carthaginian siege of Saguntum – but Carthaginian anger for the Roman appropriation of Sardinia in 238BC while the

▼ *One of the few depictions of military figures of the 2nd century BC, the 'Altar of Domitius Ahenobarbus' shows (left to right) a census, a lustrum ceremony and the levy of the army.*

TWO OF ROME'S GREATEST DEFEATS

Battle: Carrhae (53BC)
Sources: Plutarch; Cassius Dio
Opponents: Roman Republic against Parthian Empire
Location: Carrhae, Upper Mesopotamia
Romans: 40,000–50,000
Parthians: 10,000
Result: Decisive Parthian victory. (Romans 20,000 killed, 10,000 captured; Parthians 50 cataphracts killed)
Progress: Crassus and his son Publius arrogantly underestimated the Parthians and paid the ultimate price. The Romans were humiliated when, with their cavalry lured away by a feigned retreat and then destroyed and having been attacked by horse archers, they formed protective *testudos* that were shattered by the Parthian heavy cataphracts and then finished off by the archers.

Battle: Teutoburg Forest (9AD)
Sources: Tacitus; Suetonius; Cassius Dio
Opponents: Roman Empire against a confederation of Germanic tribes
Location: Lower Saxony
Romans: 20,000–36,000 (three legions and auxiliaries)
Germans: 12,000–32,000
Result: Decisive German victory (20,000 Romans killed)
Progress: Tricked and betrayed by the cunning German leader Arminius (who grew up in Rome as a hostage and knew its ways), Varus thoroughly prepared his army and his own oblivion by blindly following Arminius into the Teutoburg Forest without scouts or reconnaissance. Trapped in heavily wooded, swampy terrain that made manoeuvring impossible, the Romans were set upon from all sides and completely destroyed.

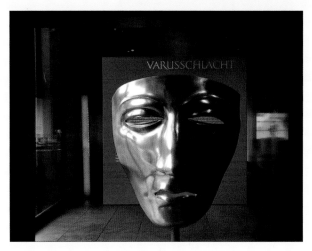

▲ *The Romans' defeat in the Teutoburg Forest is remembered in the Varusschlacht museum with this outsize recreation of a cavalryman's mask.*

► *Coins found on the site of the Battle of Teutoburg Forest, and displayed at the Varusschlacht (Varus battle) museum at Kalkriese, a likely site of part of the battle.*

Carthaginians were putting down a war with the mercenaries they had used but remained unpaid after the First Punic War. Hamilcar Barca, Hannibal's father, undertook the conquest of Spain 'with the object of using the resources thus obtained for the war against Rome.'[4]

If the Romans had thought the First Punic War hard, the second was even worse. In 218BC, having crossed the Alps with a large army, Hannibal inflicted a series of crushing defeats on the Roman Army as he attempted to split the Romans and their allies. That he wasn't able to do so save for some southern cities after Cannae and Sicily, combined with the clever delaying tactics of Fabius 'Cunctator' (delayer) and the threat to Carthaginian territories in Spain meant that Hannibal couldn't be reinforced: these were the factors that allowed Rome to hang on in spite of its heavy initial losses.

As was the case in so many of the wars fought by Roman's citizen army, the experienced troops of the first war had returned and it took some time to train them and mould them into an effective fighting force. The Romans raised as many as 11 legions in 217BC but in the field had suffered losses to Hannibal at Trebia (218BC), Lake Trasimene (217BC) and Cannae (216BC), and in Spain (in 211BC) to Hannibal's brother Hasdrubal.

The longevity of the Punic Wars also stretched the Romans' allies: in 209BC Livy reports their representatives telling the Roman consuls: 'before they reached the last stage of depopulation and famine, to refuse to Rome what the necessities of their situation would very soon make it impossible to grant … There were at the time thirty colonies belonging to Rome. Twelve of these announced to the consuls through their representatives in Rome that they had no means from which to furnish either men or money.'[5]

Some 17 years later, however, Rome had managed to weather the storm and a brilliant home-grown general, P. Cornelius Scipio won the *agnomen* Africanus by finally defeating Hannibal at Zama (202BC) near Carthage. In all, the

▲ *A Carthaginian coin with Melkart (Hercules) on the obverse, probably with the features of Hannibal Barca.*

sources suggest that Rome lost 300,000 men in the successful war that had started so disastrously. The Romans had shown that they might be slow starters, but they were dogged. Livy said about the war: 'And yet, great as was their strength, the hatred they felt towards each other was almost greater.'[6] The two sides fought to the finish and Rome had more men than Hannibal and in the end that showed.

THE THIRD PUNIC WAR

The doggedness of the Roman military system was shown in the first two Punic Wars. After them Rome showed its ruthlessness. Between the second and final war against Carthage Rome conquered much of Greece and 146BC saw both Carthage routed at the end of the Third Punic War and Greece in Roman hands, with both Carthage and Corinth utterly destroyed. In the latter, the male population was put to the sword and the women and children sold into slavery. Corinth was refounded by Julius Caesar, but the viciousness of the Roman actions in 146BC showed a hard edge that put booty ahead of other considerations.

THE PRICE OF PEACE

The period of peace between the end of Greek wars and the start of the Dalmatian Wars in 156BC had a weakening effect on the Roman Army. Indeed, the Senate was pleased to get Rome embroiled in a war after 12 years of peace – Polybius 'described it as a useful opportunity to keep Roman armies fit in times of general peace' (Dzino, 2005). Its success in Dalmatia (the war ended in 155BC with the Dalmatae's capital destroyed) ensured a Roman victory. It was becoming obvious, however, that Roman interests now spanned a large enough area that a militia army was going to struggle to maintain its commitments.

MARIAN REFORMS

It is Gaius Marius who is credited with the next significant changes to the Roman war machine, though it's likely that some of his innovations had their genesis earlier, particularly the development and use of the cohort rather than the maniple – the first use of cohorts was by P. Cornelius Scipio in Spain (as identified in Livy).

Marius was a mould breaker, a new man who used new methods, and it's not surprising that he latched on to this new tactical approach and perfected it. The Marian reforms are summarised thus:

- He created a standing army, provided with clothing and weapons by the state, although it must also be said that deductions were made from the soldiers' *stipendia* to cover these costs. Few people would have chosen to enter the army for the pay.
- Recruitment for this army was thrown open to any citizen who volunteered, irrespective of property, qualifications or poverty. This meant that most of the army was made up of men who had signed on for a career; conscription was only used *in extremis*. Conscription had been difficult for some time, mainly because people didn't want to serve for many years away from Rome – especially in Spain, where the loot was poor and the guerrilla fighting tough. The army had certainly opened its doors to poorer citizens over the years and Gabba talks about the fact that the army had been 'proletarianized' before Marius.
- Once a man had served his time, he got a pension and a grant of land. On top of this, men from the Italian allied states (Etruria, Picenum, etc.) who served were granted Roman citizenship. Poor people could see Marius' veterans getting land in Africa and north Italy and wanted something similar. The problem with this was that it made the men much more supportive of a good commander (who could make them rich with booty and land) than the state (which gave them nothing). This would cause big problems in the 1st century BC.
- Tactical changes from manipular legion to cohort legion (see p133–4). This meant that each legion was composed of 10 cohorts, each cohort of six centuries, each century of 80 men. On top of these, officers, NCOs, artillerymen, engineers and artificers swelled the legion's numbers.
- Improved training: physical, with daily full-pack route marches; fighting, through combat training.
- Improved logistics: Marius made the soldiers

responsible for carrying their own kit (which is why they became known as Marius' mules – see p93). This added to their flexibility, speed of movement and readiness for action. Each legion's baggage train was supervised by slaves (*calones*).
- The command structure of the legion started with a consul, proconsul, praetor or *propraetor*, the first two able to command more than one legion. The officers were *legati* – senators – and tribunes; the NCOs centurions, *optiones* (chosen by the centurions; *optio* =

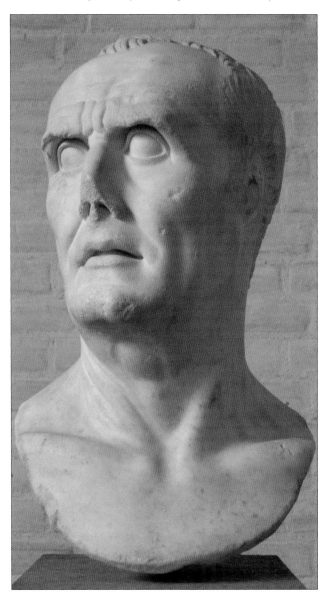

▶ *Said to be of Gaius Marius, this bust was found at Tusculum (modern-day Frascati).*

JULIUS CAESAR'S CAMPAIGNS

Campaign in Gaul (58–51BC)
- Against the Helvetii 58BC: Battle of the Arar, Battle of Bibracte
- Against the Suebi 58BC: Battle of Vosges
- Against the Belgae 57BC: Battle of the Sabis
- Against the Veneti 56BC
- Over the Rhine 56BC
- Campaign in Britain: 55 and 54BC
- Campaign against the Eborones: 54–53BC
- Campaign against Vercingetorix: 52BC Battle of Alesia

Civil war (49–45BC)
- Crossing the Rubicon 49BC
- March on Rome 49BC
- Hispanian campaign 49BC: Battle of Ilerda
- Greek, Illyrian and African campaigns 48BC: Battle of Dyrrhachium, Battle of Pharsalus
- Egyptian dynastic struggle 47BC
- War against Pharnaces 47BC: Battle of Zila
- Campaign in Africa 46BC: Battle of Ruspina, Battle of Thapsus
- Second Hispanian campaign 45BC: Battle of Munda

◄ *Statue of Julius Caesar on Mussolini's Via dei Fori Imperiali in Rome, which carved its way over important sites including the forums of Trajan, Augustus, Caesar and Nerva.*

choose) and signallers. Marius cut back the standards and flags and concentrated on the eagle.

The Social War (91–88BC) helped foster the Marian changes. The war was fought by the Republic against its Italian allies whose rebellion mixed a desire for Roman citizenship on the one hand, with the desire of many Italians to be rid of the hegemony of Rome. The ultimate victory went to the former, although it took much bloodshed before it did. Once accomplished, the additional pool of citizens available for military service was considerably larger (the census in 115–114BC shows 394,336 registered; that for 70–69BC documents 910,000). Their undivided loyalty to Rome may not have been as strong as that of citizens of the past, but it certainly improved recruiting options. With so many men available, and the poor volunteering for the army as a profession, so the wealthy began to reduce their involvement other than in command positions. The soldiers wanted booty and gave loyalty to a good, charismatic commander, as Sulla and Caesar both proved when they asked their soldiers to follow them against other Romans (Sulla against Norbanus at Capua in 82BC and Caesar crossing the Rubicon in 49BC).

The Marian reforms had produced an effective fighting force. This would be taken one step further by Julius Caesar, whose army was welded together by long years of war.

CAESAR'S ARMY
The army of Julius Caesar was victorious in the bloody civil war that followed his campaign in Gaul. A veteran army, flexible and well led, at its core were seven legions that had fought with him for nearly 15 years: VII, VIII, IX, X, XI, XII and XIII. (Altogether, 27 legions fought for Caesar at one time or another.) Included is the special Legio X Equestris, his favourite legion, which got its *cognomen* after legionaries were mounted to take the place of Gallic auxiliaries he did not trust in a meeting with King Ariovistus in 58BC.

Caesar's veterans were bound to him not just by the time they had served or his charismatic leadership, but also by the promise of land when they were pensioned off and suitable rewards – donatives or booty. On more than one occasion – from the Rubicon through to his African campaign of 46BC – he had to reason with and cajole troops who were not yes men and needed more than Caesar's name to make them take up their swords and fight. Caesar was helped by the seasoned officers and staff he had built up, whose political life and future positions were linked closely to his. The Republic armies from Marius onwards may seem to have been the hired henchmen of important leaders but that's not quite all of the story. Veterans are less likely than new recruits to be overawed by big names and more likely to extract what they want in return for their service.

THE ARMY OF THE PRINCIPATE

The army of the Principate took over where Caesar had left off. A completely professional army, it was based on two major components: the legion and the *auxilia*. We cover the legions, composed of Roman citizens who had signed up for 16 years' service with a further four years as veterans, in much more detail later on.

AUXILIA

Throughout the Imperial era, a large component of the Roman Army was made up of *auxilia*. This supply of manpower was brought about because all the Empire's allies were required by treaty to provide troops when required. During Vespasian's rule, for example, some 80,000 troops were involved in his campaigns in Judea. Of these, only 20,000 were Roman legionaries.

The auxiliary troops were divided into two groups – the cavalry was organised into wings (*alae*), and the infantry units were sorted into cohorts (*cohors*):

- Infantry cohorts of 480 men (*cohors peditatae quingenariae*)
- Part-mounted cohorts added 120 horsemen (*cohors equitatae*)
- Double-strength cohorts with 800 infantrymen (*cohors peditatae milliariae*)
- Double-strength cohorts with 800 infantrymen and 240 cavalrymen (*cohors equitatae milliariae*)
- Cavalry *ala quingenariae* of 512 men
- Cavalry *ala milliaria* of 768

Although most soldiers joined up when they were young – contemporary records show that the average age was around 22 – they typically served for the same length of time as the legionaries' years, and so usually left in their 40s.

SPECIALIST FORCES

Many of the *auxilia* were horsemen. The Romans were not natural horsemen, and most of the better cavalrymen hailed from northern Europe and Africa. It has been said that the biggest weakness of the Roman military machine lay with the relative paucity of its cavalry. This depended on the fitness of its horses for its survival, and so while pack animals were generally given low-grade fodder, the logistical supply system was set up to ensure that the mounts were provided with a high-quality diet. Modern estimates suggest that under normal conditions they would have been given daily about 2.5kg (5.5lb) of hard fodder such as barley and about 7kg (15.5lb) of dry fodder, most of which would have been hay. They also needed a lot of water – around 25–30 litres (5.5–6.5 gallons) a day in temperate climates, but more when it was hot and dry. It is thought that the barley was carried by mules from the supply train, whereas the hay was collected locally. The horses used by the cavalry not

DEPLOYMENTS OF IMPERIAL *AUXILIA*

Paul Holder's detailed analysis of known deployments of Imperial *auxilia* around AD130 showed these numbers for units from Britannia to Mauretania:

Alae (mill)	88 (7)
Cohortes (mill)	293 (30)
Total aux units	381
Aux infantry	152,260
Aux cavalry	71,468
Total	223,728

Britannia had 56 units, Dacia 43, Syria 55 and Mauretania 40.

▼ *Tombstone of a Roman auxiliary trooper from Cologne, dating to the second half of the 1st century AD. Note his long* spatha, *introduced to the Romans by Celtic* auxilia.

▲ *Caracalla as he liked to be represented: as a soldier. He spent both time and money on his legions but that didn't stop his assassination by a disaffected soldier near Carrhae.*

▶ *Arch of Caracalla at Volubilis in Morocco. The Severan dynasty originated in north Africa and the city governor raised the arch to honour the emperor in 217.*

his sons, 'make the soldiers rich'. Herodian said, 'In gratitude for his deliverance and in return for the sole rule, he promised each soldier 2,500 denarii and increased their ration allowance by one-half. He ordered the praetorians to go immediately and take the money from the temple depositories and the treasuries. In a single day he recklessly distributed all the money which Severus had collected and hoarded from the calamities of others over a period of eighteen years.'[7]

Second, he provided a bigger pool of recruits for the legions. Surprisingly, from the times of Augustus and Tiberius there were fewer Roman citizens willing to enlist in the Roman legions. There were several reasons for this. Military service in the legions was harsh and not particularly attractive as the soldiers had to serve long years before they could retire; discharge bonuses were unsatisfactory; the pay barely sufficient; and there was little possibility for career advancement. Because they didn't want to serve in the legions, citizens began to enlist in the *auxilia*, mainly the cavalry because the pay was better. Vegetius said about *auxilia palatina* of the later Empire, 'There is also another reason why the legions have become weakened: the fatigue of military service is greater in them, just as the arms are heavier, the assignments more numerous, the discipline more rigorous. To avoid all this, most hurry to take an oath in the auxiliary troops where they sweat less and earn wages more rapidly.'

There was also one further element to the Roman Army: the use of external 'barbarian' units, of which there were three main types:

- *Numeri* – irregular auxiliary units (later a *numerus* is a regular infantry unit in the Dominate's *limitanei* or border forces).
- *Foederati* – entire tribes were paid to supply warriors to fight with the Romans. As an example, Alaric led a band of *foederati*.
- *Dediticii* – specialised units such as Caracalla's bodyguards. He enjoyed wearing one of their cloaks (*caracallus*) from which he got his nickname.

only had to carry their riders, but their weapons, armour and rations too. The extra weight thus imposed is not known, but informed estimates suggest around 40kg (88lb).

Other specialist auxiliary troops included archers (*sagittarii*), camel corps (*dromedariorum*), lancers (*contarii*), slingers (*funditores*) and scouts (*exploratores* or *numeri*).

CITIZENSHIP FOR (ALMOST) ALL

In AD212, Caracalla dropped a bombshell on the Roman world, changing one of the key elements of Roman life: citizenship. For so many years an issue, at a stroke his *Constitutio Antoniniana* edict of AD212 granted citizenship to almost all freemen in the Empire – although a clause excluded the *dediticii,* those whose country had been conquered but who had remained free, and former slaves who were identified as a threat and weren't allowed with a hundred miles of Rome. The reasons for the edict have been much debated.

First, and most obviously, Caracalla increased revenue that was needed to fund the army. Septimius Severus had said to

RAPID RESPONSE UNITS

In the latter years of the Principate, with problems seemingly on every border, it became essential to have a fast, mobile force that could act as a military fire brigade. Septimius Severus' Legio II Parthica was such a unit. Based near Rome, it was available to be used as necessary around the Empire and spent most of its time in Syria. Gallienus went one step better, creating cavalry units, the *comitatenses*, that could be dispatched anywhere in the Empire in short order – something that was taken further in the Dominate where the army was divided into the legions on the borders and mobile field armies ready to react to incursions.

THE SIZE OF THE ROMAN ARMY

Date	Legions	Men	Auxiliary	PG etc*	Total
6th C BC					19,000 (inc 1,800 cavalry)
340BC	2		2 + cavalry		40,000 (inc 4,800 cavalry)
280BC	8		8 + cavalry		90,000 (inc 10,000 cavalry)
212BC	23				128,000 (inc 13,000 cavalry)
44BC	37				Difficult to assess because many understrength; at least 300,000
27BC	60				Difficult to assess because many understrength; at least 300,000
AD14	25	125,000	125,000	10,000	260,000 (inc 30,000 cavalry)
AD24	25	125,000	125,000	5,000	255,000
AD107	30	165,000	224,000	15,000	400,000 (inc 70,000 cavalry)
AD135	28	154,000	224,000	15,000	390,000 (inc 70,000 cavalry)
AD166/167	30	165,000	224,000	15,000	400,000 (inc 70,000 cavalry)
AD211	33	182,000	250,000	20,000	450,000 (inc 75,000 cavalry)
AD 3rd C crisis	36	200,000	300,000+		500,000+
AD275	37–38	209,000	250,000	20,000	480,000
AD305	53–56	265–280,000	250,000	24,000	540–550,000

* Praetorian Guard, Urban Cohorts etc

THE BORDERS OF THE EMPIRE

Whether they were primarily a military defence system or designed to control passage of people and goods, the borders of the Roman Empire would be difficult to police today, let alone 2,000 years ago when the fastest method of transport was a horse. However, remarkably, the Romans tried to do just that.

In the north of Britain, Hadrian's Wall – or for a brief time the more northerly Antonine Wall – was the start of a complex border system that encompassed much of the Empire.

Elsewhere, making the most of natural features, the Germanic and Raetian limes (the word gives us 'limit' but wasn't used by the Romans) started at the North Sea and ran along the banks of the Rhine to the Danube: from Lugdunum Batavorum (Katwijk, Netherlands) to Castra Regina

▼ *The Roman naval base at Flevum – possibly Vechten in North Holland – expanded to support Germanicus' punitive raids on the Germans. It included ship sheds and slipways. It was well placed at the northerly edge of the Empire's border.*

(Regensburg, Germany), a length of 550km (340 miles). However, there's a 300km (185-mile) gap between the two rivers from Mogontiacum (Mainz) to Castra Regina and this had to be filled with a ditch, mound and palisade, watchtowers and fortresses (there's a reconstruction at Saalburg). From there, it followed the Danube along Noricum, Pannonia and Illyricum to Dacia, Moesia and the Black Sea – although Dacia, on the north bank of the Danube, was a province for nearly two centuries.

In Africa, the *Fossatum Africae* – African ditch – dwarfs Hadrian's Wall. Mentioned in the AD312 *Codex Theodosianus*, there is some doubt it existed but the idea was championed by French archaeologist Jean Lucien Baradez, who

▶ *Watchtowers shown on Trajan's Column. The border was not simply a military boundary, but in Pannonia and Dacia it performed an important military function, as a tripwire for invaders.*

conducted aerial surveys that provided evidence of a frontier barrier made up of ditches, embankments and watchtowers. He identified four main segments – Hodna or Bou Taleb (100km/62 miles), Tobna (50km/31 miles), Gemellae (60km/37 miles) and Ad Majores (70km/43 miles) – and the obvious similarities between it and other Roman limes suggested an African barrier up to 750km (465 miles) in length. Conjecture it may be, but the idea of a customs barrier is certainly feasible: the *portorium* (duty on imports, mostly on luxuries such as spices, precious stones, silks and other fabrics, ivory, animals and slaves) was an important source of revenue, and those who collected it – the *portitores* – were as reviled then as they are today.

SHIFTING BOUNDARIES

The limes changed over the years: the Romans left Dacia, for example, in AD275, although Constantine the Great campaigned there in AD328, and walls and barriers were pushed north of the Danube. In Britain and Gaul, the threat of invasion from the Saxons led to a line of Saxon Shore forts being built on both sides of the English Channel. Those in Britain named in the *Notitia Dignitatum* came under the *Comes Litoris Saxonici per Britanniam* (Count of the Saxon Shore in Britain): Branodunum (Brancaster), Gariannonum (Burgh Castle), Othona (Bradwell-on-Sea), Regulbium (Reculver), Rutupiae (Richborough), Dubris (Dover Castle), Portus Lemanis (Lympne), Anderitum (Pevensey Castle) and Portus Adurni (Portchester Castle). There are others that were probably included, and many watchtowers.

ARMING THE FRONTIERS

It's difficult to put a figure on the numbers of men involved in these defensive structures. As is obvious from an analysis of the forts and watchtowers along Hadrian's Wall, not all were fully manned all the time. However, in times of trouble – and there were increasingly more of them from the 2nd century AD – they required a lot of manpower. It's no coincidence that most of the Roman legions spent much of their time along the borders. Indeed, as time wore on these units became *limitanei* or *ripenses* as the military reorganisations led to frontier armies.

▶ *The limes push out in a salient north of Mainz and then head south towards the Danube. This is at Idstein in Germany.*

▼ *Reconstruction of a watchtower on the Rhine in the Netherlands between Kesteren and Wageningen. There were legionary fortresses at Nijmegen and Xanten.*

THE LEGIONS

Nothing epitomises our view of the Roman soldier more than the legions. These were the building blocks of the Roman Army. From the ordinary legionaries to the *primus pilus* centurion, the *aquilifer* with the legion's eagle standard to the *cornicens* with their horns, the images still speak to us.

▲ *Legio II Augusta's symbols were capricorn (left) and the winged horse Pegasus. This is from Hadrian's Wall – the legion was in England from AD43.*

Under the Republic, Roman legions were part of a citizen army that was chosen from its population as needed to fulfil the state's requirements. Because they supplied their own weapons, the rich were heavily involved and it was only as the Republic grew in size that the opportunity to serve was extended to poorer citizens. Originally signed up for campaigns, this also altered over time as the fighting took place further away from Rome and for longer periods.

There were initially two legions – one for each consul – but this number soon grew, particularly at time of need. During the first Punic War there were 20. The legions were numbered as they were created and if they overwintered for any reason, the numbers and personnel could be changed. The legions were not longstanding: the men fighting were always citizens and there was no professional standing army.

By the time that Caesar was fighting in Gaul, things were changing. There were still conscripts who had to serve for a maximum of six years, but there were also volunteers who had signed up for 16. These volunteers allowed Caesar to increase the size of his army from his original four legions (VII–X): by 52BC he had 12. During the civil war against Pompey, this number grew to over 30 – and at the end of the war, Caesar incorporated the defeated Pompey's legions into his own army. Some of these legions would form the basis for Imperial legions.

Mark Antony raised a number of legions for his war against Octavian. Around autumn 32BC/spring 31BC he minted – probably at his base at Patrae (Patras, Greece) – coins that named his 23 units: legions, his Praetorian Guard and Cohors Speculatores (the latter were scouts, messengers or spies, usually to be found in each legion). Most of the coins were silver denarii (with a poor level of silver); there were gold aurei for 11 of them. All had a galley or a naval theme on the obverse; the reverse carried an eagle between legionary standards (save the Cohors Speculatores, which carried three standards). The units identified are: prima, II, III, IIII/IV, V Alaudae, VI Ferrata, VII, VIII, IX, X, XI, XII Antiqua, XIII, XIV/XIIII, XV, XVI, XVII Classica, XVIII Lybica, XIX/XVIIII, XX, XXI, XXII, XXIII, Cohors Praetoria, Cohors Speculatores.

Augustus, after the final battle of the war against Mark Antony, had some 60 legions. He reduced these to 28 by various means, incorporating some of Antony's into his own, retiring others.

These are the 28 legions that were

◄ *Detail from the sarcophagus of tribune T. Flavius Mikkalos (1st century AD). Note the helmets: Mikkolos is being handed a broad-brimmed crested one by an officer wearing similar. The man at right has a plumed Montefortino helmet.*

set up by Augustus, most founded before the Principate with the probable founder in brackets:

I* Germanica (Caesar)
II** Augusta (Augustus)
III Augusta (Augustus)
III Cyrenaica (Antony)
III Gallica (Caesar)
IV Macedonica (Caesar)
IV Scythica (Antony)
V Alaudae (Caesar)
V Macedonica (Augustus)
VI Ferrata (Caesar)
VI Victrix (Augustus)
VII Claudia (Caesar)
VIII Augusta (Caesar)
IX Hispana (Augustus)
X Fretensis (Augustus)
X Gemina+ (Lepidus)
XI Claudia (Augustus)
XII Fulminata (Lepidus)
XIII Gemina+ (Caesar)
XIV Gemina+ (Caesar)
XV Apollinaris (Augustus)
XVI Gallica (Augustus)
XVII*** (Augustus)
XVIII*** (Augustus)
XIX*** (Augustus)
XX Valeria Victrix (Augustus)
XXI Rapax (Augustus)
XXII Deiotariana (Caesar)

* Originally named *Augusta*, its title was withdrawn/unit was disbanded under Augustus and possibly reconstituted under Tiberius. Earned this *cognomen* after AD9. Disbanded after the Batavian Revolt.
** Originally named *Sabine*.
*** Destroyed in AD9 in the Teutoburg Wald. The actual numbers of these legions are unknown other than Legio XIX.
+ Three legions named *Gemina* – twin – may well have been formed from the amalgamation of other units.

There are a number of sources for information about the legions – three giving us full lists. The first source is Tacitus, who identified the number of legions in AD23 in Book 4 of his *Annales*:

Rhine: 8	Egypt: 2	Moesia: 2
Spain: 3	Syria: 4	Dalmatia: 2
Africa: 2	Pannonia: 2	

He notes that the two legions in Dalmatia were not too far away from Italy should it require sudden aid. The capital was garrisoned by three city and nine Praetorian cohorts.

The second source is an inscription found on a column base – the Colonetta Maffei – in the Forum in Rome (ILS 2288). This dates to Marcus Aurelius' reign (AD160s), showing the legions and where they are located. Since it is given as a clockwise list starting in Britain, it's obvious there are two later additions: II and III Italica (formed *c.*AD165–166) and Septimius Severus' three Parthian legions (formed AD197). I and III Parthica served in the east but II Parthica was based in Albanum, Italy – although it spent much time in Syria (as shown by epigraphic material in Apamea). In the 130 or so years between Tacitus and this column base inscription, deployment differences emerge. There are fewer legions in Hispania, Egypt and on the Rhine but more in the Balkans and on the Danube (note the inclusion of II and III Italica, raised by Marcus Aurelius around AD166); three in Britain; and a number in the east.

▲ *Part of the tombstone of Titus Calidius Severus, centurion of Legio XV Apollinaris who died in Carnuntum aged 58 after 34 years' service – 25 years in cohors I Alpinorum and then, having become a Roman citizen, for nine years as a centurion in the XVth. The detail shows scale armour (*lorica squamata*), vitis (staff of office), crested helmet and greaves.*

▼ *Reproduction of a bronze statue of Marcus Aurelius, on the top of the Capitoline Hill. He raised two legions – II and III Italica – to fight against the Marcomanni. Legio II's emblem was Romulus and Remus with the she-wolf to identify that the legion was founded by Aurelius and co-emperor Lucius Verus. Legio III Italica was stationed on the Danube for much of its long life.*

▲ *Typical tactics: the legionaries advance with drawn swords as they attack in a tight formation.*

Britain: 3
II Augusta (Isca (Augusta) – Caerleon, Wales)
VI Victrix (Eboracum – York, England)
XX Victrix (Deva – Chester, England)
Germania Superior: 2
VIII Augusta (Argentorate – Strasbourg, France)
XXII Primigenia (Mogontiacum – Mainz, Germany)
Germania Inferior: 2
I Minervia (Bonna – Bonn, Germany)
XXX Ulpia Victrix (Vetera – Xanten, Germany)
Pannonia Superior: 3
I Adiutrix (Brigetio – Szöny, Hungary)
X Gemina (Vindobona– Vienna, Austria)
XIIII Gemina (Carnuntem – Bad Deutsch-Altenburg, Austria)
Pannonia Inferior: 1
II Adiutrix (Aquincum – Budapest, Hungary)
Moesia Superior: 2
IIII Flavia (Singidunum – Belgrade, Serbia)

VII Claudia (Viminacium – Kostolac, Serbia)
Moesia Inferior: 3
I Italica (Novae – Svistov, Bulgaria)
V Macedonica (Troesmis – Turcoaia, Romania)
XI Claudia (Durostorum – Silistra, Bulgaria)
Dacia: 1
XIII Gemina (Apulum – Alba Iulia, Romania)
Cappadocia: 2
XII Fulminata (Battalgazi-Melitene – Eskimalatya, Turkey)
XV Apollinaris (Satala – Sadak, Turkey)
Syria: 3
III Gallica (Raphanaea – Baarin, Syria)
IIII Scythia (Zeugma – Belkis, Turkey)
XVI Flavia (Samosata – Samsat, Turkey)
Judea: 2
VI Ferrata (Legio – Megiddo, Israel)
X Fretensis (Hierosolyma – Jerusalem, Israel)
Arabia: 1
III Cyrenaica (Bostra – Busra, Syria)
Egypt: 1
II Traiana (Nicopolis – Alexandria, Egypt)
Numidia: 1
III Augusta (Lambaesis – Tazoult-Lambèse, Algeria)
Hispania: 1

▲ *A re-enactor models a full-face mask and helmet. There's debate about whether these 'parade' or 'sport' helmets were ever used in battle.*

VII Gemina (Legio – León, Spain)
Noricum: 1
II Italica (Albing, Austria)
Raetia: 1
III Italica (Castra Regina – Regensburg, Germany)
Mesopotamia: 2
I Parthica (Singara – Sinjar, Iraq)
III Parthica (Resaina – Ra's al-'Ayn, Syria)
Italy: 1
II Parthica (Castra Albana – Albano Laziale, Italy)

(Source: Dessau, Hermann: *Inscriptiones Latinae Selectae*; accessed online and Bishop, M.C. (2012) – location information.)

The third source, from the late 2nd/early 3rd century AD, Cassius Dio lists the same legions (without Severus' three *Parthica* legions) identifying the following – very much the same information with minor differences. He also identifies who raised the original legion (emperor in brackets).

Britannia Inferior: 1
VI Victrix (Augustus)
Britannia Superior: 2
II Augusta (Augustus)
XX Valeria Victrix (Augustus)
Germania Superior: 2
VIII Augusta (Augustus)
XXII Primigenia (Dio identifies Augustus but he's in error: this legion was set up by Claudius)
Germania Inferior: 2
I Minervia (Domitian)
XXX Germanica (renamed Ulpia) (Trajan)
Pannonia Superior: 2
X Gemina (Augustus)
XIV Gemina (Augustus)
Pannonia Inferior: 2
I Adiutrix (Galba)
II Adiutrix (Vespasian)
Moesia Superior: 2
IIII Flavia (Vespasian)
VII Claudia (Augustus)
Moesia Inferior: 2

▼ *Xanten (Colonia Ulpia Traiana) archaeological park. Nearby was the two-legionary fort Vetera I, where at least one of Varus' legions was stationed.*

I Italica (Nero)
XI Claudia (Augustus)
Dacia: 2
V Macedonica (Augustus)
XIII Gemina (Augustus)
Cappadocia: 2
XII Fulminata (Augustus)
XV Apollinaris (Augustus)
Syria: 3
III Gallica (Augustus)
IIII Scythica (Augustus)
XVI Flavia (Vespasian)
Judea: 2
VI Ferrata (Augustus)
X Fretensis (Augustus)
Arabia: 1
III Cyrenaica (Augustus)
Egypt: 1
II Aegyptia (renamed Traiana) (Trajan)
Numidia: 1
III Augusta (Augustus)
Hispania: 1
VII Gemina (Galba)
Noricum: 1
II Italica (M. Aurelius)
Raetia: 1
III Italica (M. Aurelius)
Mesopotamia: 2
I and III Parthica (Severus)
Italy: 1
II Parthica (Severus)

What these lists don't show is the way that elements of these legions – vexillations, so called because they carried the *vexillum* flag – were distributed as necessary through the Empire, sometimes as bodyguards or to put down rebellions.

Many of these legions survived after the Principate, for the next two centuries. They had created long-term bases with legionary fortresses – such as Isca (Caerleon), Deva (Chester) and Eboracum (York) in England, or Bonna (Bonn), Mogontiacum (Mainz), Castra Regina (Regensburg) and Vetera (two fortresses in Xanten) in Germany. The *Notitia Dignitatum* (a record of all the appointments in the Empire dated to AD395 for the east and AD420 for the west) shows 24 of these 33 legions remaining, unmoved, for nearly 200 years. However, many new legions had been created – over 180, some of which would have been created from detachments of the original legions. They were smaller and divided into those that were frontier garrisons (called *limitanei*) and field armies (*comitatenses*).

THE PRAETORIAN GUARD

Of all the Roman soldiers, the Praetorians were the most unusual. Elite, camped just outside Rome – until the Aurelian walls incorporated their fortress into the city walls – it's hard not to think of politics when one considers them. They have gone down in history as having raised emperors, assassinated emperors and even sold the Imperial seat to the highest bidder.

Inside Rome's sacred *pomerium* (the religious boundary that surrounded Roman cities), weapons could not be carried. The city was policed by the *cohortes urbanae* (urban cohorts – police force) and the *vigiles* (mainly watchmen and firefighters). The early emperors had a German bodyguard. Around 500 strong, made up mainly of Batavi (chosen because they had no political interests in Rome), it was dismissed by Galba in AD68 (which may well have contributed to the revolt of the Batavi in AD69). It was replaced by the *equites singulares Augusti*, a very similar body recruited from Roman auxiliary cavalry units.

The emperors also had the Praetorian Guard. Originating from the escorts used by senior magistrates or army commanders (praetors) of the Republic – Antony and Octavian had personal retinues, too – Augustus founded the Praetorian Guard as a personal security unit and it was there for the personal use of the emperor until it was disbanded by Constantine in AD312.

PRAETORIAN POLITICS

Housed on the doorstep of the city, it is unsurprising that it became involved in politics – although to what extent the rank and file were involved in this is debatable. Sandra Bingham, in her absorbing 1997 thesis on 'The praetorian guard in the political and social life of Julio-Claudian Rome', argues that this may well have been overstated. The fact that Tacitus identifies the commander of the Praetorians as being the third man to swear allegiance to Tiberius on his accession underlines the importance of the leader of the Guard, the Praetorian prefect, but the Guard itself was, more often than not, loyal to the emperor. Gibbon, however, summed up the traditional view of the guards as politicised:

> 'Such formidable servants are always necessary, but often fatal to the throne of despotism. By thus introducing the Praetorian guards as it were into the palace and the Senate, the emperors taught them to perceive their own strength, and the weakness of the civil government; to view the vices of their masters with familiar contempt, and to lay aside that reverential awe, which distance only, and mystery, can preserve

◄ *This relief, now in the Louvre, depicts Praetorians of around AD50. Note the footwear – ankle boots (*calcei*) rather than* caligae *(sandals) – the eagle standard, and the thick helmet crests.*

▲ The base of the Antonine Column, dedicated to the emperor in AD161. The Praetorians are in the centre surrounded by horsemen. Note the muscled breastplate of the officer (at left) and standard bearers.

towards an imaginary power. In the luxurious idleness of an opulent city, their pride was nourished by the sense of their irresistible weight; nor was it possible to conceal from them, that the person of the sovereign, the authority of the Senate, the public treasure, and the seat of empire, were all in their hands.'[8]

Certainly, it didn't take long for the Praetorians to be associated with intrigue, treachery and politics. Tiberius' Praetorian prefect – the fifth to hold the position – Lucius Aelius Sejanus, built up his position with Tiberius hoping, Tacitus maintained, for the highest office, poisoning Drusus, Tiberius' son and heir. When Tiberius decamped to Capri, he left Sejanus in charge, sharing the consulship with the emperor. The most powerful man in Rome, ultimately he was denounced to the emperor by Drusus' mother, Antonia, and strangled.

Sejanus' successor, Quintus Naevius Sutorius Macro, was then implicated in Tiberius' death and was arrested on Caligula's orders. He subsequently committed suicide. Three years later, the seventh Praetorian prefect, Marcus Arrecinus Clemens, was closely involved in the murder of Emperor Caligula. Although the Senate proclaimed the return of the Republic, Claudius was placed on the throne – and all viewers of the BBC's *I, Claudius* will remember Derek Jacobi being found hiding behind the curtains. It makes a nice story, but it's more likely that Claudius was involved in the coup, as Caligula exhibited the signs of murderous insanity Suetonius talks about.

PRAETORIAN PREFECTS DURING THE JULIO-CLAUDIAN DYNASTY

Dates	Name	End
Augustus (27BC–AD14)		
2BC–?	Publius Salvius Aper	
2BC–?	Quintus Ostorius Scapula	
?	Publius Varius Ligur	
Tiberius (AD14–37)		
?– AD15	Lucius Seius Strabo	
AD14–31	Lucius Aelius Sejanus	executed
Caligula (AD37–41)		
AD31–38	Quintus Naevius Sutorius Macro	suicide
AD38–41	Marcus Arrecinus Clemens	murdered Caligula
AD38–41	Lucius Arruntius Stella	
Claudius (AD41–54)		
AD41–43	Rufrius Pollio	
AD41–43	Catonius Justus	
AD43–50	Rufrius Crispinus	banished and, later, executed
AD47–50	Lucius Lusius Geta	
Nero (AD54–68)		
AD50–62	Sextus Afranius Burrus	possibly poisoned
AD62–65	Lucius Faenius Rufus	executed after Pisonian conspiracy
AD62–68	Gaius Ofonius Tigellinus	suicide after execution order
AD65–68	Gaius Nymphidius Sabinus	killed after pronouncing himself emperor

KEY POLITICAL EVENTS IN PRAETORIAN HISTORY

There are many more such stories of the Praetorians' involvement in politics, for instance:

- AD65 – involvement in the Pisonian conspiracy.
- AD68 – Gaius Nymphidius Sabinus attempted to have himself proclaimed emperor, saying he was Caligula's illegitimate son. The Praetorians killed him as Galba neared the city.
- AD69 – the Year of the Four Emperors, the Guard assassinated Emperor Galba.
- AD192 – the Emperor Commodus was assassinated in a conspiracy led by the Praetorian prefect Quintus Aemilius Laetus. His successor, Pertinax, was subsequently assassinated by the Guard in AD193 – in spite of the huge donative he gave them: Cassius Dio says it was 12,000 sesterces apiece. The Guard is then said to have auctioned off the Imperial position to the highest bidder as is graphically described by Dio, who was a contemporary of the events. Whether it is true or not – and Bingham discounts it – Didius Julianus paid 25,000 sesterces to each of the Guard for the position.
- AD217 – Caracalla was killed by a soldier on the orders of Praetorian prefect Macrinus, who then proclaimed himself emperor.
- AD222 – Emperor Elagabalus was assassinated by the Guard.
- AD228 – Praetorian prefect Ulpian is killed by the Guard for curtailing their privileges.
- AD238 – the Guard assassinated both emperors Pupienus and Balbinus.
- AD249 – the Praetorians assassinated Philippus II, son of Emperor Philip the Arab.
- AD306 – the Praetorians proclaimed Maxentius emperor.
- AD312 – Constantine the Great marched against Maxentius and beat him and his Praetorians at the Battle of the Milvian Bridge. With the death of Maxentius, Constantine disbanded the Praetorian Guard, dispersing those still alive around the Empire, and dismantled the Castra Praetoria.

LIFE AND TIMES OF MARCUS VETTIUS VALENS

It's certainly hard on paper to discount the Praetorian Guard's involvement in the political life of the Empire – after all, they were often used by the emperors to hold prisoners who would be later killed or forced to commit suicide – but to a great extent their involvement simply mirrored the political situation of the times. They were involved during political crises, when not just the Guard but much of the Empire was politically unstable. Between these times they served the emperors loyally, both in Rome and also on the battlefield. As an example – albeit unusually high-ranking – take the career of Marcus Vettius Valens (cited by Bingham, with translations by David Braund in *Augustus to Nero: A Sourcebook on Roman History, 31 BC–AD 68* and Duncan B. Campbell in *The Rise of Imperial Rome AD 14–193*) as shown on his tombstone in Ariminum (Rimini, Italy).

▲ *Stele remembering Pomponius Proculo, who served in Praetorian Cohort IV (given the title Pia Vindex 'faithful avenger') at the end of the 1st century* AD.

> M. Vettio M. f. Ani. I Valenti I mil. coh. VIII pr., benef. praef. pr., I donis donato bello Britan. I torquibus, armillis, phaleris, I evoc. Aug., corona aurea donat., I (centurioni) coh. VI vig., (centurioni) stat., (centurioni) coh. XVI urb., (centurioni) coh. I II pr., exercitatori equit. speculatorum, princip. I praetori leg. XIII Gem., ex trec. [p. p.] leg. VI I Victr., donis donato ob res prosper. I gest. contra Astures torq. phaler. arm., I trib. coh. V vig., trib. coh. XII urb., trib. coh. I. III pr., [p. p. II] leg. XIIII Gem. Mart. Victr., I proc. imp. [Neroni] Caes. Aug. prov. Lusitan., I patron. coloniae, speculator. X h. c, I L. Luccio Telesino C. Suetonio Paulino cos.

The career this charts is of a man – Marcus Vettius Valens – who started his military career (c.AD28) as a guardsman, distinguished himself in the Claudian invasion of Britain (AD43) as *beneficiarius* (clerk) to the Praetorian prefect Rufrius Pollo and was decorated with torques, *armillae* (bracelets) and *phalerae* (discs). Reaching his 16th year of service, he entered the reserve but returned to service (*evocatus*), with a *corona aurea* (golden crown) decoration, as was the case with many *evocati*. His progress through the ranks continued as he became centurion of the VI Cohort of Vigiles, then the Imperial messengers, followed by the XVI Urban Cohort before moving to the legions: first XIII Gemina and then as chief centurion (p. p. *primus pilus*) of Legio VI Victrix, where he was decorated again with torques, *armillae* and *phalerae* for his exploits against the Astures. Then it was back to Rome, where he took on tribuneships of the Cohors V Vigiles, Cohors XII Urban, Cohors III Praetorian and Legio XIV Gemina Mars Victrix, before his final appointment, procurator of Lusitania (southern Portugal/western Spain) – a position that could only be taken up by someone in the equestrian order. It is likely that Valens had friends in high places!

PRAETORIAN DUTIES

Until the reign of Vespasian, the Praetorians patrolled the palace and local towns helping the police and firefighters. Vespasian cancelled the guard service at the entry to the palace, but retained guards within the palace itself. They played an important role in maintaining civil order: for example, Titus Curtilius' slave revolt of AD24 was put down by a tribune and a force of Praetorians; in AD58, rioting by citizens of Puteoli upset about local government embezzlement was put down by Praetorians under Publius Sulpicius Scribonius and Rufus Sulpicius Scribonius. They policed the games, but also acted as the emperor's secret police, keeping an eye on the Imperial family (for both their protection and to ensure they didn't conspire against the emperor). They also confined and, as necessary, executed enemies of the state.

However, it's important not to forget their military assignments, the most important being:

- AD14 – after the death of Augustus, the armies on the Rhine and in Pannonia mutinied and were suppressed by two Praetorian cohorts, the Praetorian Cavalry, and Emperor Tiberius' German bodyguard.

- AD14 – in Germany, the Praetorians helped Tiberius' nephew and heir, Germanicus, to quell the mutiny and, afterwards, to advance into Germany and recover two of Varus' lost eagles.
- Under Domitian, the Praetorians fought again in Germany and then in Dacia, losing the Praetorian prefect Cornelius Fuscus, Legio V Alaudae and the eagle of the Praetorians in one misjudged expedition.
- Trajan's Dacian Wars heavily involved the Praetorians, who also served in the emperor's Parthian campaign (AD113–117).

- AD161–166 – the Praetorians fought under Lucius Verus in Parthia.
- AD169–175 and AD178–180 – Praetorians were at the front in Marcus Aurelius' wars with the Marcomanni, Quadi and Sarmatians.
- AD197–211 – Septimius Severus' new Praetorian Guard fought with him at Lugdunum (Lyon) and on into Britain.
- AD270–275 – Praetorians accompany Aurelian on his campaign against Palmyra.

CASTRA PRAETORIA

Originally dispersed around Italy – with some billeted in Rome – from the reign of Tiberius, the camp of the Praetorian Guard was situated on the Quirinal, outside Rome. In AD26, Sejanus grouped them and the urban cohorts in a large camp on the Esquiline Hill. The Castra Praetoria would later be incorporated in the Aurelian walls around Rome.

It wasn't a huge camp. There was a prison to hold defendants/those condemned to be executed (such as

Iullus Antonius for adultery with Julia, Augustus' daughter) and it had an armoury, but most of the usual camp amenities were missing; the city's would have been used. There are some two-storeyed barracks; some single. The walls have rooms for the soldiers, too. It's possible that the urban cohorts were in the two-storeyed buildings; the Praetorians elsewhere. Analysis of the arrangements shows accommodation for around 15,000 men.

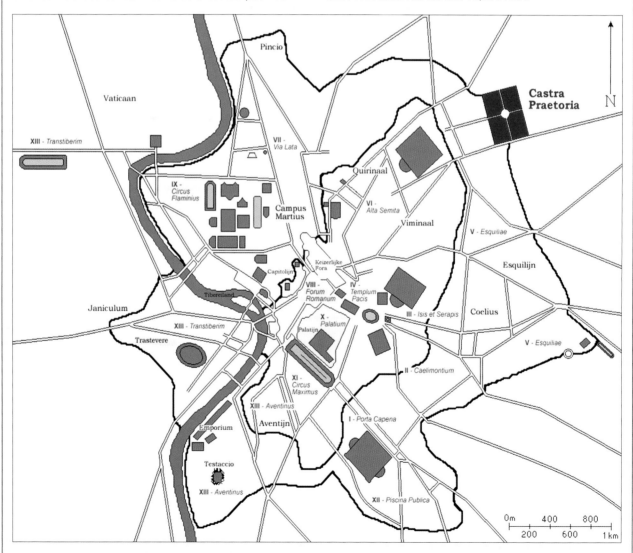

STRENGTH

Augustus' guard was initially nine infantry cohorts strong, each of 500 young men recruited in Italy. There were also some cavalry detachments (*turmae*), 30-men strong. This later increased to 1,000 per cohort, but Augustus was careful to keep down the number of soldiers visible in the capital, billeting only three cohorts there and ensuring they didn't wear armour. Instead, they often wore a toga.

In 2BC, he appointed two Praetorian prefects to run the guard and it was these prefects who would be politicised in the future. The prefects were not career military men but were chosen for their affiliation to the Imperial household.

The number of cohorts, and their size, changed over the years. After AD20–23, Tiberius concentrated them in the Castra Praetoria north-east of Rome and this probably coincided with the rise of cohort numbers from nine to 12. The number was increased to 16 in AD69 by Vitellius and then was cut back to nine (each of 500 men) when Vespasian took power, his son Titus becoming the prefect. Domitian increased their numbers to 10 cohorts.

When Trajan came to power in AD98 it has been assumed that he had the prefect Aelianus and his men killed, but as Bingham notes, Cassius Dio does not specify murder: 'He sent for Aelianus and the Praetorians … and … put them out of the way.' This probably means that they were dismissed rather than killed. Aelianus himself was probably simply dismissed from his post and sent away.

Septimius Severus replaced the Praetorians who had assassinated Pertinax with men from his own Danube legions in AD193. Lists of demobilisations suggest that by this time the cohort size had increased to nearly 1,500. So, these figures suggest an overall Guard numbering 4,500–6,000 men under Augustus; 12,800 under Vitellius; 7,200 under Vespasian; 8,000 from Domitian to Commodus; and 15,000 later. At the beginning of the 2nd century AD, Italians still made up 89 per cent of the Praetorian Guard, but Septimius Severus included legionaries from elsewhere.

▲ *Emperor Nero addresses the Praetorians accompanied by the Praetorian prefect – possibly Tigellinus or Rufus. The lettering ADLOCVT COH stands for* adlocutio cohortium, *or speech to the cohorts.*

PAY

The Praetorians' term of duty was originally 16 years – far less than the 25 years required from a legionary – reduced to 12 years in 14BC and then reversed back to 16 in 5BC. The Praetorians' pay was higher than that of a standard legionary – at least one-and-a-half times as much. As well as this, they received regular donatives, gifts or donations (see box). The Praetorians' pay increased under Domitian to 1,500 denarii per year, distributed in equal thirds during the months of January, May and September.

DONATIVES TO THE PRAETORIANS BY THE JULIO-CLAUDIAN DYNASTY		
Date	*Amount*	*Reason*
8BC	Unknown	Money granted when Gaius Caesar took part in exercises (may not have gone to the Praetorians)
AD14	250 denarii (1,000 sesterces)	Augustus' will (urbani received 500 and legionaries 300)
AD31	1,000 denarii	Tiberius for loyalty in AD31 after Sejanus' arrest
	250 denarii (1,000 sesterces)	Tiberius' will (urbani received 500 and legionaries 300)
AD37	500 denarii	Caligula's accession
AD39	Unknown	Possibly the removal of Macro (Bingham) in AD38
AD41	3,750 denarii (15,000 sesterces)	Claudius' accession. Thereafter Claudius paid 25 denarii a man annually
AD54	3,750 denarii	Nero's accession (Dio says he promised what Claudius had paid)
AD65	500 denarii (2,000 sesterces)	Restraint during the Pisonian conspiracy. Also granted the right to free grain

CHAPTER THREE

LIFE AS A ROMAN SOLDIER

It's difficult to generalise about the life of a Roman soldier when talking of an empire that lasted a thousand years and spread over a huge variety of terrains and climates. All soldiers need lodgings, supplies, weapons etc, but life would have been very different for units in Africa as compared to those manning Hadrian's Wall. And then there's the level of security. Over a thousand years of dominance the threat level in every area fluctuated: many places enjoyed the Pax Romana; many others saw it as the Roman yoke. A strong emperor usually kept the fighting to the border areas, but contested succession or civil war could see fighting take place anywhere.

◄ *Vindonissa Park in Switzerland recreates the Roman legionary camp at today's Windisch. Established at the beginning of the 1st century AD, it housed Legio XIII Gemina, XXI Rapax (during which time the fort was built in stone) and later XI Claudia. The photograph shows the centurions' quarters.*

RECRUITMENT AND POSTING

Legionaries came from all over the Roman Empire. They generally signed up in their native province but almost always served away from home – to minimise the chances of local rebels getting together with sympathetic armed and trained militia. Many volunteers came from military families living in the *vici* associated with frontier forts.

As we have seen, while all Roman citizens were legally obligated to serve in the military when called up, at various times – particularly in the early years of the Principate – this was so unpopular that voluntary recruitment prevailed except in times of dire need.

Service with the legions was considered a privilege and it conferred certain status to a man. However, many legionaries never saw Rome or even came anywhere close to it. Legionaries had to have full Roman citizenship, although exceptions were made for the sons of serving soldiers and veterans. According to Vegetius, the legions preferred recruits from temperate territories because they had proved themselves to be more reliable soldiers than men from the hotter climes. They also preferred to recruit from the countryside rather than towns, with the reasoning that country boys had already lived a harsher agricultural life and were fitter as a consequence than softly raised city lads and would cope much better with the rigours of legion life.

The majority of recruits were in their teens, mostly between 17 and 19 years old or at most early twenties, and (by AD1) signed up for 25 years, although according to Livy in extreme circumstances the army would accept soldiers up to the age of 50. Some legionaries on completing their service would sign on for a further period, so the legions could include a backbone of well-seasoned and mature soldiers.

There were three kinds of recruit:

- *Voluntarii* – volunteers
- *Lecti* – involuntary conscripts
- *Vicarii* – men coerced to volunteer in place of another

All recruiting took place in local provinces at inquests held under that governor's authority. Recruits had to be unmarried men; a married man could join up but he had to divorce his wife first. A legionary had to be free to travel and serve where and when necessary without the hindrance of emotional ties. Otherwise, he had to be of good stock and sound character, with a fit physique (no outstanding medical problems) and good eyesight.

Those excluded from the selection process are outlined in the *Codex Theodosianus* (*Theodosian Code*), which states: 'We decree that to the regiments of our most excellent soldiers there shall be given for service no man of the station of slave, no man brought from an inn or from employment in a house of ill fame, or from the class of cooks or bakers, or from that category which is debarred from military service by the ugliness of its occupation, nor shall men be dragged from houses of correction.'

UNWILLING VOLUNTEERS

Recruits were mostly voluntary, although in times of trouble conscripts could be signed up to serve in the legions whether they wanted to or not. Runaway slaves and criminals were not accepted, although that's not to say that there weren't any. Some attempted to get through the induction process and disappear into the military away from civil justice. The records mention the few that were caught, but possibly many others got away with it.

In times of war or when the legions were severely short of manpower, a *dilectus* (levy) would be called by the relevant governor. This could be activated when and where needed and would be organised by the governor in the region where the necessity arose. Otherwise, *dilectatores* (recruiting officers) were appointed in Rome and sent out to the provinces to raise recruits. A recruit could declare himself unfit for service and pay to be released, or if he was wealthy enough, he could offer a substitute to serve instead. Members of the auxiliaries were also raised from recently subjugated tribes by demanding men under the terms of the peace treaty they signed that often specified the numbers of men they had to raise for service in Roman ranks.

THE LANGUAGE BARRIER

The number of actual Romans in a legion was unlikely to be many, if any at all. During the Principate, the number of Italians in the legions generally dramatically declined; instead, legions tended to recruit from nearby communities. This must have presented a problem because the language of the legions was Latin and all administrative directions, orders, etc would have been in Latin also. Recruits must have had to learn some Latin to at least understand basic commands.

INDUCTION

Rome was run by a vast bureaucracy and the military was no exception. The induction of a recruit followed an ordered process, the criteria of which varied over time depending on the necessity to fill the ranks.

BACKGROUND CHECKS EXAMINATION

The first thing a *voluntarii* had to produce was a *litterae commendaticiae* (letter of recommendation), ideally written by a legionary veteran or an influential family friend. In this, the writer would lay out the young man's character, that he came from a good family, that he would be sure to serve faithfully and well and would be a valuable asset to the army. The probationary recruit (*probatio*) then faced a personal interview to determine whether he really was as described and that he was suitable for service. This often meant sending out letters requesting confirmation of the statements and could take quite a long time for the corresponding answers to return. During this period, the recruit carried *probatio* status – acceptable but not yet accepted. The primary enquiry was to establish that he was who he claimed to be, in particular with regard to his legal status. He had to prove he had full Roman citizenship, though the sons of serving soldiers were regularly accepted into the legions.

To join the *auxilia*, a recruit had to show he was a free non-citizen; except in Egypt, where he had to prove he was a member of the Greco-Egyptian class; native Egyptians could only be accepted into the Misene fleet. The *probatio* enquiries would show which service he qualified for – the fleet, the legions or the *auxilia* – each had their own criteria.

▲ *Tombstone of Gaius Largennius who died c.AD50 in Argentoratum (Strasbourg). He was a legionary serving in Legio II Augusta. He holds a scroll – possibly his will or his Roman citizenship document – and wears a* paenula *over his draped tunic. The sculptor has made a point of emphasising his belt by draping it over the inscription.*

MEDICAL EXAMINATION

On passing the probation, a recruit had a medical examination. 'Roman physicians examined a potential recruit's face, eyes, pulse, temperature, respiration, faeces, sputum, urine, range and motion of joints and other tests. If

▼ *The Roman fort at Lunt, near Coventry, was built c.AD60, initially for a legion. At some stage it was rebuilt to house a cohort and, during this time, a gyrus was built. This was probably a circle for training cavalry horses.*

he passed the physical examination the recruit appeared before a board of officers, which included one or more physicians. The Selection Board interrogated the recruit for his physical, mental and moral integrity.'[1] Theoretically, Vegetius tells us, he had to be around 5ft 8in (1.73m) to 5ft 10in (1.78m), but when fewer people wanted to serve, much shorter men were admitted; 5ft 5in (1.65m) seems to be the real minimum.

In fact, commanders placed much more emphasis on physical strength and fitness rather than height. 'So let the adolescent who is to be selected for martial activity have alert eyes, straight neck, broad chest, muscular shoulders, strong arms, long fingers, let him be small in the stomach, slender in the buttocks, and have calves and feet that are not swollen by surplus fat but firm with hard muscle.'[2] However, if a conscript was suspected of intentional mutilation – eg, chopping off his finger to avoid service – he was branded and forced into military labour instead.

INITIAL TRAINING

Recruits were assessed over a period of three or four months via an extensive series of physical exercises to discover how fit they were. At the same time, they started to learn legionary fighting techniques, particularly close-order drill. 'These recruits underwent an arduous basic training schedule for three or four months. There were frequent cadence marches (*militaris gradus*) of 20 miles and forced marches (*plenus gradus*) of 27 miles which they must complete in five hours carrying 60 pounds of equipment.'[3]

Initial weapons training required correct use of the *scutum* (shield) and the *gladius* (sword). First training was against a man-sized stout wooden stake using a wooden sword and a wicker shield, both of which weighed twice as much as the military issue weapons, to toughen the recruit up and make real battle conditions easier when the time came. In particular, he was taught how to use his sword to thrust rather than swinging it, as legionaries often fought in close

order. He also had to learn how to parry and cut. When they had become proficient at these, recruits moved on to training with real arms in paired sparring matches.

It was important to learn how to throw the *pilum* (spear): this too was heavier than the battle weapon to develop muscle strength. The target was the same wooden post as before. When the recruit was able to hit the target regularly he was given the battle-weight *pilum* to work with. When they were ready, recruits were paired off together to throw *pila praepilata* (leather button-tipped *pila*) at each other. Recruits were also introduced to throwing stones by hand using a sling, although this doesn't appear to be regular issue.

DRILL AND BATTLE PRACTICE

In later training, recruits were introduced to marching: both military pace (marching for tight drill) and full pace (for long marches). They had to learn how to carry heavy packs and then to march around 30km (18.5 miles) three times a month. To pass into the legion, they had to be able to march in full field pack at military pace for five hours and cover 20 Roman miles (29.6km/18.4 miles), and 24 Roman miles (35.6km/22 miles) at full pace. They also had to know how to run in full armour and jump.

As they learned the ropes, recruits took part in mock battles and were taught how to make the battlefield manoeuvres and formations: this meant learning how to move into squares, circles and wedges and how to form single-, double- and triple-line formations. When this was understood, they got to practise with the veterans, who probably did not hold back too hard. They also had mock battles using real weapons but with the points blunted by leather discs. This type of training was continued throughout their service, so the men were always sharp and well rehearsed for real combat at any time.

Even though they weren't cavalry, recruits were also taught to vault on to and off a horse while carrying a *pila* and with weapons drawn. This was first practised on a wooden horse and then the real thing. They also had to learn the basics of first aid and how to bandage wounds.

After four months of twice-daily drills, recruits were expected to be proficient with their weapons, and know how to march in time over distance, swim without struggling, take good care of their weapons and armour and erect a tent. Furthermore, they had to know how to build a camp – something the legion did every night anew when marching through hostile territory. This meant the basics of ditch digging, cutting down trees and forming defensive palisades, as well as all the other aspects of building an encampment. Anyone who failed to impress by the end of training would be sent home; the rest were accepted into the army. Even then, some recruits might have to wait until all their letters of enquiry came back with satisfactory answers.

◄ *Vegetius talks about training with heavy javelins to strengthen the arm. Certainly, the Romans practised hard to ensure precision and the ability to work in unison.*

THE MILITARY OATH

The final step was the *sacramentum* (military oath). When a number of recruits were taking it together, one of them would be selected as the *praeiuratio* to recite the complete oath, then the rest individually stepped forwards and said '*state idem in me*' ('the same in my case'). In later centuries, this oath was repeated annually on New Year's Day throughout service.

The exact wording of the *sacramentum* is unknown, but Vegetius writing in the late 4th century AD said in *De re militari* (the only surviving Roman military manual) that in part it said:

'Iurant autem milites omnia se strenue facturos quae praeceperit imperator, numquam deserturos militiam nec mortem recusaturos pro Romana republica!'

('But the soldiers swear that they shall faithfully execute all that the Emperor commands, that they shall never desert the service, and that they shall not seek to avoid death for the Roman republic!')[4]

POSTING

After the *sacramentum*, the soldier was given an advance on his pay and his posting. Up to a point, recruits could choose their legion, especially if their father had served or was still serving there.

▲ *The Roman salute – shown in David's* Oath of the Horatii *– may make a good painting, and was taken up by 20th century fascists, but has little or no bearing on reality.*

Military bureaucracy was attended to: the man's name, age, distinguishing marks or features were recorded. He was given a *signaculum* (essentially a dog tag) on a small lead tablet to wear in a small pouch around his neck and sent to his unit. If this posting was a distance away he was given a *viaticum* (road money) of 75 denarii or three aurei (gold pieces) to pay for travel, food and lodgings on the way to his new camp. Usually, a party of recruits was sent together to their unit, in which case they were guided by an officer (often a legionary centurion): he took charge of everyone's *viaticum*. Any remaining money after the journey was deposited into the recruit's account, which ultimately became his pension – from the little information available, it seems that a recruit was lucky to bank as much as one-third of this when he reached his unit.

On arrival, a letter of introduction was presented to the unit commander recommending that the new men were entered into the unit's ledger as they had passed all the necessary tests. They were each assigned their century. It is at this point that they officially became soldiers and could make their own will. This latter was a distinct privilege as sons were otherwise not allowed to do so while their father was still living, as their possessions legally belonged to their father.

FORTRESSES AND FIXED CAMPS

Regardless of the difference in size, whether it was a marching camp, an auxiliary fort or a huge legionary fortress, all Roman military installations were called *castrum* (plural *castra*). The very smallest fortlets were known as *castellum* (plural *castella*). And regardless of their size, these structures were built by the soldiers of the legions.

Army regulations required any major unit on campaign to retire to a properly constructed camp each night – as a precautionary defensive measure. No Roman *castra* were made to fight from – the Roman Army fought as heavy infantry in the open, where its superior organisation would have the most impact and an outcome could be swiftly reached. Thus the primary purpose of a *castrum* was not to withstand attack but to provide a safe staging area in which troops could prepare and assemble before deployment.

All Roman military installations essentially followed the same basic idealised template, with variations only when demanded by the constraints of time, terrain and materials available. Such a protocol maintained organisation and discipline, for every soldier knew where everything was and where he was supposed to be, whether in a legionary fortress or an overnight marching camp.

BUILDING MATERIALS

The Roman Army built in stone and turf according to availability and time, with the quicker turf-and-timber constructions used for making a temporary camp on campaign when enemy proximity required speed – the more permanent stone replacements came along later, with timber being used in both. Turf was a tried-and-tested technology for the Roman military and was considerably more robust than the modern reader might think. Revetted with timber and huge back berm earthen banks that enabled swift mass access to the top rampart and filled with cores of rubble, a turf wall was just as effective as a stone one but required rather more maintenance.

TEMPORARY CAMPS

Marching or night camps on campaign were inevitably slighter and more swiftly erected than their more permanent counterparts. Both were chosen with an eye for a good defensive position, either on high ground or in the open and sited near water, and were marked out in flags and rope lines by a specialist forward squad that was sent on ahead so that they could be laid out quickly and clearly. When the main body of troops arrived, the visible plan of the camp could then be swiftly realised.

The shape and ground plan of these night camps rarely strayed from a round-cornered rectangular playing-card shape, consisting of a wooden palisade (*vallum*) atop an earthen rampart (*agger*) built up from the earth excavated from the ditch (*fossa*) or ditches in front, with a gate on each

▼ *Long linear-built sets of defences were unusual in the Roman Empire. Two of the most significant protected the north of Britain: Hadrian's Wall and that of Antoninus Pius. The latter was primarily turf, although a number of the forts were of stone. The defences along the outside of the wall included* lilia: *pits filled with sharpened stakes.*

▲ *Aerial view of Rough Castle. The yellow line shows the path of the wall. The fort is behind and the* lilia *are opposite the front gate. Trees would not have been allowed and there would have been good sightlines from the fort.*

side leading to the camp's principal roads. Just behind the *vallum*, a road ran right around the camp and was known as the *intervallum*, enabling swift movement to any part of the defences as well as acting as a safety margin against incoming missiles. According to Belfiglio:

'A complex system of drains and sewers emptied into streams and rivers. Drinking water for soldiers and animals were taken from water upstream or separate from the waterway used for latrines. Wooden seats for latrines

which were dug to a depth of ten feet were situated over the main sewer running round three sides of the building to discourage disease-carrying insects. A smaller channel of water, fed from the water tank was for washing sponges dipped in a mixture of water and acetum (vinegar) which were used as toilet paper. Latrines also had basins for washing hands. The Romans often recycled bath water by using it as part of the flow that flushed the latrines.

The Roman army took great care to construct sanitary facilities and segregate them from water, food supplies and dining areas. When water was in short supply lime pits were used in the latrines. Roman physicians recognized that fomites could spread disease. They washed clothing, blankets, woven materials and saddles before recovered soldiers returned to active duty.'[5]

LABOURING

▲ *Roman soldiers certainly could dig: the ditches and walls of their marching camps, forts and defensive walls were all dug out by the legionaries themselves – at Masadafor example, they built a huge ramp to allow them to attack a mountaintop. While most of the defences would have been in turf, as legions became settled, so buildings were rebuilt in stone.*

▶ *A typical playing-card-shaped camp showing the usual layout, with corner towers and gates. There were usually four, but some forts on Hadrian's Wall had side gateways ahead of the wall and so were given two extra gates to relieve pressure on the southern entrance. The drawing highlights the main buildings:*
- *Granaries (*horrea*)*
- *HQ (*principia*)*
- *CO's house (*praetorium*)*
- *Barracks (*centuriae*)*
- *Stables/workshops (*stabuli/fabricae*)*
- *Note latrines (*latrinae*) and ovens (*forni*) built near the walls and drains.*

▼ *Milecastle 42 on Hadrian's Wall, south of Cawfield Crags. When in use it would have had basic accommodation, hearths and possibly even an oven. Usually garrisoned by squads of soldiers on guard duty from a local fort, milecastles controlled passage through the Roman frontier allowing travel both ways, but enabling the soldiers to levy taxes and import duties. They could also, of course, bar entry.*

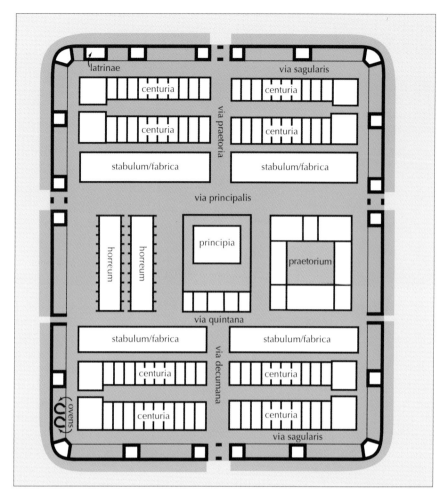

The inside of the camp was divided into four quarters by the two roads that bisected each other – the Via Principalis and the Via Praetoria, with the command and supply sections always in the centre. (Sometimes the Via Praetoria did not pierce its walls dead centre, creating three thirds rather than four quarters but with the middle third still the command and control section.) In the middle of the camp was the *praetorium*, the command centre where the praetor (first officer), the unit's standards, pay chests and command staff were housed, with the legate's tent with those of the tribunes ranged in front. The Via Principalis at this central part was used as an assembly area and parade ground.

On one side of the *praetorium* there was the hospital and on the other was the *quaestorium* (quaestor = supply officer) where the units stores and supplies were kept. The cohorts' tents occupied either side of the command section and sometimes part of this space was also left open in which to muster, hold prisoners and booty or horses and supplies.

If especially anxious and expecting imminent attack, more ditches could be dug and the gateways further protected with frontal hemispherical berms. When time was available, these ditches could be made more elaborate and deadly, with their backs cut vertically to prevent escape, an ankle-breaker bottom slot and the addition of various sharpened wooden stakes – some huge and obvious while others were more

▲ *Reconstructed assembly hall at Saalburg. In Hadrian's time the fort housed the Cohors II Raetorum civium Romanorum equitata (a 500-man infantry unit with some horsemen). The fort had an extensive* vicus *and a bathhouse outside its walls. Reconstructed in the 19th century, today it houses an excellent museum.*

trap-like, being hidden in pits covered in brushwood. Wide, deep ditches created a killing zone for the soldiers on the ramparts armed with javelins and supported by artillery.

LONG-TERM BARRACKS

In the more permanent barracks or forts, a similar plan was followed, using heavier materials and often over the top of the wooden original. The *praetorium* was built in stone and resembled a Mediterranean Roman villa. The *quaestorium* was also constructed in stone and featured the heavy-set *horreum* (granary) with its double-skinned walls and a raised floor to aid airflow and prevent the vital grain supplies from rotting. Gates in the camp walls were no longer flush with the wall but protruding, often doubled and built of stone, with towers on either side as well as at each corner of the camp, while other watchtowers also studded the walls.

Baths were usually built outside the camp because of the ever-present danger of fire, unless the fort was large enough to accommodate them. The vital bread ovens would also be built into the back of the rampart, minimising the risk of fire. Temples, too, were often built close by rather than inside the forts, along with extra workshops producing building supplies such as tiles, pipes and lime mortar.

Other changes or evolutions occurred in camp and fort construction over the course of time and reflected the shift of military emphasis away from infantry to different kinds of auxiliary troops – often cavalry or mixed units. Later forts tended to be square rather than rectangular.

▶ *Give us this day ... a small rotary hand quern to grind grain for small-scale or domestic use. Horse, or donkey, mills were used all over the Roman world; water mills are also not unknown.*

FORT AND CAMP LOGISTICS

The day-to-day smooth running of large groups of people in such installations required clockwork precision in order to succeed. Aside from the military duties of guarding the camp itself there were fuel supplies to be gathered for the ever-present bread ovens, food supplies and preparation, water for the baths and latrines, grazing and exercising of animals. The supply administration of a permanent camp was run as a business using money as the exchange medium so native tribes that supplied many of the army's needs for food, animals, fodder and construction materials accrued considerable wealth in the process.

LEGIONARY FORTRESSES

◄ One big find at Inchtuthil was a buried hoard of 10 tons of nails – too heavy to carry away but too important to let the tribesmen acquire them: 800,000 iron nails would make a lot of weapons.

Until the beginning of the 2nd century AD, when the borders stabilised, Rome's continuous expansion meant that legions moved around, needing permanent camps only for winter quarters. It was Hadrian who started fixing the borders, retrenching from Trajan's less stable advances, and this approach was maintained by Marcus Aurelius and Septimius Severus, under whose aegis reforms made legionary life more popular than it had been hitherto. The legions became fixed in their locations – with the soldiers allowed to marry – and families congregated around the camps. Because of this, the fortresses were built in stone, and some have survived. Indeed, some 85 legionary fortresses have been found – Caerleon, York and Deva in Britain – along with others that are examples of earlier, turf fortresses, such as Inchtuthil in Scotland. M.C. Bishop's *Handbook to Roman Legionary Fortresses* provides a detailed analysis of what has been found to date, where the fortresses were, what is extant and the units that can be directly related to the locations.

Of these, the legionary fortress the Romans called Pinnata Castra at Inchtuthil is virtually unique in that it was not occupied for long and has never been built over, and as such provides a most detailed ground plan. Given the time of its construction and its central location, its purpose was the consolidation of the conquest of Hibernia following the Battle of Mons Graupius (AD83–84), an aim later abandoned with the restructuring of the remaining legions within Britannia. Following the departure of Legio II Adiutrix to fight in the Dacian Wars (AD101–106), the constructors of Pinnata Castra, Legio XX Valeria Victrix, carefully destroyed it (burying almost a million potential weapon-making iron nails) and relocated to Deva (Chester), leaving Legio IX Hispana as the northernmost legion at its fortress in Eboracum (York).

Legionary fortresses, with virtually all their features eventually built in stone, were usually long-term and massive – up to 50 or 60 acres. The same was true of Pinnata Castra, which although only manned for some five years, nevertheless

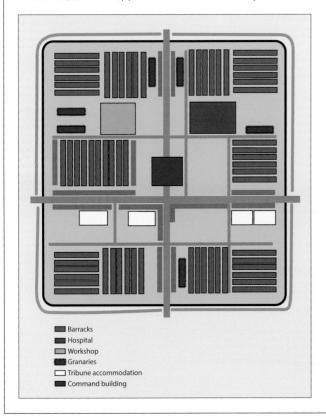

- ▮ Barracks
- ▮ Hospital
- ▢ Workshop
- ▨ Granaries
- ▢ Tribune accommodation
- ▮ Command building

▲ *Roman castra started off in the standard playing card shape with tents and, as they became more permanent, were rebuilt in wood and stone. York's famous Multangular Tower once stood at the west corner of the legionary fortress, although what can be seen today is mostly medieval.*

occupied a 53-acre site and was virtually complete, lacking only the *praetorium* (commander's private residence) and some tribunes' quarters. Built to the standard Roman Army plan, it had a turf rampart 4m (13ft) thick, revetted at the front with a stone wall 1.5m (5ft) thick, fronted by a berm of 5m (16ft) and a ditch 6m (20ft) wide and 2m (6.5ft) deep, with a counterscarp bank 6.5m (22ft) wide formed from the ditch upcast, creating a killing zone controlled from the ramparts. Each wall was punctured with a double-gated portal with bracketing towers and gatehouses. The *principia* at the centre was smaller than usual and must also have been incomplete at the time of abandonment, but contained offices and a shrine (*sacellum*) for the Imperial and legionary standards with its underlying strongroom for the legion's money. There were a large hospital, 64 barrack blocks, a huge workshop, half a dozen granaries, a gym, latrines and ovens. All the buildings were timber-framed, with wattle-and-daub walls that had been burned, and the timber removed.

QUARTERS

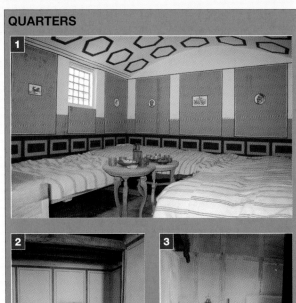

Archaeology has helped us re-create interiors of Roman forts and barracks. These are in Vindonissa (Windisch, Switzerland) and show:
1 Banqueting chamber in the officers' accommodation. Centurions, tribunes, legates and other senior officers would have had decorated rooms
2 Altar
3 Cooking and domestic facilities
4 Contubernium (squad) storeroom

DAILY ROUTINE

Units slept, cooked and ate together, and every detail of their day was planned. An occupying army does not necessarily have a great deal to do and the ordinary soldier less than most, so to prevent the men from becoming bored and potentially seeking trouble-causing distractions, their day was strictly regulated by routine.

▲ *Cheese, honey, lentils (a favourite and, rich in phosphorus and iron, fortifying, too!): the Roman soldier was better fed than his counterpart in many armies, before or since.*

A DAY IN THE LIFE OF A LEGIONARY

The legionary's day usually started before dawn.
- Get suitably dressed. Tidy room. Eat a simple breakfast, consisting of things like cold meat and cheese (depending on region).
- Morning muster parade and roll call, after which they were given any news concerning the emperor, the Empire or the local province, plus any announcements. They were told of their general orders/assignments for the day, given the watchword for the day and then dismissed. Individual soldiers moved to a smaller muster before the centurion to get their individual orders for the day – eg guard duty, latrine cleaning, escort duty, etc.
- It is known that Roman commanders drilled their men hard. In fact, the Jewish historian Josephus declared that one would not be mistaken to call 'their exercises unbloody battles, and their battles bloody exercises.'[6] The amount and rigour of drill would have varied according to the enthusiasm of the individual commanders, but it would have been a regular activity, possibly even daily for ordinary legionaries, to keep them fit and sharp.
- After *cena* (second meal of the day in late afternoon) a legionary had time to himself unless he had been assigned guard duty. Most likely, he went straight to the bathhouse for a good relaxing clean-up and gossip.

Within the fortress, legionaries slept in closely packed lines of barrack blocks. Each *contubernium* (eight-man squad), lived cheek by jowl in two rooms of about 4.6sq m (50sq ft) each. They all slept together, probably in bunk beds, in one room, and used the other room for relaxing and storing their kit.

When awake, their days were packed with activities. The remnants of a duty roster from one of the Egyptian legions dating from the late 1st century AD shows that beside each man's name is his assignment, whether it be cleaning the latrines, out on patrol duty, on leave or guard duty, etc. In this way, the commander knew where everyone was supposed to be at any given time.

BATHHOUSE

Good hygiene was very important for Roman soldiers and the communal bathhouse (*thermae*) provided the facilities, but it was also the main social centre of the fort.

Located outside the fortress wall because of the danger of fire, the *thermae* is where soldiers came to bathe and relax but also play games (dice and coins), buy refreshments (evidenced by chicken bones and shellfish remains) and generally gossip and pass the time of day. Soldiers also lifted weights there and probably followed light exercise routines.

▼ *To the Romans baths were social places: even families were allowed in as attested by toys and jewellery found in the drains of the baths at Cilurnum (Chesters). There's an altar, too (to Fortuna). In Deva (Chester), a large legionary bathhouse was completed during the reign of Vespasian (c.AD79) linked to a large exercise hall.*

▲ *Glannoventa, today's Ravenglass, started life as a fortlet built around the time of Hadrian (c.AD122). The settlement was in the firing line (literally: archaeology shows evidence of destruction by fire in 197, 296 and 367) as the southern edge of the Hadrian's Wall/Cumbrian coast defences. The remains of the fort and an extensive* vicus *are limited to the baths, some of whose walls are 4m (3ft) high. Glannoventa is about 16km (10 miles) from Hardknott on the road to Galava (Ambleside).*

Thermae would have been noisy places with the high ceilings and waters amplifying the noises of talking, laughing and arguing as well as the yowl of pain as injuries were massaged and hair plucked. Sufficient numbers of coins have been found in the *frigidarium* to suggest that soldiers paid for food, masseurs, hair removal and bath oils there. Some archaeological evidence found in the bath drains suggests that dental (teeth have been found) and medical care (scalpels) were also provided.

Because it was outside the fort, civilians could also have used the facilities; some sites have revealed entry tokens, which suggests that trusted civilians were allowed to share the baths. Men and women were forbidden to bathe together, so it is probable that certain times were exclusively reserved for women, depending on the demand. The commanding officer had his own private baths in the *praetorium*.

How the thermae were constructed

The *thermae* consisted of a number of thermally different rooms set in series one after the other. They varied in size and facilities depending on the muster and importance of the fort, but they would have been symmetrical, with flagstone floors – made from local stone wherever possible – and walls between each zone to keep the climates controllable. The heating was provided via an underfloor hypocaust system. The vaulted ceilings were supported by thick walls and the whole covered with topical frescoes and decorative stone carvings. Mosaics often decorated the walls and floors, their quality and extent depending on the importance of the place. *Thermae* would have their own slaves whose purpose was to keep the baths hygienic.

PLAN OF A TYPICAL *THERMAE*

- *Apodyterium* – changing room with cubicles or shelves to hold belongings.
- *Frigidarium* – cold room. Contained at least one *piscina* (cold plunge bath) and a number of *labrae* (circular stone wash basins) in arched alcoves. A central drain running the length of the room took away the waste water.
- *Tepidarium* – temperate room. Heated via a hypocaust with the cooling air from the *caldarium*.
- *Caldarium* – hot room. The dry heat was provided by a hypocaust system under the floor. The room also held *alveii* (plunge baths) filled with hot water and a number of *labrae*. The floor would be too hot to walk on with bare feet.

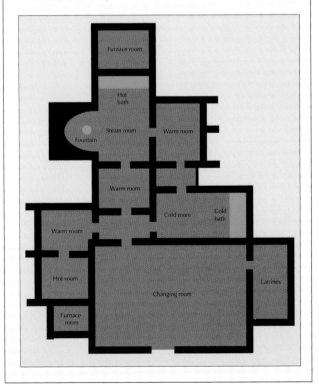

◄ *Armies march on their stomachs and field kitchens were as important to the Romans as any other army. The Roman soldier ate large quantities of bread (there are ovens built into the walls of their forts), and collected their rations and cooked them by squad. There were hard tack biscuits (*buccellatum*) such as are found in most army rations, and porridge (*pulmentum, made from wheat), salt beef and cheese – and, of course, the ubiquitous garum fish sauce, the Romans' ketchup. They drank wine (*vinum*) and* posca *– a sour wine/vinegar and water mix.*

How the hypocaust worked

Water for the *thermae* was piped through wooden or clay pipes from the main fortress system into a *castellum aquae* (reservoir) reserved specifically for the baths.

This remarkably effective heating system was powered by wood or coal open-burning fires in the *praefurnium* (the room under the *caladarium*), over which was a water-filled boiler sitting on iron supports. A stopcock controlled the temperature of the water. The hot gasses from the boiling water were ducted through flues under the floor of the *caldarium* where they heated the room and the waters. The now cooling but still very warm air then siphoned off through arches into the *tepidarium* and up through the walls and across the ceiling vaults through a *tubulatio* (linked system of pipes) of *tubuli lateraci* (hollow box-shaped bricks). This elaborate method of heating all the surfaces of the room prevented condensation forming and dripping on the occupants. The gasses then vented out through chimneys or holes at the eaves that in turn created a draught that drew and distributed the warmth through the rooms.

It is likely that slaves or soldiers on punishment duty drained, cleaned and refilled the baths every night. Waters from the hot room were sluiced into the drain for the *frigidarium* and because this was done by candlelight, many items, such as coins, nail cleaners, *strigils* and glass pieces of oil bottles, were missed and these have given archaeologists insight into the life of the *thermae*.

Using the thermae

Most soldiers seemed to have bathed in the afternoon after a day's work and it could have been that bathing hours for women (if provided) would have been in the morning. Night bathing appears to have been rare.

After taking off his clothes in the *apodyterium*, the soldier entered the *frigidarium* where he removed most of the dirt and sweat from his body using a *strigil*, a curved metal hand tool. He then moved into the comfortable warmth of the *tepidarium*, which is probably where most people lingered, chatting, maybe snacking and drinking and enjoying the sociable atmosphere. Later, he moved on to the dry heat of the *caldarium* to make his body perspire – the heat of the floor would have been so blistering that he would have had to wear wooden clogs to stop his feet scorching. Romans often used oil to further cleanse their bodies, using a *strigil* to remove it afterwards. He then probably returned to the *tepidarium* to continue talking.

Games were played outside the baths in the south-facing *palaestra*, an enclosed courtyard.

Latrines

Communal latrines were provided as part of the *thermae* facilities. They consisted of open, stone-built structures. The men sat in line on wooden seats with the waste dropping down into a shallow channel that was kept continually flushed with running water. Sponges on sticks were used for cleaning, washed with a mixture of water and *acetum* (vinegar) and replaced for the next customer. Slaves, and probably legionaries on fatigues, cleaned the latrines every day, probably overnight.

MONEY

Legionaries were not particularly well paid, but they were regularly paid a *stipendium* (usually, though not always). It appears that this *stipendium* was not intended to be an income but simply provided to cover a legionary's expenses, and any money he acquired or saved would go into his pension.

Caesar set the *stipendium* at 300 sesterces, paid three times a year, probably on 1 January, 1 May and 1 September. Around the beginning of the 2nd century AD, Domitian increased legionary pay to 1,200 sesterces annually; a century or so later Septimius Severus increased the pay again, this time to about 2,400 sesterces. This was increased by 50 per cent by his son Caracalla, an indication of the rapid inflation hitting the Roman Empire in the 3rd century AD. Cavalrymen received a better salary, probably because they had to feed their horses as well.

In actuality though, legionaries did not receive these amounts because the legion deducted at source various expenses – for clothes (issued), weapons (issued), food (issued) and compulsory savings. Nevertheless, a careful soldier who didn't gamble or fritter away his money could amass a comfortable sum to retire with, particularly if he was lucky enough to benefit from a good share of booty. The Vindolanda letters indicate that there was some form of credit offered, so a man could pay off his debts over a period of time. There were also times when the money was not available to the legion and poor or even complete lack of pay was a documented grievance in many a mutiny.

The table below shows the significant changes during the Principate, and also the difference between the ordinary soldier and the centurions. Much of the information comes from work done on tablets found at Vindonissa in Switzerland.

WOMEN

The ideal was a celibate army whose entire loyalty was to the emperor and military service, so theoretically women did not exist for the Roman military. The authorities did not want emotional ties to women and children to impede the mobility of the army and distract individuals' attention from their duty. The reality, of course, was rather different.

Only the centurionate were allowed wives; all lower ranks were barred from matrimony. The letters found at Vindolanda fort in northern England show that commanding officers had their wives living in their forts beside them. Similarly, senatorial governors and even legionary and auxiliary commanders would take their wives with them to their provinces. The

▲ *The Roman system of currency developed over many years, individual emperors minting their own coins which – often debased – lasted for a long time, but there were many, many changes to the way they looked, what they were made of and what they were worth. Of the many denominations, the best-known are probably the* Aureus *(a gold coin initially worth 25 denarii; by AD301 it was worth over 800) replaced by Diocletian's* Solidus *in AD301; the* Denarius *(worth 10 Asses), a silver coin produced 267BC–mid-3rd century AD by which time it contained half the silver it had done; the* Sestertius, *a big bronze coin in the days of the empire worth 2.5 Asses (ie 0.25 of a* Denarius*); and the* As, *made of bronze or, latterly, copper.*

exception was for equestrian officers because they only served for a short time with the army and were not considered professional soldiers. The only stipulation for them was that they were not permitted to marry women from the province in which they served.

The pay of the Roman army (sesterces per year)[7]					
Rank/Unit	Augustus	Domitian (AD84)	Severus (AD197)	Caracalla (AD212)	Max. Thrax (AD235)
LEGIONS					
Miles legionis	**900**	**1,200**	2,400	3,600	**7,200**
Eques legionis	1,050	1,400	2,800	4,200	**8,400**
Centurio legionis	13,500	18,000	36,000	54,000	108,000
Primus ordo	27,000	36,000	72,000	108,000	**216,000**
Primus pilus	54,000	72,000	144,000	216,000	**432,000**
AUXILIA					
Miles cohortis	**750**	1,000	2,000	**3,000**	**6,000**
Eques cohortis	**900**	1,200	2,400	3,600	7,200
Eques alae	1,050	1,400	2,800	4,200	**8,400**
Centurio cohortis	3,750	5,000	10,000	15,000	30,000
Decurio cohortis	4,500	6,000	12,000	18,000	36,000
Decurio alae	5,250	7,000	14,000	21,000	42,000
HORSEGUARDS					
Eques singulares Aug.		(2,800)	5,600	8,400	16,800
Decurio eq. sing. Aug.		(14,000)	28,000	42,000	84,000

Emperor Augustus attempted to prevent marriage at even the highest level, forbidding senatorial officers to take their wives with them to their provinces, but this was generally ignored. His own stepson, Germanicus, a prominent member of the Imperial family, was a prime example as his wife, Agrippina, accompanied him everywhere and two of their daughters were born in Koblenz.

In practice, of course, men did form lasting relationships with local non-Roman women (*peregrinae*) and were often unofficially married to them. This became especially true after AD2, when most of the legions and auxiliary units were based permanently at a fixed location and only moved away if sent on campaign or in an emergency of some sort. The authorities tended to turn a blind eye to such liaisons as the result was invariably children accustomed to military life, and sons who were easy and willing recruits into the ranks. Sons of auxiliaries were ineligible for the legions. A little female company also helped to prevent discontent among the rank and file. In fact, Claudius granted soldiers the privileges of married men so they could avoid the penalties of the unmarried.

It became the practice for a soldier to declare unofficially in front of witnesses that he was the father of a particular child, so that in time, when he completed his service, that child was indisputably eligible for citizenship.

Some men kept paid mistresses in the *vicus*, while others had women who were wives in all but name. They still were not allowed to marry, but could form long-term relationships with local women. However, any subsequent children were technically illegitimate, so could not inherit their father's estate. This injustice was corrected by Emperor Hadrian in AD119, when he granted such offspring the right to inherit their father's possessions.

▲ *The Roman roads were the arteries of the empire, allowing speedy troop movements, swift communications and, most importantly, strong supply lines. Towns built up around the staging posts as exemplified by Letocetum (Wall) on Watling Street in Staffordshire near the junction with Icknield Street. An important nodal point, a town grew up at this point with baths and* mansio *(place to stay) for official travellers.*

A growing community

Around AD197, Septimius Severus allowed soldiers to live with their wives – a legal recognition of the widely practised existing situation. It is unlikely that this meant that families could live within the forts though. The only visible change is that the *vici* around the forts and the *canabae* (villages) got much bigger at this time. They were getting bigger anyway as local economies grew around settled Roman forts, but the ruling would have encouraged a more stable society generally. In the long term, the legal change meant that soldiers were more likely to develop strong ties to their region and become extremely reluctant to move away to new postings. By then, the collective camp was so large that it was extremely difficult to move anyway. Rome responded in the 3rd century AD by marshalling a mobile field army to use as a strategic reserve when needed.

Although a legionary could marry a woman, everything depended on her legal status. A soldier with citizenship marrying a woman with citizenship made a *matrimonium iustum*. If only the soldier was a citizen, the couple could only contract a *matrimonium ex iure gentium*. However, both grants made inheritance for wives and children easier. When in AD212 or 213 Caracalla granted citizenship to all free peoples throughout the Roman Empire, both marriage and inheritance became much more straightforward.

LEISURE AND LEAVE

Depending on their posting, legionaries could have quite a bit of free time, especially if they were in permanent quarters. Some units in the east had so much leisure time that individuals developed their own business ventures. In fact, at many periods of Roman history there must have been large numbers of legionaries who never fought in battle.

In a fort in the evening – if not on duty – legionaries were able (within reason) to do what they liked. They could deal with their mail and send home letters, or go to the bathhouse, a temple or into the *vicus* where all manner of attractions were on offer. The taverns there were more expensive than in camp but did provide more amenities, including women for hire.

Occasionally, official entertainment was laid on and paid for by the Imperial authorities in Rome – particularly if they were actively trying to gain the legion's support for something like a power grab. Otherwise, the entertainment could be paid for by the legionary legate or personally by the provincial governor if they wanted to mark an occasion with festivities. Such diversions would include plays and theatrical entertainments, especially mimes. Other popular shows were more physical, such as gladiator fighting or military games (often inter-unit matches), and wrestling bouts.

LEAVE

Legionaries were entitled to up to a couple of weeks' annual leave when, if they lived near enough, they could go home. But this was only with the permission of senior officers (usually his unit commander), who didn't always grant it. There was no specified amount or number of days' leave; instead, time off was by arrangement with senior officers, usually in exchange for a cash payment to be officially relieved from normal duties and fatigues for a time. According to Tacitus, at any given time, up to a quarter of a military unit could be absent outside the fort, on leave in peacetime or in camp but excused duties. Some of the laxer companies allowed men to stay overnight outside the fort.

◥ *Vindolanda had a well-established* vicus, *as did most forts. The buildings outside the walls included the houses of wealthy citizens. There would have been bars and shops, places of worship and a bathhouse.*

▶ *The Romans were unabashed by sex. Augustus passed a law prohibiting soldiers from marrying – not relations with women. So, female camp followers abounded, many of them female slaves. Records show many memorials to soldier husbands from wives, many of whom were freed slaves. The ban on marriage was lifted by Septimius Severus in the early 3rd century* AD.

RELIGION AND GODS

Religion was of huge importance to the Roman soldier – as it was to the vast majority of people at the time. The official Roman pantheon was never fixed: it proved adaptable enough to absorb the gods of other nations and Roman soldiers enjoyed a number of cults, such as the double axe-wielding Jupiter Dolichenus.

▲ *The radiate head of the sun-god, Sol, from the temple of Jupiter Dolichenus. It was found reused on the floor of Coria's east granary. Sol Invictus (the Invincible Sun) became an official cult in 274 thanks to Emperor Aurelian. Sol was described as Dominus Imperii Romani (the official god of the Roman Empire) during his reign. Interestingly, the day of Sol Invictus' birth – dies natalis Invicti – was 25 December.*

SUPERSTITION AND SACRIFICES

All Roman soldiers were deeply superstitious and each legion had an augur – a priest who foretold the future through the examination of natural phenomena and the entrails of a sacrificed animal.

Making a sacrifice – the *lustratio* – to the gods was therefore a fairly regular occurrence in the Roman Army, serving to purify the army before battle, appease the gods, and provide both entrails for the augurs and fresh meat for the soldiers. Oxen, sheep and pigs were the most common sacrificial animals.

Sacrifices were also held after victory. A papyrus dated around AD223–227 from Dura-Europus (a city beside the Euphrates in what is now Syria) includes a partial list of sacrifices performed between 3 January and 23 September by the military unit stationed there. It shows 24 days when cows or oxen (sometimes both) were sacrificed.

Roman soldiers worshipped a huge range of deities, although the most important centred around the Capitoline Triad of Jupiter – often referred to as Jupiter Optimus Maximus (greatest and best) – Juno Regina and Minerva. Their worship was regulated by official calendars such as the Feriale Duranum. The other important god was the god of war, Mars (and later Hercules). Others included the personification of victory, Victoria, and deities such as Fortuna, Honos, Disciplina, Urbs Roma, Virtus, Pietas and Bonus Eventus.

Because the military were recruited from around the Empire, soldiers continued worshipping deities local to the region they came from originally and took with them to their new posting. For example, Mars Thincsus was worshipped by Germans based in Holland, and Tungrians brought their goddess Viradecthis to Birrens. Additionally, soldiers often took to the local deities of their new posting – these in time all became Romanised deities or assimilated gods – *interpretatio Romana* – for example the local northern British deity Cocidius was elided with the Roman Mars to become Mars Cocidius, and the German deity Donar merged into the aura of Hercules for German-raised soldiers. They shared attributes so could be worshipped together as one god.

Referred to as Jupiter Optimus Maximus Dolichenus – as exemplified on altars found at Lambaesis in Algeria (the first, dating to AD125) and Carnuntum (the capital of Pannonia Superior) – Jupiter Dolichenus is a good example of a Roman cult that flourished in the 2nd and 3rd centuries AD and was of particular interest to the military: of 260 names on inscriptions associated with Jupiter Dolichenus, 90 are soldiers.

THE CULT OF THE SIGNA (STANDARD)

Usually, every cohort had its own standard – a flag, banner or pennant bearing a totemic animal or other symbol that represented the identity of the unit to which it belonged. The most important of these standards was the *aquila* (eagle), which was to be venerated and protected at all costs. The loss of a legion's eagle was almost synonymous with the loss of the legion: it was traditionally (but not always) followed by the disbandment of the legion concerned. For this reason, the *aquila* was guarded by the first cohort and was personally looked after by the *primus pilus*.

Originally made of silver, the *aquila* was by the time of the Republic made of gold or silver-gilt and was mounted on a long pole with a sharp butt that could be nailed into the ground. On manoeuvres, one man carried it, but it never left the winter quarters unless the entire legion moved out. In

◄ *The cult of the standards was promoted by officers to establish unit cohesion. The standards were kept in a shrine – in this case in the* principia *treasury of the reconstructed fort at Saalburg – that would have been guarded day and night. Note the eagle in the centre. The standard to the left of the eagle has the unit's title above the* phalerae *and a wreath surrounding the* manus*. To the right of the eagle is the standard of Cohort VII.*

camp, it was kept in a small, dedicated chapel in every legionary headquarters alongside the various other legionary *signa*, which were stored in rooms each side of the shrine. Also in the chapel was a statue of the current emperor, in a position of honour.

MITHRAISM

The god Mithras was an eastern emissary of light sent to earth by the cosmic deity Ahura Mazda (the Light). His cult was second only to that of Jupiter Dolichenus in importance to the military. Mithras is always shown in the centre of the cosmos, surrounded by stars, and is frequently depicted on Roman altar stones as pinioning down a divine bull (a symbol of fertility) with one hand, grasping its nostrils while the other plunges a blade into its chest to spill its life-giving strength on to the earth. Known as tauroctonous (bull slaying) or tauroctony reliefs, they also depict evil entities – known as the Ahriman (the Dark), possessors of the powers of darkness and disorder – a serpent, raven, dog and scorpion (always stinging the bull), trying to prevent the divine blood reaching and nourishing the ground. In the background, the gods Sol and Luna (Sun and Moon) are often present.

Mithraism was a highly secretive dualistic cult or religion that played with the balance of light and dark – good versus evil. There are no authenticated contemporary accounts about its proceedings so it remains largely unknown and mysterious despite its early widespread popularity. Most of our knowledge comes from interpreting the sparse information inscribed on altars and contested interpretations of temple mosaics and occasional graffito. It is now generally thought that Mithras was not even Persian as the Romans believed.

Anecdotally, Mithraism reached Rome via Cilician pirates in the 1st century BC, took another century to take root across the Empire, peaked in the 4th century AD, then disappeared as Christianity took hold. Rome seems to have remained its epicentre, although more than 400 Mithraeums (temples) have been found scattered across the Empire from east to west.

◄ *The tombstone of Felsonius Verus,* aquilifer *of Legio II Parthica from about* AD218. *The image is of a standing soldier wearing a* sagum *(cloak), a sleeved tunic, a belt with ring buckle and holding a standard with an eagle in a cage. Another tombstone, that of Titus Flavius Surillonus,* aquilifer *of Legio II Adiutrix, has a naturalistic eagle atop a pole. It's possible that these were live mascots – but also that they were simply a different representation of an eagle standard.*

This was primarily an officer-level militaristic cult and worshippers were exclusively male; they believed in honour, duty and sacrifice – traditional military values. Backing this up is the fact that mithraeums are found at military establishments and in major trading centres like Rome and London, where it is thought that the merchant class contained devotees.

The Mithraic cult believed that a follower could win true happiness in the afterlife through extensive secret initiation, worship, personal merit and honourable behaviour. Symbols of the zodiac – Scorpio and Taurus are the most important – and the Sun is frequently depicted on Mithraic reliefs and frescoes around the walls, as well as depictions of other associated gods in the temple.

The shrines are generally a short walk outside the fortress and are strikingly similar in form wherever they are found. They are invariably small, only able to contain a maximum of 40 people, and resemble a windowless sunken cave with a narrow central isle flanked by two raised side aisles with the main altar positioned at the head. The altars themselves are often dedicated (usually

by officers) to the 'Unconquered Sun'. Mithraea could contain more than one altar, plus cult reliefs and frescoes. At the entrance stood two figures dressed as Persians (the Gemini twins): Cautes standing upright with a torch and Cautopates standing in reflection with an inverted torch symbolising darkness. Lit by torchlight, the elaborate ceremonies progressed through seven grades of physical and spiritual initiation for new members, which many scholars believe were linked to the planets. Here, initiates would also feast and worship well away from the prying eyes of non-believers.

The core of the cult was the secretive mysteries, men who only achieved that status after passing through all the extensive initiation ordeals. There is considerable speculation about how these initiations proceeded, but nobody actually knows.

Theodosius outlawed all pagan sects in late AD3 and Mithraism was officially abolished, though doubtless continued illegally for a period of time. When the cult died out, the temples were shut down and buried, then lay forgotten for centuries.

▼ *Ostia Antica, Rome's ancient port, had 16 Mithraea – the highest known concentration. This one at the Baths of Mithras dates to the early 3rd century* AD. *It was designed to portray the cave where Mithras killed the sacred bull.*

FESTIVALS

Knowledge of festivals primarily comes from the *Feriale Duranum*, the calendar of events of the Cohors XX Palmyrenorum at Dura Europos in Syria in early AD3. While this document only refers to this cohort, the same festivals were almost certainly celebrated in military units across the Roman Empire. The festivals probably included military marching/manoeuvres and after the sacrifices, music and feasting.

- *Natalis aquilae* – 3 January: the most important annual festival that celebrates the founding of the legion. (This might mean that each legion celebrated its birthday on different days.) It was dedicated to Jupiter Optimus Maximus, the chief protector of the Roman state and chief deity of the Capitoline Triad (with Juno Regina and Minerva). An ox was sacrificed to Jupiter, a cow each to Juno and Minerva.
- *Missio honesta* – 7 January: when time-served veterans were honourably discharged
- *Rosaliae signorum* – 10 and 31 May: decoration of the military standards
- *Quinquatria* – 19 March: festival dedicated to Minerva
- 21 April: festival to celebrate the founding of Rome
- 26 April: festival dedicated to Marcus Aurelius
- 9 June: festival dedicated to Vesta
- 12 July: festival dedicated to Julius Caesar

There would also be celebrations for the reigning emperor's birthday, to local gods and to popular army figures, such as Germanicus.

MEDICINE

Legionary forts, particularly the large ones, almost always had hospitals within their confines, as well as specialist medics who would go on campaign with their legion. Roman medicine was heavily based on Greek precedent, but Roman military medical techniques and medicine greatly improved on the original.

HOSPITALS

Covering an area of some 560sq m (6,000sq ft) and with space for 250–500 patients, a Roman hospital was clean and well lit, quiet and well ordered. Romans clearly understood the importance of hygiene – medical tools were routinely cleaned, sharpened and sterilised – and any wounds were regularly assessed.

Cleanliness was of particular importance, as Belfiglio notes: 'Hygiene and sanitation were regularly practiced in all

▼ *The hospital* (valetudinarium) *at Vircovicium (Housesteads). Medical care was essential for soldiers, and was provided by a separate corps of the army from Julius Caesar's time onwards. Other densely garrisoned areas also had major legionary hospitals such as those recorded at Haltern, Novaensium-Neuss, Bonn, Vetera (Germania Inferior), Vindonissa (Germania Superior), Lauriacum (Noricum), Carnuntum (Pannonia Superior), Inchtuthil (Britannia Inferior), Caerleon (Britannia Secunda), and a huge one at Novae (Moesia Inferior).*

military encampments, especially hospitals. Roman physicians took steps to reduce sepsis and separated sick and wounded soldiers in the hospital wards to minimize contagions from spreading among patients. In the event of epidemics, isolation wards were set up in tents near the hospital. Roman Army camps were situated near streams or rivers, away from marshes, swamps and standing water. The hospital bath area was attached to a gymnasium for exercises or massages.'[8] In the event of epidemics, isolation ward tents could be set up near the hospital.

Alongside these cornerstones of good practice were many techniques and medicines that are still in use today (see below). For instance, their missile extraction and amputation techniques were still in use as late as World War One.

As patients started to recover, they would be encouraged to try light exercise – as they are today. To keep their morale up, their commanders would visit the hospital to praise and encourage their recovery, showing an understanding of the benefits of positive thinking and boosting self-esteem.

MEDICAL MANUALS

The Romans knew about medicine, as is evident from the wealth of written sources: Cornelius Celsus (1st century AD), who wrote a manual of wound surgery, Pedanius Dioscorides (AD40–80) who compiled an extensive catalogue of medicinal products and their uses, Claudius Galenus (AD129–c.199) compiled a systematic approach to medical procedure and Flavius Renatus Vegetius (4th century AD) who discussed sanitation and hygiene at military encampments and preserving the health of soldiers. Theodorus Priscianus (4th century AD) wrote a study about skin diseases and wounds and Quintus Gargilius Martialis (3rd century AD) specialised in dietetics, including foods useful to helping wounds heal and those possessing analgesic properties. Pliny the Elder (AD23–79) recorded a valuable collection of pharmaceutical formulas.

▶*The Greek god of medicine, Asclepius, carried a rod with a serpent twined round and had many daughters, including Hygieia – the goddess of health, cleanliness and sanitation. The Romans incorporated the god as Aesculapius.*

During battles, when the hospital was overwhelmed with triaged soldiers, the medics appreciated that speed was important. Consequently, the treatment of the merely sick could be delayed under such circumstances – the acutely wounded took priority.

FIRST AID ON THE MOVE

On campaign, the medics would wait in tents behind the fighting units ready to treat battle wounds. They did what they could on site then sent the wounded back behind the lines to hospital. Most legion injuries (if not killed outright) occurred to the unshielded right side, especially to the leg.

Hygiene was taken just as seriously in these makeshift hospitals as it was back at base, as Belfiglio describes: 'Every night while others slept, a detachment of soldiers performed hospital police duties. The detail cleaned the entire hospital, including the kitchen, baths, latrines, surgical suite, walls and hallways. They used a mixture of Ammoniacum juice, water and vinegar as a cleansing agent. The *medicus tesserarius* (hospital officer of the watch) monitored cleanliness by inspection after the work was completed. A *medicus decanus* (task master) ordered the specific tasks of workers on the policing detail. A separate detail cremated dead soldiers outside the camp walls.'[9]

TREATING DISEASE

There was no cure for infectious diseases and viruses in Roman times. Instead, soldiers who contracted a communicable disease received bed rest, isolation and symptomatic treatment in the hushed, calm environment of the legion hospital. Sleep was recognised as an invaluable

healer and hospitals were kept suitably quiet to facilitate this. Rainwater was preferred for use in liquid medications and if unavailable, spring water was used; Romans appreciated the importance of a clean source.

Treatments depended on the severity of the problem and many of the remedies are still in use in more refined versions even today. The doctors also appreciated that the dosages and application of medicines depended upon the patient's size, age and physical condition.

Galen and Celsus discussed the common problems of high fever and dysentery, both of which were especially prevalent during epidemics and could lead to death. Convalescent staff sponged fever patients with tepid water and *acetum* (vinegar) and gave them a draught containing the powdered bark of the willow tree (*Salix alba*). When the fever was dangerously high, the patient's head was kept cool with ice or cold compresses, and his body kept warm with blankets. Physicians controlled dysentery through medicine and diet. Galen prescribed the juice of Stinking St John's Wort (*Hypericum hircinum*) and mastic (*Pistacia lentiscus*) for diarrhoea. Celsus prescribed a compounded mixture called kolikon for dysentery. The recipe contained costum, anise, castoreum, parsley, pepper, poppy, cyperus, myrrh and honey mixed together in warm water.

Inflammation was treated with ice and the application of a solution of cupric acetate. Constipation was treated with castor oil (*Ricinus communis*). Non-pharmaceutical intervention included oral water rehydration therapy and eating plain foods such as boiled eggs, baked chicken and vegetables, toast, oatmeal and barley.

Soldiers experiencing mild pain were treated with the use

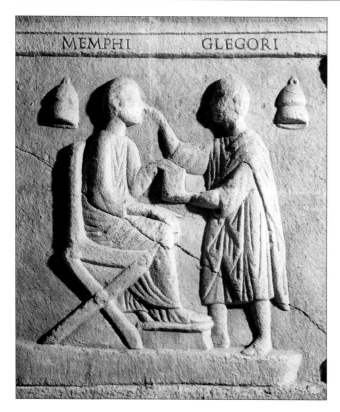

▲ *This 2nd century* AD *relief shows an ophthalmologist examining a patient. The Romans may not have had our level of knowledge but they had a practical understanding of many elements of medicine. Indeed, medical instruments found in Britain show the Romans carried out procedures such as head surgery and cataract operations. In* Medicine and Health in Roman Britain *Dr Nick Summerton says, 'Archaeological finds of eye medicine stamps, representations of eyes together with a sickness report from the Roman fort at Vindolanda suggest that eye diseases were a particular concern within Roman Britain.'*

of a local anaesthetic such as henbane seeds (*Hyoscyamus niger)* combined with opium (*Papaver somniferum*) in an ointment mixed into lanolin or with broadleaf plantain (*Plantago major*). The powdered inner bark of the slippery elm tree (*Ulmus glabra*) was used for coughs. For persistent coughing, patients were given red wine mixed with horehound (*Marrubium vulgare*), a type of mint.

Soldiers in severe pain could be given a draught of mandrake (*Mandragora officinarum*). Badly injured men and post-operative patients (including amputees) would have been given a draught of opium to lower their temperature, reduce their pain and help them sleep.

Ideally, patients needing sleep or de-stressing would have been administered *Withania somnifera* (also called ashwagandha, winter cherry or Indian ginseng) in the evening to help them sleep. However, this was not always available as it had to be imported from India via the Silk Road. As an alternative, Celsus recommends a mixture of mandrake, opium seed and the seeds of henbane mixed in red wine.[10]

MEDICAL STAFF

- *Capsarius* – a medical corpsman who had received training to render advanced first aid and field dressings to wounded legionaries. In particular, he treated sword cuts, using bandages made of linen and wool and ointments, all of which he carried in a leather pouch called a *capsa*. First, he cleaned the wound using either antiseptic vinegar, wine or olive oil, then he stitched and bound it with a linen bandage. Bad wounds had tourniquets applied and/ or were cauterised with a hot iron. Also contained in the first aid kits were dried aloe for use as an anti-haemorrhagic, and henbane seeds (*Hyoscyamus niger*) in an ointment prepared with wool fat (lanolin) for pain. *Absus* (sick or wounded soldiers) who were unable to walk were evacuated by stretcher or wagon pulled by horses to the field hospital (*valetudinarium*).
- *Medicus* – a trained doctor with the equivalent of a centurion's rank. He dealt with the trickier arrow wounds and used specialist equipment to extract barbed arrows and spear heads. He could also staple severed tendons together.
- *Medici ordinarii* – ordinary medical staff. These were ordinary soldiers and *immunes* who were excused usual duties in exchange for medical help. However, their muster probably included senior officers as well, who would have had different ranks and functions. Their equipment included scalpels, forceps, retractors, knives and saws for amputations, and other specialised equipment.
- *Optio convalescentium* – physician's assistant.

▼ *A selection of Roman Army medical instruments.*

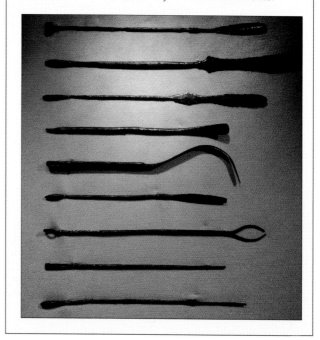

PUNISHMENT

All armies are built on discipline and rules, and each administers punishments to those who transgress. The Roman Army was no exception. Although our knowledge of its rules is patchy, it is indicative of its strict regime that one of a centurion's marks of office was the *vitis* vine stick with which they administered swift, on-the-spot punishment to recalcitrant legionaries.

In a well-known story Tacitus mentions one centurion, Lucilius, during his description of the Pannonian mutiny: 'Camp humorists had surnamed him "Fetch-Another", from his habit, as one cane broke over a private's back, of calling at the top of his voice for a second, and ultimately a third.'[11] Indeed, so ingrained into military discipline was the centurion's *vitis* that 'our first visual evidence of the vitis as well as a portrait of a centurion: an epitaph from the mid-first century BC to Minucius Lorarius. "Lorarius" translates as "flogger".'[12] To push this point home he is shown with his right hand holding the switch.

Few specific details of Roman military law survive in the writings of antiquity until late in the history of the Roman Empire. In AD429 – well outside our period – Emperor Theodosius II ordered a compilation of all the Empire's laws since the Christian rule of Constantine began in AD312. The resulting *Codex Theodosianus* compiled all existing military and civil laws and legal decisions into one vast collection that went into force on 1 January AD439. The military section, although comparatively short, does give an insight into rules, regulations and punishments that must have pertained.

MILITARY PRIVILEGES AND PUNISHMENTS

Soldiers enjoyed levels of privilege not granted to ordinary civilians. In particular, they were exempt from state-sanctioned torture and condemnation to the mines as punishment. It also seems, judging by a complaint from the satirist Juvenal, that they had their legal affairs sorted out much more quickly. He also complained that ordinary citizens were unlikely to win a claim against a legionary. If the latter did commit a crime or misdemeanour, they were investigated in camp by a tribune who imposed punishment based on his own and the field commander's comments and feelings about the matter. Huge emphasis was put on military honour and obedience, and lack of obedience was mercilessly punished.

In peacetime, crimes and misdemeanours were punished less severely than in wartime. Mitigating factors included rank, service record, character and previous offences. New recruits and first offenders were usually given more leniency at the discretion of the commander.

◄ *Reproduction of the tombstone of Marcus Caelius at Saalburg (top). Caelius died in the Teutoburg Forest with Varus. Caelius carries a* vitis *and a number of decorations:* corona civica, *two* armillae, *two* torques, *five* phalerae *on harness and possibly two* phalerae *above his shoulders. A centurion of the Ermine Street Guard (left) is similarly equipped, although he is less likely to have used his* vitis.

TYPICAL PUNISHMENTS

- Theft – flogging
- Rape – nose cut off
- Desertion to the enemy in peacetime – reduction in rank for cavalrymen and dishonourable discharge for legionaries
- Allowing a standard to fall into enemy hands – ultimate punishment was disbandment
- Stealing weapons – flogging
- Stealing the pack animals – one or both hands cut off
- Losing or casting down weapons or shields during battle – if an entire unit turned and ran from the battlefield it could be decimated but in practice this happened only in cases of extreme cowardice or mutiny. Decimation meant one in every 10 men was clubbed or stoned to death by the other members of the cohort. The punishment for the survivors was to be put on barley rations instead of wheat. An insubordinate unit was made to camp outside the fort; if they mutinied they could be disbanded.

TYPES OF PUNISHMENT FOR LEGIONARIES

Discipline was harsh in the legions and punishment could be completely arbitrary depending on the attitude of the commander. They included beating, clubbing to death, execution, *munerum indictio* (extra duties, such as cleaning latrines and fetching water and wood), fines, *militiae mutatio* (loss of privileges or demotion to inferior service), *gradus deiectio* (reduction in rank) and *missio ignominiosa* (dishonourable discharge). However, *pecuniaria multa* (fines) and loss of pay were the commonest punishments.

Capital crimes included risking the security of the legion in any way, such as by conspiring against the commanders, treason, insubordination, violence, hitting an officer, leaving your post – failing to keep the night watch properly invoked the death penalty by *fustuarium* (being clubbed to death) – hitting an officer, stealing from fellow soldiers, homosexuality, giving false evidence, running away from battle, pretending to be ill to avoid fighting, entering the camp unconventionally (i.e. over the walls), loose talk about the fort or legion, and joining or simply giving information to the enemy. The death penalty was also invoked cumulatively for three lesser offences committed at different times. If found guilty of a capital offence, the army commander's lictors carried out the punishment – hanging, beheading, burning alive, consignment to the arena to face almost certain death, cudgelling (*fustuarium),* foot whipping (*bastinado*) and decapitation *(decollatio).* However, the death penalty was rarely applied; instead, other severe sanctions were usually ordered.

Corporal punishments (*castigatio*) included reduction in rank, dishonourable discharge, flogging, fines (*pecuniaria multa*), extra duties, body mutilation or humiliation. The latter included standing outside the fort without wearing a belt so the dangling tunic made the man look ridiculous.

DESERTION

Desertio was a flagrant offence punishable by death. It was a violation of the sacred military oath the soldier took on joining the legion. Despite this, it was a common problem. By AD3, for instance, Roman frontier soldiers had largely assimilated with local populations so in times of war many, especially new recruits, melted away into the civilian population.

If a commander set a harsh regime it led to desertion. Interestingly, soldiers who went AWOL were questioned about their motives and could be treated considerately If they had a genuine reason for abandoning their post. Mitigating circumstances would also be considered, as would the man's rank, character and previous record. Forgivable reasons included illness, family problems and pursuing a fleeing slave. Voluntary returnees were treated more leniently. If a number of legionaries deserted together but returned within a specified time they were often split up among other units but could avoid corporal punishment. If, however, a legionary deserted to join the enemy (*transfuga*), he would be accused of treason and put to death if caught.

When a deserter was caught after being AWOL for a long time, he was deported and deprived of Roman citizenship. Under civil law, a convicted deserter was also required to return all the money he had earned or acquired during his service. Someone who aided and abetted a deserter (a *receptarores*) was punished as well.

AUXILIA PUNISHMENTS

The *auxilia*'s training and punishments were essentially the same, but discipline could also be maintained by a unit's own tribal punishment system. During the Republican era, army discipline was stricter and the punishments harsher. The voluntary recruitment of Imperial legions could partly explain this, and the evolution of influence – whether an emperor's need to keep the army loyal or a general's bid for ultimate power. The increased variety and nationality of recruits across the legions and *auxilia* was also a factor.

▼ *Decimation (reducing a legion by executing 1 in 10) is one of those punishments that fascinates modern readers. Its documented occurrences are few, perhaps the best known being that inflicted by Crassus on the men who fled from Spartacus. Appian suggests he decimated two legions.*

ROMAN MILITARY RANKS

All armies have ranks, and the Roman Army was no exception. The officers and NCOs may not have had pips and stripes but that does not mean that any man in the legion wouldn't have known their place, to whom they reported and who was in command. Just as in a modern army, it was these officers who kept the ordinary soldiers disciplined.

Differences in accommodation, pay, clothing, armour and weaponry: the officer class would have been obvious in any legion. There was some change over time. The position of *Praefectus castrorum* – for much of the Principate the third in command – increased in importance as legions became more fixed in position. This was also one of the few positions that could be filled by someone who had been a top centurion, thus raising them to the equestrian ranks.

▼ *Typical representation of a centurion wearing a tunic and a* paenula *cloak. He holds his* vitis – *the vine stick that acted as both a staff of office and a cudgel – while he pours an offering on an altar.*

Just as in a modern army it was the senior NCOs – the centurionate – that provided the backbone. They seem – other than the *Primus pilus* – to have held the same rank but been ordered by their years of service. There were around 60 centurions in a legion. Beneath them, the soldiers also had their own specialism, hierarchy and range of duties. They broadly fell into a number of categories, the chief being *immunes*, who specialised in particular jobs (eg architect, sword cutter, baker, etc).

THE *IMMUNES, DISCENS* AND *EVOCATI*
Immunes ('exempt')
These were the men of a legion whose specialist knowledge in their particular technical fields made them more valuable than the average basic *miles gregarius*. As such, they were therefore exempt from many of the tedious tasks of day-to-day army life. *Immunes*' status was reached through having served first as an ordinary legionary for several years, then having undergone a period of the relevant specialist training. Their salaries were usually larger than those of the ordinary soldiers.

Discens ('learning')
This was a term for any legionary in training for an additional specific technical role and as such would have had to have time to learn and practise. All specialist ranks required this extra training from the existing masters of each art, such as

---

LITERACY AND NUMERACY

The level of literacy across the military is much debated. The Romans were very bureaucratic, so a proficient level of reading and writing was the minimal requirement for many positions in a legion. This could mean writing in Latin (sometimes Greek as well) and mathematics.

The *signiferi* were in charge of the legion's savings and the *signifer* of each century was responsible for their money and therefore was required to be completely literate. Other offices within the legion needed to be numerate and literate: officers almost by definition had a good education and therefore would have been both numerate and literate.

In charge of clerical duties was the *cornicularius*, a senior non-commissioned officer, in rank directly below the centurionate. Some ordinary soldiers were literate and numerate and they were probably recruited from the start to work as *librarius* (clerk).

RANK NAMES AND ROLES

- Consul – two consuls were elected every year by the citizens of Rome. They had both military and civic duties to undertake, but primarily they commanded the armies
- *Praetor* – this was the commander appointed to lead a legion or grouping of legions
- *Legatus legionis* – drawn from the senatorial class, this was the primary legion commander
- *Laticlavian tribune* – second-in-command of the legion; lesser (angusticlavian) tribunes (there were five of them) would serve as junior officers
- *Praefectus* – third-in-command of the legion; various prefects did different things. The *praefectus equitarius*, for instance, was in charge of a cavalry unit
- *Primus pilus* – both commanding centurion for the first cohort and the legion senior
- *Centurio* – basic commander of a century (*decurio*) – one of a legion's cavalry officers in command of a unit (*turma*). Promotion to legionary centurion was ultimately down to the approval of the emperor in Rome, but most were men promoted from the ranks of the legion
- *Decurio* – commander of a cavalry *turma*

- *Optio* – second-in-command for the centurion, and responsible for battlefield discipline
- *Aquilifer* – the bearer of the eagle standard (*aquila*) for each legion
- *Signifer* – a military administrator who handled financial matters but also carried a standard
- *Imaginifer* – the bearer of a standard showing the emperor's image
- *Cornicen* – a horn blower or signaller
- *Tesserarius* – watch commander who controlled the passwords
- *Decanus* – commander of an eight-man *contubernium*, equivalent to a corporal
- *Milites/Munifex* – the legionary foot soldier
- *Tirones* – a new recruit, subject to a minimum of six months' rigorous training

Other positions
- *Beneficiarius* – someone given a special task; carried a spear with a distinctive spearhead
- *Frumentarius* – in charge of food acquisition/supply
- *Metatores* – surveyors who laid out the marching camp
- *Speculatores* – spy

an engineer (*architecti*) or artilleryman (*ballisarius*), a surveyor (*mensorem*), an eagle bearer (*aquilifer*) or other standard bearer (*signifer*), trumpeter (*buccinator*), medical orderly (*capsarius*) and craftsman (*fabrum*).

Evocati ('summoned')
In the time of the Republic, an *evocatus* was a soldier who had reached retirement age but was induced to remain in service by the Senate or their commander due to critical events, such as Catiline's appeal for Pistoria and Pompey persuading his veterans to remain for the Battle of Pharsalus in 48BC with the temptation of glory and booty. After Augustus, an *evocatus* was a soldier who has served his full military service, obtained his honourable discharge (*missio honesta*), received his retirement sum payment from the Imperial Treasury (*aerarium militare*) and who had then voluntarily re-enlisted – usually at the request of an old commander or consul. (Auxiliary *peregrini* were given citizen certificates and land on which to settle.)

As veterans, *evocati* were higher ranking than ordinary serving legionaries, being automatically granted *immunes* status. They were often but not always made centurions and were entitled to chastise juniors with the *vitis* vine staff. There were also Evocati Augusti – made up exclusively of retired Praetorians, called back to serve again at the emperor's behest.

PROMOTION
Soldiers could have very different careers even within the same legion, as some arms of service offered more opportunities for promotion than others. Theoretically, an able recruit could rise

to the ranks of the *principales* and even to the centurionate, but in practice the man had to already possess a good level of education and have higher influence from family and friends to advance up the ranks. A man from a good background going into the Guard generally remained in a superior position and able men could reasonably expect to be promoted to a centurionate in a legion and maybe higher if they had a good military career, an influential family or sheer luck. For men in the auxiliary, there were fewer opportunities: the best he could hope for was the auxiliary centurionate.

▼ *The emperor addresses the troops – an* adlocutio. *On the dais (top right), Marcus Aurelius and his staff; listening below, the rank and file; to the left centurions, standard bearers and* cornicens. *From the column of Marcus Aurelius.*

SLAVES AND SERVANTS

The Roman empire was built on slavery. Slaves supplied labour in the worst of conditions, in the mines, as farm labourers and as domestic slaves. They also worked as highly skilled, unpaid specialists: clerks, secretaries, doctors, teachers. Many of these slaves were taken prisoner on campaign and sold to traders who followed the army.

The sheer number of slaves in Roman society as a whole makes it difficult to determine how many there were in the legions and what they did. (Even though the Romans held regular censuses because nobody knows for certain who they actually counted, though almost certainly not slaves.)

The question of the proportion and numbers of slaves serving in the legions has to be based on analysis of surviving documents. Most of the slaves in the Roman Empire were captured enemies – the spoils of war – it has even been suggested that the acquisition of slaves was a significant rationale behind some campaigns. Most of these captured people would have been put to service on the land but many would have been retained for army work. Such workers were regarded as being so unimportant personally that they rarely feature in any contemporary documentation, all of which makes their contribution to legion life all the more difficult to ascertain.

One way of helping sift out the slaves in a unit is the use of single-named soldiers (as opposed to the usual *tria nomina*), and that these are in fact slaves of their military unit. Slaves were specifically forbidden from serving in the ranks, although it is documented that a few managed to bluff their way in. It

▼ *The Romans take Dacian army captives – as shown on Trajan's Column. Their fate, almost certainly, was to become slaves or to fight in the arena as gladiators.*

also seems that some may have achieved this with collusion from their owners, who provided them with supporting 'evidence' that they were citizens so that they could serve as substitutes in their place. If this was discovered, the owners were severely punished. The slaves were executed.

Although in normal circumstances slaves were forbidden to serve in the military, in times of extreme manpower shortage the rule was lifted. Suetonius, in his work on Augustus remarked, 'only twice did Augustus enlist emancipated slaves as soldiers … [they] were recruited from the households of rich men and women and immediately freed, whereupon they were placed in the front line, but kept separate from the freeborn and given different weapons.'

Voluntary enslavement

It is supposed from the writings of Tacitus among others, that the ranks of the *lixae* (camp followers) were filled with conquered people desiring Roman status. To this end, some foreign men volunteered for public slavery in the Roman legions so that after long service they would become citizens, but also during that time they had the opportunity of being trained in a skill or profession such as clerical work (it is known that some units used slaves for administrative jobs), logistical skills or a profession such as doctor.

The role of slaves

Calones (military servant; sing *calo*) or *lixae* were the servants of Roman soldiers and they are generally thought to have been slaves. There is only fragmentary evidence about these public slaves – the *servitia castris* – but skilled slaves were undoubtedly important for the day-to-day administration tasks. The quaestor, for example, managed the unit's money and would have been assisted in his office by literate and numerate slaves. He would also have dealt with logistical duties and possibly the direct dealing with outside suppliers, while the unskilled slaves laboured with all the physical housekeeping and cleaning duties around the fort or military camp. The Vindolanda letters have thrown some light on legion slavery and suggest that slaves were responsible for at least partially organising the commander's household. It is also impossible to tell whether all the slaves attached to military personnel were personal property (of the officers) or belonged to the unit. They probably worked as personal attendants, batmen and grooms for the soldiers, but no evidence actually supports this. *Capsari* (hospital orderlies) were most likely public slaves and it is even thought that some *medicus legionis* (army doctors) were public slaves.

BENEFITS AND REWARDS

Bravery in battle, a victorious campaign, promotion: all soldiers like medals, honours and rewards, and the Roman soldier was no different. Individuals and units were happy to acquire titles or awards, and to share the spoils of battle. Generals and emperors hoped each campaign would allow them a triumphal procession in Rome.

HONOURS

Honours and decorations were a vital component of a legion's prestige. Honours were sought after as they conferred status within the unit and the awards themselves added dazzle and spectacle to the uniform and the overall appearance of the legion. They were covetable trophies that inspired the men and were always given in the emperor's name. Some emperors were much more forthcoming with rewards than others, with Trajan in particular considered generous with his benevolence.

Dona – decorations

After a successful battle or on completion of a victorious campaign, the commander held a ceremonial parade in front of the whole army at which, among other things, he distributed the loot. Particularly heroic efforts were noted and individual honours were given for bravery and initiative. The entire spectacle was designed to reinforce the feeling of pride in the legion and to encourage and inspire particularly the youngest soldiers to feats of bravery.

The highest awards were crowns – generally only given to senior officers. Otherwise, the most prestigious awards were:

- *Corona civica* – for saving the life of a Roman citizen or allied soldier. Given if the saved citizen recognised the act of bravery and made a crown of oak leaves and acorns for the hero. It conferred many social privileges on the man for the rest of his life.
- *Corona aurea* – gold crown awarded mainly to centurions for killing an enemy in single combat and holding his ground until the end of battle.
- *Corona muralis* – gold crown decorated with turrets, presented for being the first legionary over the walls of an enemy city.
- *Corona vallaris* – gold crown decorated with *valli* (entrenchment uprights) for being the first legionary across enemy ramparts.
- *Corona obsidionalis* – grass crown for relieving a besieged garrison. A rare decoration that carried enormous prestige. The grass was collected from the battle site, bound into a wreath and presented by the rescued army to the victorious general.
- *Hasta pura* – small, blunt commemorative silver spear – awarded to centurions and *primus pilus* and above, for acts of courage.

Usually only awarded to citizen soldiers:

▲ *A centurion's* phalerae. *These military decorations were usually made of silver – as here – or, rarely, of gold and bronze. As well as being worn by soldiers, they are also in evidence as part of horses' harnesses, and on standards.*

- Large gold torque (necklace) – awarded for valour.
- Small gold torque that hung on a leather harness near the shoulder – awarded for valour.
- *Armillae* (gold armbands worn on the wrist) – awarded for valour.
- *Phalerae* (embossed discs) – worn on a harness over the uniform and analogous to modern medals.
- *Vexillum* – a miniature version of the battlefield standard mounted on a silver base.

Under truly exceptional circumstances these decorations could be awarded to auxiliaries. However, auxiliary soldiers were not recognised individually. Instead, their unit could be rewarded with an honorary title such as *Torquata* or *Armillata*. For really exceptional service, an entire unit could be granted a *civium Romanorum* – immediate Roman citizenship – but only for those serving at the time.

TRIUMPH

A triumph was always held in Rome in front of the entire populace – emperor, Senate and citizens. It was the ultimate

recognition of a legion's valour and usually only granted to an emperor or a really successful general.

The celebration had to be requested, usually by the emperor, but could only be granted by the Senate. Depending on the popularity of the general with the senators, this could take a while. Initially, the victorious general had to be declared an *imperator* by his own troops (a title he would hold until the end of the triumph), and he and his army had to wait outside the gates of Rome so as not to influence the decision while the Senate debated whether the triumph was merited. When the decision was 'yes' (they were never going to say 'no' with a dangerous, fully equipped, triumphal army of battle-hardened veterans waiting outside the gates), all the temples in the city opened their doors, garlanded their shrines with flowers and lit dense clouds of incense to perfume the air. The actual triumph could last up to two days and comprised parades, sacrifices and celebrations. A general who had won a triumph for an emperor was often awarded *ornamenta* – triumphal decorations.

To qualify (usually) for a triumph, several criteria had to be met:

- More than 5,000 enemy must have died in battle.
- The campaign must be over and definitively won.
- The Roman Empire must have become more powerful as a result of the victory – usually winning new territory over which Rome now had dominion.

▲ *Marcus Aurelius was granted a triumph in AD176 after his success against the Sarmatian and Germanic tribes. Here he celebrates his triumph entering Rome at the start of the parade.*

▶ *The triumphal procession would sing songs of victory and bawdy ballads of conquest, all aided and cheered on by the thronging crowds who had a holiday for the duration. The expenses for the triumph were covered by the Senate.*

TRIUMPHAL ROUTE THROUGH ROME

- Temple of Bellona to the Porta Triumphalis
- Through the city to the Circus Flaminius
- To the Circus Maximus
- To the Roman Forum and along the Sacred Way
- Up the Capitoline Hill
- To the Temple of Jupiter Optimus Maximus

The triumphal procession

The parade mustered outside the city near the Temple of Bellona in the *Campus Martius* (Field of Mars) where the *imperator* addressed his troops with a rousing speech praising their exploits. They then processed to the Porta Triumphalis (a gate used only for triumphal processions) where the *imperator* entered the city to the sound of trumpets announcing his arrival. The entire Senate greeted him before he set off in his high circular triumphal chariot pulled by a quadriga (four horses) with his male offspring and senior officers flanking him on horseback. He wore the traditional purple robe of Jupiter, embroidered with gold, over a flowered tunic, had his face painted red to emulate Jupiter's ancient statue, and balanced a laurel (sweet bay) wreath on his head. In his right hand he brandished a laurel bough and in his left he held an ivory sceptre. Julius Caesar was idolised by the crowds and by his men, who gave him the status of a god, so to mitigate this and remind him of his mortal status, behind him stood a slave holding a golden crown over his head and murmuring '*Respice post te! Hominem te esse memento! Memento mori!*' ('Look behind you! Remember that you are mortal. Remember that you must die!')

▲ The Triumph of Julius Caesar *by Andrea Andreani, 1599. Although painted hundreds of years later, this painting conveys something of the colour, chaos and booty of a typical Roman triumph.*

▼ *Every April hundreds of actors take part in the annual Grands Jeux Romains in Nîmes amphitheatre. This is a scene from 2013, a historical re-enactment of the Battle of Alesia, c.52BC, during the Gallic Wars where Julius Caesar was victorious.*

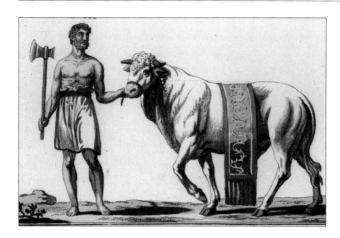

▲ *At the Temple of Jupiter white bulls (or oxen) were sacrificed to the gods. The animals were washed and prepared for their role with gilded horns, decorations and garlands (*serta*).*

All the way, the crowds cheered and roared on the spectacle. Preceding the *imperator* through the streets were cartloads of showy booty collected on campaign, the more the better. This could include statues, piles of coins, unusual plants, strange animals (ideally elephants) and even enemy ships – in short, anything that looked good and was impressive. Next, followed the captive enemies in chains or cages, particularly their war leaders, as savage and exotic as possible.

Throughout the procession, musicians played music and laughing and singing would have filled the air. White bulls and oxen wandered along the route on their way to sacrifice at the temple of Jupiter. Last, but by no means least, in the parade was the legion itself. Marching through Rome, singing ribald and obscene songs to ward off evil, they roared their battle success and brandished their laurel-wreathed spears, cheered by crowds of Romans, as everyone enjoys the holiday. Depending on the campaign, the whole parade could last over a day or even two.

At the Temple of Jupiter, the *imperator* made a sacrifice to the god to thank him for his support and munificence. Jupiter himself was then celebrated and petitioned to continue the prosperity of Rome. Sacrifices included several pure white oxen and the *imperator*'s golden crown. He then called the

---

OVATIO (OVATION)

This was a lesser triumph, granted to a general. It could be held following victory over a minor enemy, for example over rebelling slaves or fighting pirates. For this, the commander, wearing a wreath of myrtle and a purple-bordered robe, entered Rome on foot or horseback. The Senate would not necessarily attend and his army was also unlikely to be present. A sheep was sacrificed at the Temple of Jupiter instead of a bull. During the Republic, there were 25 known ovations, followed by a further seven during the Principate, with the last being that for Domitian in AD93.

---

final parade, awards and commendations were made and the booty was shared out. Prayers were said, and finally everyone dispersed.

Having marched away, the legion had leave to celebrate for a good week or so. The captives, by stark contrast, were usually strangled later in the Forum or somewhere quiet, well away from the festivities. Alternatively, prisoners could be held back to perform in the Colosseum games that were usually held as part of the festivities, where they died in front of the cheering masses.

RETIREMENT AND PENSIONS

After full service of 25 years, legionaries became citizens of the Roman Empire. By then, many of them were in their mid-40s, though this of course depended on how old they were when they signed up. Legionaries also had the option to sign up for further service. The man's details were logged at the records office on the Capitoline Hill in Rome and could be verified on request.

The *praemia militia* lump sum of his pension or land grant changed over the years. The initial Augustus pension of 12,000 sesterces (increased to 20,000 by Caracalla) equated to 12–14 years of income: plus any monies (booty etc) that he may or may not have managed to save. Throughout his service, the legionary earned money but he didn't always manage to save it, much of it going on his food, clothing and equipment; only what was left over went towards his pension.

The veteran also received various prerogatives and privileges – *emeritum* – that also changed over time. These are too specific to enumerate here, but as examples:

- Augustus granted (and this was confirmed by Domitian) veterans – and their close families – exemption from tolls.
- Claudius made soldiers the equals of married men – that meant tax benefits.
- Constantine confirmed exemption from taxes on trade up to 15 solidi (gold coins introduced by Diocletian).

Going it alone

For a veteran of 25 years, leaving the legion could be a shock. He was no longer constrained by authority and for the first time had to manage his own everyday affairs – he hadn't had to find his own food and lodging for all that time, let alone all the other necessities of living comfortably. This often proved too much and many men re-signed for further service, meaning some served many decades in the legions.

Others with a business mind set up services to their former unit and made a profitable living using their connections. Alternatively, some made friends with existing businessmen and were invited to join the enterprise (for an investment).

After serving in an area for a good number of years, many retired legionaries simply moved into the local *canabae* (village) so as to be near old friends and colleagues and perhaps to live permanently with his unofficial family, or marry the mother of his children. After 25 years, he may have had a son who had enlisted with the nearby unit anyway.

▶ *On retirement, bronze military discharge certificates were issued to those without Roman citizenship. After Caracalla opened citizenship to all in the Empire by the* Constitutio Antoniniana *of 212AD, they ceased to be issued except for certain units that employed people from outside the empire. For more information see pages 146–7.*

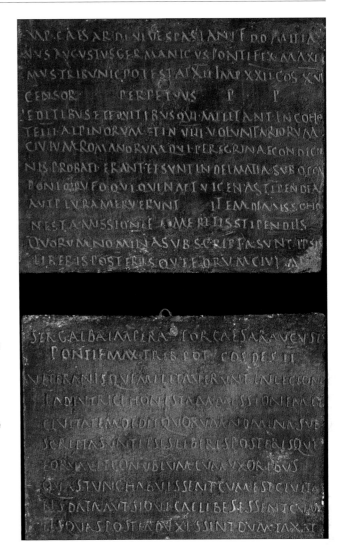

Studies have shown that to the age of 42 veteran soldiers enjoyed better health than civilians, but that after that their survival rate steadily shrank below civilians'. This has been put down in part to the long-term effects of old war wounds and injuries, but also to the decline in their living standards as their pensions were spent. Veterans seemed to have better, longer lives if they moved to live in a *vici* or *canabae* in a frontier zone where the military presence was considerable and veteran associations flourished.

Keeping the retirees sweet

Under Marius, retired legionaries en masse were offered land in newly conquered territory. For the Roman Empire, this meant that a veteran fighting force was on hand to encourage the locals not to revolt against Rome. Augustus planted 28 such colonies in Italy, mostly for veterans of the civil war. However, most of the later colonies were founded in the provinces or in underpopulated areas. The intention was to colonise new territories with Romanised men who would raise Roman families, but veterans often preferred instead to return to the lands where they served with the legion, or where they had originally come from. Many also had little interest in raising families, so left no heirs to work the land. A lot of such settlements didn't gel as men from differing units often failed to bond sufficiently to cohere and develop a community; besides, they were soldiers, not farmers. Emperor Hadrian stopped this practice and instead encouraged local recruitment and service, and grants of money were made to veterans instead of land.

Under Augustus, in AD6 the *praemia militia* gave retiring soldiers a fixed provision. This was not an act of generosity but rather a way of quelling military veterans' unrest about their overall financial situation and their general lack of willingness to extend their service. This itemised a fixed scale of gratuities: praetorians received 5,000 denarii after 16 years' service and legionaries 3,000 denarii after 20 years' service. It was not always honoured; in AD14, veterans were complaining that they had been cheated and instead of getting the money they were owed they were given marshland or uncultivable hillsides.

Auxiliaries, praetorians and marines each received a pair of bronze plates proving their status: that they had served their term, had been honourably discharged, granted Roman citizenship and *conubium* (the right to marry a Roman citizen) if appropriate. If he were already a citizen, he still needed a *conubium* unless his wife-to-be was a citizen. This diploma also granted citizenship to pre-existing children, including daughters. This changed in AD140 when existing children lost that privilege.

DISMISSAL

There were only four ways for a legionary to be dismissed:

- *Missio honesta* – honourable discharge. The man had served loyally and well and served his emperor and legion faithfully. He was entitled to full pension benefits and all the other privileges of a former legionary.
- *Missio causaria* – honourable discharge. Given for a physical injury, ideally for being heroically wounded, but no longer fit enough to serve. This had to be assessed by a doctor via a thorough physical examination. His pension was correlated to the length of his service.
- *Missio ignominiosa* – dishonourable discharge. Given for a heinous crime that meant the man was no credit to the legion. He would most likely be severely whipped before discharge. He was stripped of all privileges, forbidden from living in Rome, barred from Imperial service of all kinds, and shunned by all decent people.
- *Mortus* – death.

CHAPTER FOUR

UNIFORMS, KIT AND INSIGNIA

Roman military equipment is represented in art as standardised, but it was by no means uniform – even within a single cohort. Over the centuries there were stylistic changes and improvements in manufacture but the technological level of military equipment remained fundamentally the same throughout the Ancient World and with no real concept of obsolescence, older items remained in service for as long as they continued to be effective. There was also local variation in the equipment manufactured in each province, either privately or, eventually, in state-run factories.

◄ *During the Principate, the bulk of the army's equipment was provided through a system of private contractors but Diocletian (AD284–305) and the emperors of the Tetrarchy (AD293–313) created Imperial arms factories known as* fabricae.

CLOTHING

The clothing worn by the legionaries wasn't uniform as we known it. Hand-made before the age of machines, there may have been an attempt at universality, but there would have been many variations in manufacture and colour, the latter depending on the strength of dye and efficacy of the fixing agent (mordants).

Almost all the evidence for clothing worn by Roman soldiers is sculptural or epigraphic, mainly in the form of gravestones and monuments – especially the invaluable Trajan's Column in Rome. It is to these representations of fabric in stone that one must turn for visual clues. However, interpreting these monuments is problematic, because of the stylisation and idealisation of the sculptors and also the traditions that maintained archaic and iconic features of appearance, fashion and equipment long after their time, for political, nationalistic or religious reasons. Nevertheless, a wide variety of styles can be observed with many local variations, explained by the unsynchronised changing of fashions in different parts of the empire and the distinctive appearance of something made or copied in a particular place. In the period of the Dominate, from the time of Diocletian (AD284–305) and the emperors of

the Tetrarchy (AD293–313) the production of military clothing was centralised in state-owned facilities located near major fabric-producing centres like Alexandria. Other army-administered weaving mills were located throughout the Empire, with examples discovered at Reims, Tournai, and Trier. These factories and their products were funded by a tax known as the *vestris militaris*, since by this time the state no longer had the resources to fund an army of the size required.

COMMON FABRICS

Most of the fabrics used by the military and society at large were either of wool or linen made from flax. When it came to dyeing, the Romans preferred to dye the fleece rather than the cloth, and because linen was so difficult to colour with the dyes they had at the time, it was mostly worn in its natural

◄ *Army tunics were made from wool and were either undyed or came in the Roman Army's identifying colour red, deriving from the madder plant* Rubia tinctorum.

▼ *Leather was the most common and vital material for the Roman Army, used in every conceivable way for clothing, covering, cording and containing or fastening and linking every kind of equipment.*

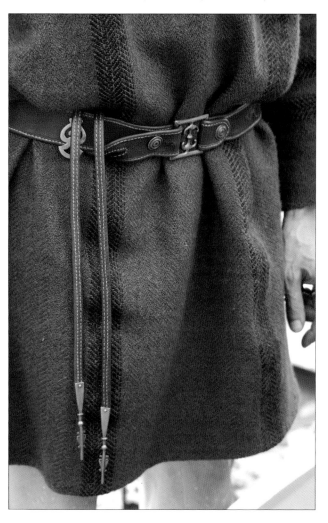

shade – greyish brown, or bleached whiter by long exposure to sunlight. Perhaps the most vital material, however, was leather, from which the Roman Army made an enormous number of objects, including dress such as kilts, trousers, cloaks, boots, belts, (baldrics), armour (petruges, fittings for all metalwork, under-armour jerkins), as well as tents, bags, shield covers and horse equipment.

To feed this continuous demand for large quantities of leather elaborate empire-wide trade networks operated, making fortunes for the patrician livestock and landowners. Just as with livestock, the military's demand for leather would have regularly exceeded its internal supply and it must have been obliged to outsource when on campaign or on the borders, and this was one of the ways the army interacted with local populations rather than just militarily.

TUNICS

A basic – often homemade – garment that came into general Roman fashion sometime in the 3rd century BC, the tunics (*tunica*) were worn by both men and women. It originally consisted of two simple, identical rectangular pieces of material sewn together with holes for the arms and the head, which came down to above the knees and was usually cinched at the waist with a belt (*cintus*). They were generally decorated with *clavi*, two coloured vertical lines either side of the neck opening. Men's tunics were (except for those of some louche emperors and patricians) worn short, but later, women's versions became longer.

The principal material was wool: even in Egypt military tunics were made from it. Linen was used for under-tunics or for the special tunics such as those for dining, the difference between rich and poor revealed by the quality of the material used and the colour it was dyed. In the army, tunics were for the most part undyed but they also wore their favourite mandated colour – the colour of the war god Mars – blood red. 'Roman Army Red' was mostly derived from madder – one of the cheapest dyes available – which would fade with washing and sunlight. The pigment was extracted from the plant by crushing and drying, with the root giving the strongest colour. The most vivid dye comes from the species *Rubia tinctorum* (common madder or dyer's madder).

The tunics depicted on Trajan's column demonstrate that they could be worn off the shoulder and tied behind the neck in a knot. Many Roman soldiers chose to represent themselves for posterity – on their tombstones – unarmoured and draped in various elaborate styles of tunic and cloak. This could be just funerary fashion or idealisation, or indeed simply that they were proud to show off their citizen status. For the most part, legionaries wore their above-the-knee-length tunics belted at the waist for both work and leisure, but in colder climes they could be layered.

Later, long-sleeved versions worn by cavalrymen rather like a collarless shirt were also used, in combination with three-quarter-length wool or leather trousers (*braccae*). On the

▶ *Tombstone from Bad Kreuznach, Germany of auxiliary soldier Annaius Daverzus who served in Cohors IIII Delmatarum. In spite of his presumed lower status, his tunic and cloak are every bit as elaborate as those of his legionary counterparts.*

▼ *A re-enactor from Tarracoviva wearing early Roman equipment: a pot helmet, chest protector, shield and spear. In the time of the early Republic, each legionary was expected to provide his own uniform, equipment and weapons, and to replace them when they were worn out, damaged or lost.*

◄ Archers wore chain mail shirts rather than Lorica segmentata *for the freedom of movement necessary in using a bow. After the Marian reforms, the State provided government-issue kit, but detailed records were kept and all equipment had to be handed back on retirement.*

KILTS

Kilts (*pteruges*) came to the Romans from Classical Greece and featured a kilt of hardened leather or stiffened linen strips and epaulettes worn underneath armour. These were presumably a single garment but perhaps a two-piece, made to cushion the soldier from his metal cuirass and avoid bruising and rubbing as well as to add some feeling of increased protection. They were worn by all ranks, although less visible leather or padded linen jerkins were also used.

PADDED UNDERCOAT

Made from two layers of stiffened or quilted linen with wool sandwiched in between, no physical examples of the *subarmarls* have survived, but it took the form of a padded undercoat made to cushion the wearer from the impact of an enemy's strike as well the rubbing and chafing of his own armour. The *subarmalis* could also be made in leather, often ending in long strips that hung down beneath the armoured cuirass but over the tunic, rather like a continuous *cingulum militare*. This type, sometimes now called *pteruges*, is portrayed as being worn by legionaries with *lorica segmentata* during the 'classic' Principate period. As generally longer ring and scale armour replaced *segmentata*, however, *pteruges* became unecessary.

CLOAKS

The outer layer for the legionaries consisted for the most part of two types of cloaks – the *sagum* and the *paenula*. Both were thick and waterproof, made from wool containing much of its natural water-repelling lanolin. Originating in Gaul, the *sagum* was already in widespread use across northern Europe and became the standard legionary cloak during both the Republic and early Empire. It was made from a simple long rectangular piece of coarse cloth, and fastened by a leather or metal clasp. It was worn over armour doubled or gathered in cold weather but was also used as a legionary's sleeping bag or bedroll and so was always part of his kit, being carried rolled up on his forked-pole *furca* (see page 93). The *sagum* was known as the war cloak, worn in symbolic contrast to the toga when the state was waging active campaigns.

The *paenula* a was semicircular or oval, three-quarter length, thick and poncho-like cape – without sleeves but often with a square hood added. It was made from felt – a cheap, coarse wool fabric that has been beaten, rolled and pressed compactly into layers that are then glued. (Wool was made into felt long before it was spun or woven). There were also leather versions. The *paenula* had various methods for fastening at the front, ranging from brooches or studs to laces and toggles.

column of Marcus Aurelius, some auxiliaries wear long-sleeved tunics under short-sleeved ones and at least one officer in attendance with the emperor on other Antonine-period sculpture does the same. The Vindolanda writing tablets reference underpants (*subligaria*) and socks (*udones*), under-tunics (*subuclae*) and under-cloaks (*subpaenulae*); as well as overcoats or cloaks (*superariae*) and waistbands (*ventrales*), which protected the wearer from the metal fittings on the back of the *cingulum militare*.

TROUSERS

Originating in Gaul and varying in length from three-quarter to full, trousers (*braccae*) were worn by some of the soldiers in the non-Roman *auxilia*. At first, these were scorned by the Romans as barbarian and effeminate, but they changed their tune when they ventured into the cold north and soon adopted them. However, outside the military and to conservative toga wearers they remained anathema and eventually towards the end of the Empire the Emperor Honorius issued a decree prohibiting men from wearing them in the city of Rome – it was impossible to legislate for the entire Empire. *Braccae* were made from wool or leather, with laces at all ends with which to loosen and tighten them.

▲ *Tombstone of an unknown soldier found at Camomile Street in London. He wears a* paenula *cloak that has two buttons and at least one other toggle-type fastener.*

▲ *A* beneficiarius, *a soldier given special duties, and distinguished by an elaborate lance. He wears a long cloak called a* caracalla.

The *cucullus* or *caracalla* was an ankle-length hooded cape adopted from the Germans, becoming popular with the legionaries and an emperor, whose nickname it became.

The British *birrus* (*birrus britannicus*) was a famously warm and waterproof type of hooded cloak made from hide and fleece. It was also called a *cucullus* and was popular among the legions serving in Britain. Undercloaks (*subpaenulae)* and overcoats or cloaks (*superariae*) were also used, proving that a legionary had a more sophisticated wardrobe than we tend to think.

There are other military cloaks, too, including a version of the *lacerna* (long, open and weatherproof made from dark wool) and the *abolla* (thick cloth folded double, held with a brooch and draped over one shoulder), that appear to be similar but not identical to the *sagum*. From sculptural evidence, the *paenula* was favoured by legionaries when active, for it could be worn gathered at the shoulders, leaving the arms free for work, while the longer *sagum* was for keeping warm when static (guard duty), during very bad weather and when sleeping.

The *paludamentum* was a long cloak worn by senior officers and any of the legionary command group, though not in combat. It fastened at the shoulder and was usually dyed crimson or scarlet. After the reign of Augustus its use was restricted to emperors, who were often portrayed wearing the *paludamentum* on statues and coinage.

SCARF

Knotted around his neck, the legionary wore a short scarf known as a *focale* or a *sudarium* (sweatcloth). Again, the material used could vary from linen to wool according to climate, which would determine whether it was worn to keep its wearer warm or to mop up sweat, though both types prevented the chafing caused by wearing armour. There was probably a great deal of colour variation in the *focale* – a small and personal enough item to be made at home, given as a gift or just improvised from anything available, such as a worn-out tunic. As anyone who works or walks a lot outside will know, a cloth, flannel or kerchief is one of the most useful things one can have, with an almost infinite number of uses.

ACCOUTREMENTS

Each legionary needed hardy footwear to help him cover the miles he marched and a range of accoutrements: to carry his gear and from which to hang his weapons. Most of these were made from leather with metal buckles and decorations, often in the camps or *vici* that built up around them, sometimes in larger factories (*fabricae*).

◄ *Based on his tombstone, P. Flavoleius Cordus of Legio XIIII Gemina from Mainz wears a* paenula *cloak. It is fastened on the right shoulder with a brooch in an 'eastern' manner.*

BELT

The belt (*cingulum militare*) was an ostentatious, highly metalled, wide leather belt, often ornamented with metal decorations and embellishments, with an added curtain of vertical leather strips (usually between four and eight) that hung down at the front. Each strip was decorated with ornate cast or stamped discs of tin or bronze punctuating its length and finished with a pendant (*pensilium*).

Traditionally accepted as an item of body armour designed to protect the soldier's lower abdomen and groin, practical experiments with re-enactor reconstructions have shown that the *cingulum* gave no protection whatsoever in combat, instead becoming a hazard that could hamper movement. Its purpose was surely more decorative – worn as a mark of pride and status.

The distinctive swaying rhythm and the clanking sound they must have made, along with hobnailed boots, armour and weapons, would have transmitted the unique aural and visual signature of Roman soldiers. Wearers of the *cingulum militare* often had their dagger (*pugio*) also attached to it on a frog. A conventional *cingulum militare* would not have been practical on horseback and was not used by the *auxilia* (cavalry, auxiliary infantry had them).

As time went on such belts went in and out of military fashion. Republican legionaries wore a much plainer belt with no aprons and the early imperial decorated aprons were already in decline after the 1st century AD. Belts become more elaborate again in the 3rd century AD. A less ostentatious *cingulum* was also used and in the 1st century AD the sword and dagger were sometimes carried using two crossed belts. In the 2nd and 3rd centuries AD the baldric and the *cingulum* were sometimes joined as one – a waist belt with an added shoulder loop.

BALDRIC

The *balteus* was a type of baldric – a leather belt worn over the right shoulder hanging down to the left side of the waist, used to carry the legionary's *gladius* and make it easy for him to draw when carrying his *scutum* (shield). Centurions and other higher ranks wore their swords attached to their waist *cingulum*. *Baltei* could also be individually highly ornamented.

BOOTS

On their feet, the legionaries wore heavy duty, openwork, flat-soled hobnailed boots called *caligae*. (Tribunes and legates wore low-cut sewn boots called *calcei* made of soft leather usually without the hobnails.) *Caligae* had a middle sole and openwork upper part that were cut from a single piece of leather, with a heavy outer sole then attached using clinched iron hobnails and an inner added to protect the feet from the nail ends. The hobnails gave the boots grip – except on very smooth surfaces where they slipped easily – and also made the boots last longer and so made them perfect for marching. *Caligae* usually had a central lacing system from the centre of the foot up to the top but there were different regional styles in the strapwork. The open leatherwork allowed for coolness in the Mediterranean climate but in colder climates, additional socks or wool wadding were used.

By the 1st century AD, a closed-boot version called *calcei* was replacing *caligae* – especially in the colder parts of the Empire. The more partially open *carbatinae* was used for hotter climates. The *campagus militaris* was a fully enclosed boot rather like a modern walking boot. The increasing role of

▼ *Hob-nailed openwork boots – the basic footwear of the Roman Army. The nails held the boots together and made them last a lot longer. Roman legionaries were known as* caligati *('sandalled men').*

cavalry encouraged the use of a longer – to just below the knee – closed boot and in cold weather puttees or gaiters (leg wrappings) made of fabric, leather or fur were worn to keep the lower legs warm.

SATCHEL

Each legionary had a *loculus* ('little place') for his personal effects – a money pouch, a comb used to clean out lice, bronze tweezers, a sewing/leather-working kit, a piece of flint and a steel used to start fires, gambling dice and gaming counters, herbal medicines, lucky charms or keepsakes. It consisted of a rectangular leather bag or satchel about 45 x 50cm (18 x 20in) made from a single piece of hide, reinforced with diagonal straps, with a central bronze stud to fasten its lid and two rings on either side enabling a carrying strap. It was carried as part of the assemblage on the shoulder pole known as the *furca*. Some *loculi* were just a simple circle or oval of leather thonged on the outside edge to make a more bulbous shape.

MARIUS' MULES

The Marian reforms had reduced the lengthy and cumbersome supply train that slowly followed a legion everywhere it went. There were still mules (about 640 for a legion) and some transport carts, but with the paramount importance of soldiers being self-sufficient and to speed up movement and toughen the troops, Marius decreed that legionaries should carry a lot of their own kit on a forked pole called a *furca* as they marched and it was for this that they were nicknamed Marius' mules (*muli Mariani*).

Fastened to the *furca* was the soldier's marching pack (*sarcina*) that would contain a satchel (*loculus*) with a few personal items, money and small tools. Next, a cloak rolled up with perhaps some other spare clothing, a net bag for three days' supply of basic foodstuffs (including *buccellatum* – a dried hardtack that lasted indefinitely), a water or wineskin, a cooking pot and a mess tin (*patera*). He also had to carry a few stakes, a wicker basket, and either a mattock, a mezzoluna-bladed turf cutter or sickle, a pickaxe (*dolabra*) or a spade. These entrenching tools enabled the construction of the ditches and ramparts of their route camps and the turf-and-timber defences of forts, but also in overcoming any obstacles they might encounter when on the move. All this as well as his military equipment! How did he manage it?

It seems from recent finds that Roman shields with their canvas or hide surfaces provided protection from the elements; rings fitted on the inside near the rim enabled them to be hung on the legionary's back with the *furca* then able

▲ *Ermine Street Guard legionary re-enactors in full 'classic' kit.*

to rest on its upper rim and its different elements hanging behind it on the other side, cushioned by the softer ones. This would stop the hard elements of the assemblage digging into a soldier's back. He could then use one arm to shoulder the *furca*, leaving the other hand free or swappable for relief. Helmets were hung or fastened in front to the chest armour.

▼ *Winter kit – note the leg warmers and cloaks – for route marching in colder climes, showing just how much leather went into the making of a legionary's equipment.*

DEFINING DRESS FEATURES

The most distinctive of all military clothing was worn by the legion's commanders and signallers. On a battlefield without long-range sharpshooters, there was no need for commanders to hide. Quite the opposite: they needed to to stand out, and deliver their orders clearly so that they could be seen and acted upon.

COMMAND GROUP DISTINCTIONS

The command group of a legion stood out in more distinctive armour than the standard legionary – often a highly ornamented, hammered-bronze muscle cuirass that idealised the human physique (*lorica musculata*) or else a high-quality scale armour vest (*lorica squamata*), ornamented shin greaves and extravagant crests or plumes atop their elaborate helmets. They wore their swords not on baldrics but on either side at the waist since they did not carry a shield.

Very senior commanders sometimes wore white cloaks and plumes, while the legate could be identified immediately in the field by his distinctive helmet and body armour, his scarlet cloak (*paludamentum)* and scarlet sash (*cincticulus*).

▼ *Line up of a legion's command group with standard bearers. A mass of glittering metal, left to right:* vexillarius *or* vexilifer, optio centuriae, cornicen *(bugler),* centurion, imaginifer *(carrying the imago of the current emperor), and the* signifer *with the cohort's standard.*

The centurions definitely stood out from the men with their awards and decorations, with the most senior being the most decorated. His armour was not *segmentata* but *musculata* or *hamata* (mail armour). Round his neck and across his breast he wore his medals (*phalerae*) – shining gold, silver, or bronze sculpted discs. He wore his sword on a belt not a baldric, and his *cingulum militare* would be of the very highest quality. His helmet's crest was transverse – the opposite way to a legionary's longitudinal one, and it had a different-coloured crest. As a symbol of his authority and a non-lethal weapon of reprimand, he carried a vine stick (*vitis*) instead of a shield, and rather than marching he rode on horseback.

OTHER MARKS OF RANK

Each centurion chose an *optio* from his own century as his second-in-command. The *optio* wore the standard legionary kit with the addition of a more recognisable helmet crest and carried a long staff at least as tall as himself called a *hastile*, used to control and discipline the soldiers. This would have been his standout feature.

▲ *Standard bearers – two* vexilifers *or* imaginifers *flanking an* aquilifer *– on a metope from the Adamklissi Tropaeum, Dacia (modern day Romania). Protected and revered standards were also crucial communication devices with which to organise the troops.*

▲ *A* vexillum *– the identifying standard of a* vexillatio *(a temporary task force detachment) of the illustrious Legio XX Valeria Victrix, founded by Augustus in 31BC. It is carried by a* vexilifer, *who was one of the* signiferi *(signallers) of a Roman legion.*

▲ *The tombstone of Genialis Clusio,* imaginifer *of Cohors VII Raetorum, from the mid-1st century AD, carrying an image of the emperor or one of his family. Note the claws of the bearskin draped over his left shoulder.*

The *evocati* of the legion would have been instantly recognisable, partly because they were often centurions themselves but also because of their awards and medals, perhaps older classic equipment but above all because of their age, experience and attitude.

The *immunes* of each legion must have also been easily identifiable because of their rank, but above all their knowledge and experience would have set them always in a certain position both socially and wherever their specialisation was located in a camp, fort or army.

Rewards for achievements similar to medals could be worn by any who had won them, including gold neck torcs and armbands, small silver *hastae* (spears) and arrows.

STANDARD BEARERS

To enhance unit identity, display allegiance and to lead or rally the troops, the legion had a series of standards, which were revered and used at all important events – battles, parades, rituals and ceremonies. These were carried by bearers who were marked out from other soldiers by the animal heads and skins that they wore on parade and in battle – usually a lion, wolf or bear – with the mouth of the beast open and the teeth showing across the top of his helmet. Wearing a lion skin was the *aquilifer* – bearer of the legion's silver eagle standard and a position of great prestige, for upon him rested the responsibility for the safety of the sacred symbol of the legion, whose loss could bring disgrace and even disbandment (see page 70).

Next, came the *imaginifer* – standard bearer of the emperor's image and proof of the legion's loyalty to him – then the *signifers* – trusted men, one for each century, who bore its unique centurial signum totems and symbols and also looked after their unit's pay and savings.

The standards were revered and used at all important events – battles, parades, rituals and ceremonies. Besides the standards, sound was used as a signal. In the noise and din of battle commands had to be clearly understood and three different types of wind instrument were used for specific purposes, with the trumpet the most commonly used on a day-to-day basis. One horn, the cornu, was used for anything to do with the legionary colours and the heavier buccina horn was used as a mark of the legate commander's authority. All Roman soldiers were deeply superstitious and each legion had an augur – a priest who foretold the future through the examination of natural phenomena and the entrails of a sacrificed animal.

Exactly who wore animal skins, which animal skins and when is a subject of debate. There is ample evidence on the depictions that have survived that animal skins were worn – as with the imaginifer above. Indeed, Polybius mentions wearing of skins and there is some numismatic evidence back as far as the 3rd century BC, however, whether they were worn uniformly and how much 'choice' there was is difficult to say. Also, there were differences between types of unit – especially when praetorians, imperial guards and the auxilia are taken into account. There is evidence of skins worn without helmets, and of *signiferi* going bare-headed.

What can be said with some certainty is that lion skins seem to have been used primarily by the praetorians, with or without helments and that legion and *auxilia signifers* used bear or wolf – although they can also be found bare-headed.

CHAPTER FIVE

ARMOUR
AND
WEAPONRY

As with their clothing, Roman armour and weaponry appears to
be uniform but we must always remember that it came from a
society that did not enjoy the machinery and expertise that we
have, 2,000 years later. The arms and armour identified on
statuary and artistic representations were just that: shorthand to
provide the informed viewer what they were seeing. In fact there
was a considerable variation with old and new as the legions
used what equipment and materials that they had to hand.

◄ *Today, informed by Hollywood and re-enactors, this is what we think of as
being the definitive Roman soldier, wearing* lorica segmentata, *carrying a* scutum
and short sword, wearing a red tunic and sandals.

ARMOUR

Rome's early forces were warrior bands of farmers conscripted only as part-time soldiers for the duration of the relatively short summer fighting season of ancient times. As they became more formalised from tribal warriors into citizen soldiers, their equipment underwent changes, influenced in no small part by the equipment used by the enemies they came across.

▲ *This re-enactor shows what a Republican heavy infantryman would have worn – not a great deal different to later* auxilia. *His shield hasn't reached the rectangular stage, and his sword is carried in a baldric. The* cingulum militare *didn't come in untill the early 1st century AD. His helmet is of the Montefortino style.*

▶ *This is what a centurion of Claudius's army would have worn around AD43. M. Flavonius Facilis's mail and equipment are interpreted from his gravestone found in Colchester. He served with Legio XX Valeria Victrix.*

Prior to the Marian reforms *c.*107BC, soldiers had to pay for their own arms and armaments, which were based on the Greek and Etruscan hoplite model of breastplates, helmets and greaves to go with their spears, shields and side swords. With only the wealthiest able to afford the whole assemblage, the Roman *triplex acies* (triple line) formation was based partly on the amount of equipment and therefore social rank and partly on the fighting experience of each man.

The troops of the phalanx all had some degree of armoured protection; only the front skirmishing *velites* wore none at all, being unable to afford any, except perhaps a helmet of hardened leather. Scale mail was known but was rarely the equipment preference of the phalanx. The Romans absorbed other Italic influences in their combats with Sabines and Samnites but also with the encroaching Gallic Celts, from whom they learned of chain mail. Then, in the end phase of the Roman Republic, the Marian reforms created a standing army by fundamentally altering recruitment and making the state responsible for providing the arms and equipment. It was in this period that armour became more standardised, with state-issued laminated-steel plate armour eventually replacing what an individual could afford, whether of steel or bronze, plate or mail.

THE SEGMENTED CUIRASS

The distinctive cuirass that is most associated with a Roman legionary in popular culture is called *lorica segmentata*, of which there were three or four variants – usually differentiated by their thickness and number of the hoops as well as differences in the fittings. (The name is in fact a later one that was applied when it was rediscovered in the 16th-century Renaissance – the Romans called it *lorica laminata* or just *lorica*.)

The exact origins of *segmentata/laminata* armour are unknown, even though thanks to it being the first Roman mass-produced cuirass it has left plenty of monumental and archaeological traces (even if only in small pieces). However, it is possible that its iconic but somewhat idealised appearance on Trajan's Column has made it more definitive than it actually was, or perhaps it was especially iconic to the Romans – for it differentiated them from the foreign *auxilia*. That said, it was never the armour of officers or elite formations and when taking into consideration the many other depictions of legionaries in scale and chain mail armour, its assumed prevalence must be questioned.

Whatever its origin and usage, it was undoubtedly light yet strong, packed down compactly and was cheaper and easier to produce than either scale or chain mail. Now, except for his arms and his face, the legionary's upper body was completely armoured, protected by a cuirass of independently moving segmented armour made in an intricate arrangement of hoops, strips and plates of face-hardened steel that were held together with ties and sometimes riveted to a leather jerkin. Those on the torso were hinged at the back and hooked at the front to be lace-fastened, with the main chest plates usually fastened by buckle, while the two hooped shoulder guards were attached separately last of all. The strips were arranged horizontally on the body, overlapping downwards, and when worn with a padded jerkin and *pteruges* (leather under-protection for the hips and shoulders) this armour was both comfortable and very strong.

The downside was that it did not cover the arms or the groin, it was high maintenance and it didn't last very long compared to other types of armour, for it corroded easily – especially the fittings – which were usually made of thinner brass. Despite this, *lorica segmentata* began to replace the older equipment in legionary formations around the time of Emperor Tiberius (AD14–37) and was being issued as standard legionary equipment by the time of the Claudian invasion of Britain in AD43. With its stout shoulder protection it fared well against the Gallic Celts' downward-slashing strokes from their long swords, but less so against the two-handed Dacian *falx* (weapon with a curved blade), which could reach past the *scutum* to vulnerable arms and legs or even penetrate the *scutum* and the armour itself. In an attempt to counter this, shields were made heavier and metalled on their rims and troops wore leg greaves and segmental armguards (*manicae*).

Perhaps for this reason, among others, by the time of the civil wars of the 3rd century AD, *lorica segmentata* was becoming more rare.

SCALE ARMOUR

Of the other two main types of Roman armour – chain and scale – both of which existed before the introduction of the *segmentata* cuirass, historians and re-enactor forums endlessly debate which would have been the most effective. The answer really depends on the mode of construction, for both could be produced in more complicated, time-consuming and so expensive ways, or be worn in doubled layers, and at key points that increased their capability. The oldest-known armour to the Romans, as it must indeed be the oldest type of all, was *lorica squamata* or scale armour. This was made up of any number of small plates of metal of varying size and composition attached to each other with wire or rivets and sometimes sewn on to a quilted fabric undercoat or else worn on top of one. Its use had travelled westwards from the Middle East, where it was worn by warriors of many different cultures.

High-quality *lorica squamata* was more flexible than the *segmentata*, resembling a fish's seamless overlapping scales with each lower edge rounded. However, the fact that it was being produced in various sizes by craftsmen of varying ability meant that it could be much more primitive, consisting of larger, squarer plates attached to an undercoat without being

▲ *An image of the Roman soldier in the Dacian Wars at the turn of the 1st century AD from Adamklissi. He wears scale armour over two rows of* pteruges, *a manica on his sword arm. Note the Phrygian cap and double-handed* falx *swords of his Dacian opponents.*

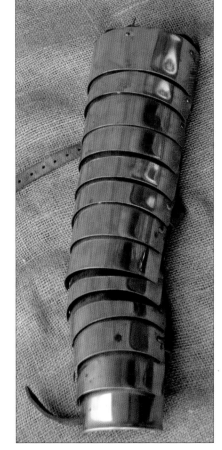

▶ *A modern reproduction of a* manica – *literally a sleeve.*

▲ *A standard-bearer with* squamata *scaled armour, which was made of either bronze or iron. His sword hangs on a baldric on his right, and he wears a bearskin.*

▲ *The soldier of the 3rd century* AD *often carried an oval shield, wore mail and a helmet with more pronounced cheekguards, and used a thrusting spear.*

properly overlapped, and therefore much more vulnerable to penetration. Plates were usually of bronze or iron, initially wired together but later riveted and reinforced in a variety of ways – by overlapping more of each plate or by more back riveting and wiring on the inside. *Squamata* was generally heavier than the chain mail known as *hamata* and usually cheaper to produce. It was in use for the whole of the Roman period.

CHAIN MAIL

Chain mail, *lorica hamata* (*hamata* = hooked), was invented by the Celts. It consisted of alternating rows of riveted bronze, iron or steel rings of two sorts – solid punched-out rings that were joined by alternating open-linking ones, which could be either butted or riveted shut, with each ring being connected to four others at either side, above and below. It was stronger when riveted shut, but riveted ring mail takes longer to make than butted. How long it took also depended on other things: the type and size of wire used, the weight and aspect ratio of the rings, the complexity of the weave and the speed of the weaver.

Made properly, high-quality *hamata* gave superb protection. Like scale, it could be worn either over a cushioning undergarment or sewn on to one, and the shoulders often had

a double layer for added protection, with the neck edged in leather to prevent chafing. There were several versions of *hamata*, for its versatility enabled it to be modified to suit both infantry and cavalry. It reached down to the upper thighs and was usually sleeveless, though it could be short-sleeved and later long-sleeved, knee-length and with a hood.

This mail had many advantages that ultimately made it the armour of choice – for it continued to be produced right up to the age of gunpowder weapons. It was flexible but strong, allowing comfortable movement, and the constant friction of the rings against each other kept them rust free. It was easy if time-consuming to make, to modify to fit, and to repair – and easily recycled and reused. Criticisms of *hamata* centre on its expense in terms of time, for it could take months to laboriously make and join up more than 20,000–30,000 rings. Yet despite this, from the time of its appearance, *hamata* remained in constant use by Roman armies throughout the Roman and Byzantine periods.

TORSO-SHAPED CUIRASS

Any of a command group could wear the *lorica musculata*, a cast-bronze or iron torso-shaped cuirass, made in two pieces –

front and back – that mimicked the human physique with visible details of idealised musculature, but often having other myths and motifs traced on them. *Musculatae* featured in the many representations of officers and generals, but especially emperors – who wore the most highly ornamented and gilded versions.

ARMOUR PREFERENCES

During the Principate, *lorica segmentata* defined the difference between Roman legionary and foreign auxiliary, especially the cavalry, who were always equipped with either *hamata* or *squamata*. This suited the needs of horsemen much better than the more cumbersome *segmentata* and native styles acted as a defining characteristic of a particular unit. After the demise of the *lorica segmentata*, *hamata* was reintroduced and became the standard-issue state armour by the 4th century AD.

Of the legion command group, centurions, who led from the front, tended to favour the *hamata* mail for real combat although it seems they might also have worn high-quality *squamata* or even a basic *musculata*. Legates and tribunes preferred high-quality *squamata* – for it could be etched, polished and would glitter. Its surface plates allowed for considerable variation and there must have been commonly adopted styles, but also expensive bespoke ones, as it was often individually patterned.

A style now known as *lorica plumata* (feathered) was a hybrid combination of *squamata* and *hamata* with scales resembling a bird's plumage in front attached to chain mail rings behind. It was very expensive to produce and very high-maintenance. Such exclusivity was worn only by the most senior ranks.

PUTTING ON A SHOW

It was originally thought that the very best and most showy armour was worn only on parade or for displays and not in action, but it seems that this was not the case. Close-quarter archaic battles contained many theatrical elements as a way of communicating various qualities or making a statement. On a personal level, if it might be your last day on earth and you might meet the gods then you would want to look your best. It is now believed, then, that armour once thought to be the preserve of the parade ground was used sometimes in battle, worn along with medals and decorations earned from previous conflicts. This fitted in with the prevailing trend: to stand out and show your quality was part of the individual warrior concept that the Romans kept and cultivated. Experience counted and battle glory was a path to higher status.

What's more, distinctive weapons, armour, helmets, crests, plumes, coloured cloaks, painted shields, flags and standards all had a purpose beyond display. As well as cultivating esprit de corps and unit pride, they brought instant identity on the battlefield.

Undoubtedly, however, there was some armour that was made purely for show and ceremonial purposes – for instance, extremely fine ring mail, or tiny scale and lamellar mail that would not withstand a hard thrust, as well as

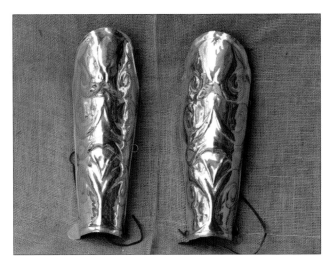

▲ *Greaves were certainly worn by both legionaries and – as with this beautiful pair – centurions.*

full-face cavalry 'sport' helmets and highly elaborate stylised armour for the riders and their mounts in their tournament displays. Some things that make you look good in an exhibition don't help in a fight, and even get in the way. Yet full-face helmets *have* been found on battlefields so, despite this, it seems that some did see action.

▼ *'Sports' or 'parade' helmets and facemasks may have been worn in combat although there's not a great deal of evidence either way.*

CAVALRY ARMOUR AND WEAPONS

Although the early Roman Army reflected Greek and Etruscan influence with its heavy infantry preoccupation, over the course of the Roman period the cavalry arm developed steadily to virtually outgrow the infantry itself in importance. This gave rise to the need for additional and different armour, both for the horses and their riders.

With the creation of the *auxilia*, Rome tapped directly into the expertise of native specialists in the equine field – tribes who lived and fought on horseback. At times, certain equipment to facilitate mounted combat was state-supplied, but tribal levies often kept their own specialist items of kit, in weapons, armour and dress. This depended on the origin of the individual *ala* (wing), but standard kit would include chain or scale mail, a smaller shield than the *scutum* (usually round, flat or dished, but it could be any shape), a longer sword (the *spatha*) and some kind of spear. The type of spear was dependent on the type of unit: light cavalry such as mounted archers would have short throwing spears (*akontes*) and darts (*plumbatae*), while heavier cavalry used a lance called a *kontos*.

Unless a foreign helmet was used as a recognition feature of a particular unit, cavalry helmets were similar to those of the infantry, sharing the bowl, peak and crest as well as the neck and cheek guards, but sometimes with larger ear guards. They were also usually more elaborate in design, as were the fittings for their horses. Besides these metal versions, there were also more basic attempts to provide the horse with protection using leather. The very same designs that we see in the surviving metal *chamfrons* (face protection for horses, with cheek, nose and eye covers) have also been discovered in leather (at Vindolanda). This implies a transition path to metal but also that horse armour was much more prevalent than had previously been supposed and it was not merely the preserve of the heavy cavalry.

▲ *This beautifiul chamfron dates to the 2nd or 3rd century* AD *and shows Mars standing on a giant.*

▼ *Roman cavalry at 2017's wonderful 'Turma' exhibition along Hadrian's Wall. Note the draco standard behind the front right-hand horseman.*

COMBAT vs DISPLAY

So to the perennial question about the most elaborate Roman plate cavalry armour: was it ever worn in combat? Some stunning, if rather theatrical, assemblages have been found, especially the full-face helmets, but also armour for horse and rider. To a modern eye it screams parade or display, but Iron Age warfare had an element of theatre as important context and this remained so for most armies up until the 20th century. You were *supposed* to be seen. Undoubtedly, the amount of armour potential increased and was therefore used on a day-to-day basis – but some of the most delicate *must* have been kept for the *hippika gymnasia* and other special civilian event displays. (A grave at Tell Oum Hauran in Syria contained a cavalryman buried with two almost full sets of equipment, including two helmets, one for battle and a best for parades.) There were also heavier, thicker helmets made of iron with a detachable face mask, which were definitely used in combat, for cataphracts came similarly equipped.

TYPES OF CAVALRY

Apart from elite bodyguard units, cavalry was either light or heavy – and the heavy cavalry got heavier. After a long period of exposure to primarily eastern cataphracts (Armenian, Sarmatian, Parthian) Rome had begun to recruit such heavy armoured cavalry formations into its own military from native levies and mercenaries. The first recorded deployment of Roman auxiliary *equites cataphractarii* was the *ala I Gallorum et Pannoniorum catafractata* in the reign of Hadrian (AD117–138). Later, with the creation of the mobile *comitatenses* (rapid reaction forces) by Gallienus (AD253– 268) to cope with the multiple threats facing the Empire,

▶ *Cavalryman of the late 2nd century AD. Note scale armour, horse eyeguards and florid designwork on the helmet and greaves.*

the emphasis was on having a balance of types within the critical cavalry element – light, heavy and archer.

CATAPHRACTS AND THEIR ARMOUR

Cataphracts were always high-calibre troops – a strike force not a melee one, where, lacking the manoeuvrability of lighter cavalry, they proved cumbersome and vulnerable. They needed to be used at the right moment and supported by other types of unit (horse archers, light cavalry, slingers) and defended by infantry. They were used mainly in the East where they were more suited to the terrain, and Diocletian created state-run factories (*fabricae*) at Antioch, Nicomedia and Caesarea, which specialised in producing armour for them. The cataphracts continued to evolve after the demise of the Western Roman Empire, into the Byzantine period and beyond, and were the precursors of the European medieval knight.

The sheer quantity and quality of the cataphracts' metallic accoutrements demanded a huge investment in training and equipment to be able to do the job. From the end of the 2nd to the 5th centuries AD, the *cataphractarii* were the armoured punch of the cavalry, man and horse both armoured in iron, bronze or alloy lamellar armour. Usually, this consisted of copper-alloy scales sewn on to padded linen backing, though iron scales on to leather and other permutations have also been found. The horse was completely protected on its visible upper parts, leaving the lower legs, belly and underside of the neck and throat free. The tripartite chamfron had a central panel running down the nose and two cheek panels that had two small colander-like hemispheres covering the horse's eyes.

The rider similarly wore scale armour that hung down almost to his knees like a demure skirt, cinched in the middle to take some of its weight on his hips, with greaves to protect his shins. He sometimes had additional pectoral protection in the form of a breastplate and an extra layer of mail across the shoulders. His helmet could be full-face, almost Corinthian style, with a nasal plate, but alternatively a curtain of lamellar scales could hang round the back of the head from cheekbone to cheekbone with a detachable nasal guard. He couched a long (over 3m/9.8ft!) two-handed *kontos* lance to outreach all opponents, so wore his shield double-hooped on the left forearm. His charge impact was enabled by his saddle, for at this time the Romans did not have stirrups. Roman saddles consisted of two sets of usually wooden horns at each end of a wood frame over which leather was stuffed, stretched and stitched, in order to cushion both the man and the animal. Horses were controlled with a bridle and a bit, but partly by the legs – especially when the weapon required two hands. Secondary armament was a sword, but sometimes a mace.

SHIELDS

The exact source of the distinctive Roman shield known as the *scutum* is a matter of much debate. Shields already had a long history by the time of its appearance, their exact origins lost in the prehistoric period, but they evolved inevitably to counter the use of hand weapons, short-range bows or slingshots, by blocking or intercepting attacks.

The exact source of the distinctive Roman shield known as the *scutum* is a matter of much debate. This is partly due to their rarity in the archaeological record, because of their organic nature and fragility, especially in damp soils. With a single exception, real archaeological evidence is just the remaining metalwork, but there are representations of shields on monuments and memorials and descriptions of them by various authors of the Roman period (Ammianus, Cassius Dio, Livy, Polybius, Plutarch, Virgil). The *Notitia Dignitatum* also illustrates the shield patterns of many Roman Army units at the start of the 5th century AD.

EARLY SHIELDS

The very earliest shields were made from wood, hide or wicker and could be almost any size, but with the coming of the Bronze Age (3000–1200BC), parts of the shield began to be made from metal. The shield front was reinforced with a convex bronze bowl inverted in its centre, known as a boss (where the handhold was fixed), and the face began to be covered in flattened bronze.

As Rome grew, it came across different cultures that influenced the army's development: the Etruscans, Greeks and, especially, the Celts, with their skills in metalworking for weapons and armour and their love of horses and cavalry.

The strongest initial influence was from the dominant culture of Greece, with the hoplite phalanx as the model. Early Republican forces had a variety of shields according to what each man could afford, made from combinations of planks of wood dowelled and glued together, then faced in hide. Called a *clypeus*, they were round, varied in size and were based on the Greek *aspis* model.

▼ *Early shields would have been similar to those seen on Greek illustrations, round and made of wood.*

As the phalanx changed to the maniple and the Romans fought other central and northern Italic peoples (Samnites, Ligurians and Celts) they were influenced again in turn by various styles, such as an ancient Italic oval shield that originated in the prehistoric Villanovan Apennine culture of the 15th–14th centuries BC and other oblong European shields with metal bosses used by the Celts.

THE EVOLUTION OF THE *SCUTUM*

At some point in the 6th–5th centuries BC, Rome made another military synthesis inspired by the

▲ *During the Republic, shields were oval, although becoming more rectangular. They were made from plywoood, curved, with metal edging and a central boss.*

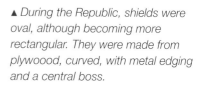

enemies it was coming up against and evolved the *scutum*. At first, this was oblong and slightly convex in shape, but by the 1st century BC it had developed into a relatively large semi-cylindrical shield, approximately 1m high and 0.5m wide (3.25 x 1.6ft), with a depth from its curve of about 30cm (1ft) and weighing about 10kg (22lb). It was made up of layers of laminated wood glued together at right angles then steamed into a curved shape and completed with the addition of a protruding central iron boss that protected the hand and gave the shield an offensive capability. The outer edge was rimmed in metal, while the face was covered in leather or canvas and dyed or painted Legionary Red and then emblazoned with Jupiter's crossed thunderbolts (as seen on Trajan's Column), combined with individual legion and cohort badges, identifying numbers and colours.

After meeting the Dacian *falx* at the end of the 1st century AD, *scuta* became thicker and their metal rim edges denser to cope with these heavy cutting weapons, but it remained a versatile shield that offered very good protection.

LATER SHIELDS

By the end of the 3rd century AD, however, the *scutum* seems to have disappeared as oval and circular shields once again came to the fore. These had never gone out of use among the *auxilia* and the cavalry, and as the structure and composition of the Roman Army changed in the 3rd century AD, so too did its budget and its requirements. Cash-strapped by civil wars, multiple border raids and latent instability, and following the granting of Roman citizenship to all free inhabitants of the Empire (mainly for tax reasons), which meant that the distinctions between the army and the *auxilia* no longer existed, the emphasis was now on equipment that was cheaper to produce but that would be just as effective as the old classic legionary kit.

Shields therefore became round and flat, or slightly dished and edged in rawhide. Smaller oval laminate shields (1m/3ft across and bigger than a dustbin lid), still with an iron boss and reinforced edging, allowed for greater ease of movement and a wider field of vision. They were used with a spear as the primary weapon against the increasing amounts of enemy cavalry, with a *spatha* (sword) as a secondary armament. These new weapons also reflect the change to a more mobile form of warfare, with the emphasis no longer exclusively on heavy infantry, and thanks to their simplicity they could be rapidly mass-produced in the state-run *fabricae*.

THE SCUTUM IN ACTION

The *scutum* was the shield of the Roman legions during the heyday period of the Principate and as such the classic shield of the Roman legionary. It evolved simultaneously with the *gladius* and *pilum* for fighting as a cohesive unit. Used in unison, each one protected both its bearer and the man to his left, and by locking or overlapping shields, various formations could be made – from a shield wall to a still more protective *testudo*. Aggressive use of the *scutum* was to punch forwards with the boss – used en masse shields could 'kettle' enemy soldiers into an ineffective huddle, as modern riot police do to protesters today.

CAVALRY SHIELDS

In the early days of the Republic, the Roman cavalry was provided by the aristocracy, who paid for their own equipment, and few carried shields. As time went on the recruitment property standards dropped and more commoners were involved. Shields were carried more and more: smaller round shields made of hide over a metal frame called a *parma*, or an even smaller buckler-like *parmula*. By the time of the Punic Wars, the *auxilia* and allies were providing most of the cavalry and oval shields began to come in. By the time of the Principate, most cavalry shields were oval or hexagonal, although the light cavalry, the Numidians or Mauri, used the smaller, lighter shields into the 3rd century AD.

SHIELDS OF THE PRINCIPATE

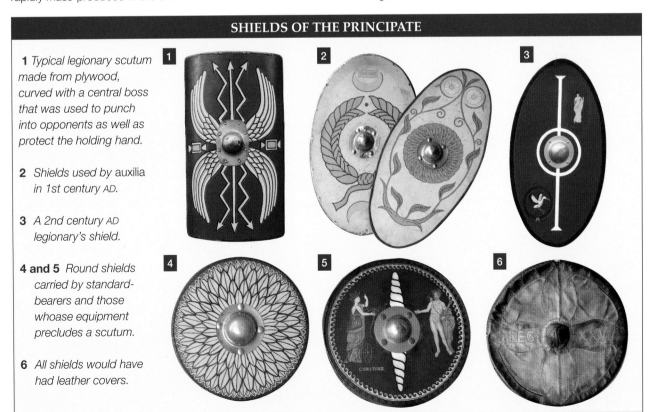

1 *Typical legionary scutum made from plywood, curved with a central boss that was used to punch into opponents as well as protect the holding hand.*

2 *Shields used by* auxilia *in 1st century* AD.

3 *A 2nd century* AD *legionary's shield.*

4 and 5 *Round shields carried by standard-bearers and those whoase equipment precludes a scutum.*

6 *All shields would have had leather covers.*

HELMETS

The helmet (*galea*) was a distinctive part of the legionary's equipment that evolved over time. The first Roman helmets were made from various materials to no common design, influenced by the helmets worn by Etruscan and Greek warriors, and depending most on the wealth and status of their owners.

Helmets could range from hardened leather to bronze or iron, and from Etruscan crested helms or Corinthian types with cheek and nose protection to plain semi-spherical or conical caps – often with a fitting for a horsehair or plume crest.

MONTEFORTINO HELMETS

At some point in the 5th or 4th century BC, Rome began to brush with the Ligurians and the Celts of northern Italy, who became the source of various designs of military equipment that the Romans would adopt as their own. One of these was the Celtic or Gallic helmet. The earliest style is known as the Montefortino (named as per custom after the place where it was found), which originated in the 4th century BC and saw use until the 1st century AD. It consisted of a hemispherical bowl made out of bronze plate, tending to become more conical towards the top, ending in a round knob like that on a tea pot lid, while at the back there was a small peak extension to protect the neck. The knobs were often shaped and decorated like a pinecone and the helmet's edge was usually thickened and featured a twisted-rope pattern. On the sides, there were riveted fittings to take the cheek guards that would

▲ *Iron helmet with crest, from Gaul, 4th century BC.*

▲ *Basic, early Montefortino style helmet: a pot with a small neckguard..*

have hung on rings and doubled as a fastening for the whole helmet to the head of the wearer. These guards must usually have been made out of hardened leather because not many metal ones have been found, but there certainly were some metal cheek guards.

By the 1st century BC, the top knobs became hollow (a bit like the top of a small bottle) in order that a plug-in crest could

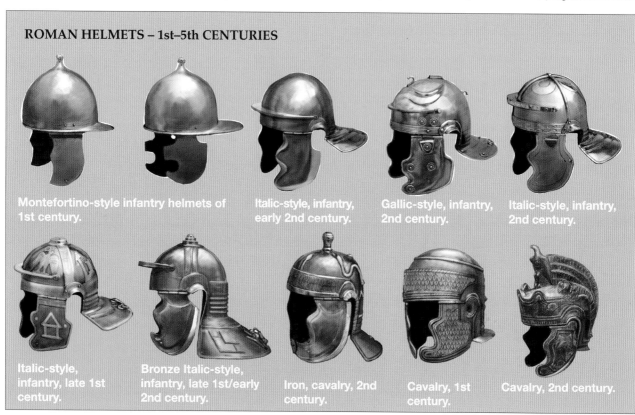

ROMAN HELMETS – 1st–5th CENTURIES

Montefortino-style infantry helmets of 1st century.

Italic-style, infantry, early 2nd century.

Gallic-style, infantry, 2nd century.

Italic-style, infantry, 2nd century.

Italic-style, infantry, late 1st century.

Bronze Italic-style, infantry, late 1st/early 2nd century.

Iron, cavalry, 2nd century.

Cavalry, 1st century.

Cavalry, 2nd century.

be mounted, and by the 1st century AD the back neck guard had become considerably wider. These early helmets were simple, practical and cheap to produce for the larger armies that came about following the Marian reforms. Montefortino-style helmets were produced over a wide area – they were worn by the Romans and some of Hannibal's Celto-Iberian mercenaries simultaneously during the Punic Wars! – and so there was considerable variation in the quality of manufacture.

COOLUS HELMETS

Another Celtic helmet that was related to the Montefortino and concurrent with it was the Gallic Coolus (from Coolus in Marne), which was in use from the 3rd century BC to the 1st century AD. Very similar in shape with a simple hemispherical brass or

▲ *Typical 'Barbarian' pot helmet (this one's Celtic).*

bronze bowl and a rounded rather than conical top, it didn't always feature a crest-holder top knob and the back neck guard was longer than that of the original Montefortino. Some later versions were made from copper alloy and spun on a lathe rather than bronze hammered into shape, with a riveted frontal ridge at the forehead and the crest-holder knobs welded or riveted on top, sometimes with additional tubes above the ears for side plumes.

▲ *The museum at Carnuntum (in Pannonia between Vienna and Bratislave) has this Weissenau type helmet used during the Dacian Wars.*

IMPERIAL-GALLIC HELMETS

The next design to appear, in use from the late 1st century BC to the early 2nd century AD, was another Gallic progression not directly derived from the Montefortino but again originating from Gaul, which is now known as the Imperial-Gallic. This helmet would become the progenitor of further subtypes, all of which we recognise today as the classic helmet of the Roman legionary. Early Imperial-Gallic helmets were some of the most heavily stylised of Roman designs, typically ornamented with elaborate bosses and raised embossed lines in contours around its different parts.

It was more sophisticated than the Montefortino and the Coolus, and was first made from iron with the decorations in brass. It had a tighter-fitting head bowl that followed the shape of the head with the ear parts cut out, dropping down at the back to a long, wide, ridged neck protector that sloped downwards. The large cheek guards were hinged for raising and were riveted to the main body. At the front, there was

now a reinforced peak riveted along the forehead and above it an embossed eyebrow design with a crest holder consisting of a right-angled foot that slid into a tube on the crown and sometimes even with an extra one on the peak. The rim of the entire helmet and the cheek protectors were edged in brass. The Imperial-Gallic was mass-produced to a high standard by Gallic craftsmen but it was also copied in other parts of the Empire, resulting in two obviously different types.

▲ *Imperial Gallic D helmet with brow and 'eyebrows'.*

▲ *Helmet found in the amphitheatre at Besançon.*

IMPERIAL-ITALIC HELMETS

The Imperial-Italic versions were less well made and more basic, lacking a lot of the Imperial-Gallic's skill in construction and often with almost no decoration. Both designs had much larger neck and cheek guards than the Montefortino and Coolus helmets, and various versions of both were produced from the 1st century AD onwards with perhaps a trend toward deeper, more sloping neck guards and wider ear guards reaching down to meet and attach to the neck guard itself, as well as the back of the helmet.

At some point in the 1st century AD, Imperial-Italic helmets began to be spun on a lathe out of a copper alloy rather than beaten out of a plate, and this produced a much more classy, even bowl using a faster and more consistent process. Then, having met the Dacian *falx* at the turn of the 2nd century AD, substantial crossbar reinforcement began to be added to the helmet's top in the style of a cross with still larger neck and cheek guards. This began as a modification while on campaign but then became standard and was also retrofitted. Brass carrying handles could be mounted at the front above the rim or at the back riveted to the neck guard, or else a hook could be riveted somewhere near the top.

ROMAN RIDGED, INCISA OR SPANGENHELM HELMETS

For some reason there is very limited archaeological evidence for infantry helmets in AD3, but at a certain point late in that century a new Roman helmet began to appear, made in a completely different way from all that had gone before it, perhaps reflecting the changing nature of the composition of the army and the increased importance of its cavalry arm. Known as the Roman ridged helmet, Incisa or Spangenhelm, its origins were in the East, from the helmets of the Sassanids and Sarmatians.

The new helmet was made in two ways – now called

▲ *Dacian re-enactors in Romania launch their attack against the Romans, the leading warrior leaping to give more momentum to the blow of his heavy two-handed falx.*

◄ *Having met the Dacian falx in battle, bar reinforcement, in the shape of a cross began to be added to the top of Roman helmets, along with still larger neck and cheek guards.*

(some even with jewels inset) and exaggerated neck and cheek guards. It is often thought that these later composite helmets were chosen for their cheapness of manufacture but there is evidence to suggest that there was a limit to the thickness of a one-piece bowl that could be produced that was circumvented by building up thicker but smaller individual pieces of iron. A thicker helmet would give more protection, further enhanced by the extra layer of the riveted top ridge that could deflect strikes. Its individual elements could be forge-heated and quenched more uniformly than could a single-piece helmet, making it less likely to shatter when struck. The explanation of expense is also undermined by the tinning of the top surface and richness of decoration of other more valuable metals, but perhaps this top layer was to cover the rivets and keep them waterproof and rust-free.

PADDING

There is very little real evidence for what the Romans used to pad the inside of their helmets. Traces of leather infer its use especially for integrating parts such as the cheek and neck

ridged and Spangenhelm – by welding iron strips together into two halves or four quarters of iron to make the core shape, then adding either a reinforced, welded and riveted longitudinal ridge that stood proud in the case of the ridged, or flatter cross-bracing across the quarters for the Spangenhelm, which was then united at the bottom with a ridged rim. Neck and cheek guards and often a nose guard were then riveted on. Sometimes, these guards were almost vestigial, implying that the helmet was worn with other chain or plate mail as part of an assemblage, perhaps even with a kind of leather underhelmet.

The ridged and Spangenhelm helmets both had a definite conical shape to them and ranged from very plain to very highly decorated, with the ridged in particular morphing into a decadent late period of especially elaborate decoration

▶ *Late period ridged and studded Spangenhelm with an exaggerated neck and cheek guards.*

MAKE DO AND MEND

By the 4th century AD the production of a lot of army equipment was concentrated in state-run factories, making certain basic styles more prevalent, but remembering that there was no real concept of obsolescence until something was irretrievably broken, there must have been a diverse array of helmet styles even within a cohort. And when viewing the bewildering variety of Roman helmets recovered there obviously was an enormous amount of repair and modification.

▶ *At some point in the late 1st century AD Imperial helmets began to be spun on a lathe out of a copper alloy rather than beaten out of a plate – a faster and more consistent process. This is a 2nd or 3rd century infantryman.*

▲ *This classic Imperial Gallic helmet, with a longitudinal horsehair crest, was worn by centurions and other officers (here an* optio*).*

guards, but felt and linen padding must have been used inside to cushion heads from metal. Their existence is implied by traces of a simple sticky resin, which would have been used to glue the fabric inside the helmets.

CRESTS AND PLUMES

Not all but many of the styles of helmet used by the Roman legionary have special adaptions for the mounting of crests or plumes. These crest knobs and tubes for side plumes appeared in the 1st century AD. The crests were originally made from horsehair and would have been natural colours since the predominantly plant dyes (madder, walnut, woad, weld and dyer's broom) the Romans used didn't work well on it. Plumes were made from feathers that could be dyed more easily and were white, red, purple or black. (Polybius tells us that legionaries of the Republican time wore three feathers as their helmet crest: red, purple or black.) Arrian details yellow as the colour of cavalry crests in the 2nd century AD. Larger avian feathers used included those from vultures, geese and swans and smaller ones like the iridescent blue, green and

◀ *Centurion's helmet with tranverse horse-hair crest.*

purple feathers from various kinds of duck. More exotic plumage became accessible the further the Empire expanded east and south – flamingo and ostrich spring to mind.

Both crests and plumes must have been gathered together into a kind of tight wooden container to hold them, a bit like a brush or broom. They attached to the helmet with a mounting plug or foot, which was then inserted and twisted into place. The fact that only metal decoration has been found, rather than metal crest holders themselves, means that they must have been wooden.

There is debate about whether the legions wore their crests and plumes in combat or just on special occasions such as parades and ceremonies, but as with medals and expensively ostentatious armour, such decoration would have a psychological effect on both the Romans, who would look magnificent, and the enemy, who might feel awed. Also, there was the practicalities of identification in battle, with the command group deliberately standing out, especially the centurions with their transverse crests.

Fighting this kind of formalised, theatrical warfare required the correct costume. Despite individual variations, the Roman soldiers did all look fairly similar and always presented themselves to an enemy in formation and there were fewer problems with snipers than experienced by officers when rifles arrived on the battlefield.

SWORDS

The primary weapon of the classic Republican and Principate Roman heavy infantry was the *gladius*. For more than 400 years, this iconic double-edged and pointed short sword was produced for the legions, with only a few relatively minor changes in size, shape and weight.

Its longevity explains its suitability as a perfect close-quarters infantry hand weapon when used en masse in formation and in conjunction with the *scutum* – a sharp stabbing sword designed for close-quarter combat and so suitable for slashing and chopping as well as thrusting with its tapered point.

▶ *The* Hispaniensis *sword evolved in the 2nd century* BC *and was adopted by the Romans during the Punic wars. It was elegantly waisted, slightly leaf shaped, its tip gently tapering to its point.*

▼ *The thicker and shorter Pompeii type sword had almost straight sides up to a short triangular point.*

EARLY SWORDS

Prior to its adoption, very early Roman swords were based on the Greek *xiphos* – 50–60cm (1.6–2ft) long, with a leaf-shaped or wasp-waisted blade in profile and diamond shaped in cross-section. Leaf-shaped blades were prehistoric in design and universal in distribution by this time, made of either cast bronze or forged iron, both of which can be shaped more easily than steel.

SPANISH SWORD

By the 3rd century BC, having had increasing contact with the Celts and Hannibal's Celto-Iberian mercenaries in the Punic Wars, the ever practical Romans chose to model their swords on what they called the *gladius Hispaniensis* or Spanish sword, though it seems more likely that its source was more Celtic than Iberian – as usual, there is debate about its exact origins. The shorter steel sword fitted perfectly with the legionary's shields, javelins and armour to make a formidable new weapons system.

The first *Hispaniensis* was the longest of the *gladius* types. The double-edged blade was slightly leaf shaped, with its tip having a gentle curved tapering to its point, between 60–80cm (2–2.6m) long, about 5cm (2in) wide and weighing approximately 1kg (2.2lb). It was finished with a wooden or bone hilt, furnished with a hemispherical guard into which the sword butted, a ball-shaped pommel at the end, and it had a knurled grip. The *Hispaniensis* was produced from around 216BC until 20BC.

MAINZ SWORD

Over the next century or two the *gladius* spawned three versions as its blade evolved to be thinner and smaller while the hilt (and pommel), made of wood, bronze or even ivory and often personalised, remained essentially the same. The next variant, produced some time in the last century BC, is called the Mainz type (after where it was found). Shorter (between 50–70cm/1.6–2.3ft), wider (7cm/3in) and lighter (800g/28oz) than the *Hispaniensis*, it had a slighter waist that flared out more at the end before the tang and at the business end it had a shorter, more angular point. Without the curve keeping its width this possibly made the end of the Mainz rather narrow and perhaps prone to snapping.

FULHAM SWORD

Soon after the Mainz sword and no doubt running concurrently with it, the Fulham type was fractionally smaller (50–70cm/1.6–2.3ft), narrower (6cm/2.5in) and lighter (700g/25oz). The Fulham sword had lost the waisting towards the hilt and now had parallel sides tapering down to a narrow

◄ *Recreated from a body found at Herculaneum (so, dateable to* AD*79) this shows a carpenter who may have been a veteran or a naval man, found with his tools of trade and with some textile evidence. He wore a sword and dagger.*

THE *SPATHA*

At first it seems surprising that the infantry should take up this weapon. The *spatha* was the sword used by the auxiliary cavalry and its adoption, as well as the use of ring or chain mail instead of the *segmentata* armour, reflected the changes happening both in Roman society but also in the technology and tactics of contemporary warfare. Heavy infantry no longer exclusively decided the outcome of a battle: instead, a more mobile all-arms and mixed-arms combat became the norm, requiring a different, often looser, approach.

It is thought that the *spatha* originated with the horse-loving, weapon-mad Celts, to whom a sword was a living thing. The practical Romans had no such spiritual relationship with their weapons – they just killed people with them (including lots of other Romans) – but then neither did they actually invent a type of sword; they just brazenly stole designs and tweaked them a bit. So it was with the *spatha*. Measuring between 75cm (2.5ft) and 1m (3.25ft), it was straight and long and lenticular in shape, generally with a longer hilt than the previous *gladius*, though at first it kept the organic composition of wood or bone and the ball pommel. Later hilts featured increasing amounts of metal and had pyramidal pommels – mainly on expensive decorative versions.

There seem to have been two main types, defined really by their length, width and end points, with one being more rounded to prevent accidental injury when mounted and so used by cavalry. The Straubing-Nydam type was long and thin while the Lauriacum-Hromowka design was wider and heavier. They were both constructed by forge-welding laminations of iron and steel plates and later pattern-welded for visual decoration on the blade itself. The *spatha* remained in use long beyond the Roman Empire and was the forerunner of the medieval knight's sword.

◄ *A 3rd-century legionary with a ridged Gallic type helmet, extended chain mail and carrying a spear and* spatha *longsword.*

point that was slightly narrower but very similar to the Mainz – perhaps with the same inherent vulnerability? Schematics of the sword would imply this but it would depend on its thickness and the quality of the steel used in its construction.

POMPEII SWORD

The final *gladius* produced is known as the Pompeii, from some time in the 1st century AD. It is the smallest (45–65cm/1.5–2ft) and narrowest (5cm/2in) and most prevalent of the four types, weighing 700g (25oz), making it the same weight as the Fulham, so it must have been thicker. It also had the same parallel sides but no tapering of the point, so the blade edges continued straight until a short triangular point at the end. The Pompeii sword is more clunky and utilitarian in appearance than both the Fulham and Mainz, lacking the elegance of the waisting and the tapering of the blade, but the parallel edges are longer, giving the sword more cutting and slashing power, while the foreshortened point must have been more solid. Its design bears the hallmarks of economy and standardisation and it must have been cheaper and faster to produce, while still achieving its purpose.

THE TRANSITION FROM *GLADIUS* TO *SPATHA*

All versions of the *gladius*, as long as they were serviceable, continued to serve side by side, since army-issued swords had to be returned to the armoury for reassignment on death or retirement. The *gladius* was produced and used well into the 2nd century AD, its variants reflecting mainly economic factors, but by the 3rd century AD they finally gave way to a longer sword that was taken up by the infantry – the *spatha*.

DAGGER

Once again, as with almost all Roman weapons, the origin of the *pugio* is much debated. The dagger is never mentioned in the older ancient sources, but archaeological evidence points to the time of its appearance being the late Republic and early Principate. It is thought the weapon might have originated first in Hispania.

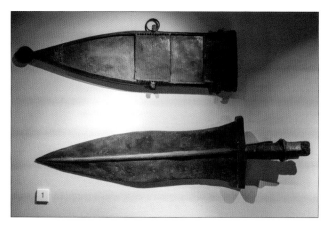

▲ *Not a utility knife, rather an exclusive status symbol for the Roman military – the fat, ribbed* pugio.

▼ *Detail of an officer wearing* lorica squamata *scale armour and showing the intricate mounting arrangements for the* pugio. *Note the* pteruges.

Pugiones were made from either bronze or iron and later steel. Early ones had a blade length range between 20–25cm (0.66–0.8ft), featuring a relatively wide leaf shape with a distinctive central groove or rib running down the centre and a flat tang. A new style emerged in the 2nd century AD consisting of a slimmer blade with a central groove and in the early 3rd century AD new versions were even larger than their predecessors – up to 28cm (0.9ft) in length and 9.5cm (0.3ft) in width.

Sheaths and hilts were composed of different configurations of metal, wood and leather and were usually highly and personally decorated with intricate inlays of precious metals, making the *pugio* a rather 'bling' showpiece as well as a weapon; indeed, it seems that it was carried as an exclusive status symbol for the soldiers, since only they had the right to wear them.

Given its size, shape and the degree of decoration it is safe to say it was definitely not a utility knife – such much duller workaday knives are found in abundance at Roman sites. It was worn on the left side suspended on rings hanging from the *balteus*.

SPEARS, JAVELINS AND DARTS

Along with bows and slings, spears, javelins and darts were the missile weapons of the Bronze and Iron Ages, although in Ancient Greece the heavy spear became a primary fighting weapon. As in many things, the Romans were adept at adopting and adapting the technology and techniques of their enemies and making them their own.

SPEAR

The *hasta* was an original weapon of the Roman phalanx based on the Greek model. It was long (at least 2m/6.5ft), with a large, sharp iron head and often a bronze point or lump on the reverse end. It was made to be held, thrust and even braced on the ground, but not thrown. It was used in conjunction with the others around it in the phalanx to present a united front of iron points towards the enemy and the *hastati* line in the *triplex acies* (see page 132) from which it took its title.

This kind of spear never left the Roman inventory, for the *auxilia* retained a slightly smaller version for its infantry while the cavalry used something similar as a lance, although in the 3rd century BC, with the adoption of the *scutum*, *segmentata* and *gladius*, the new Roman assemblage for the legionary of the late Republic and early Principate period was instead completed with the *pilum* – a kind of javelin. However, *hastae* once more regained their usefulness as the nature and composition of the army changed again in the 3rd century AD.

JAVELIN

The *pilum* originated with the Samnites and was another Roman adoption and adaption. It was lighter and smaller than the *hasta* though still a heavy javelin, with its weight providing penetrating power. It was predominantly for throwing, though it could also be thrust at opponents. Picking off individual targets or hurled en masse in a barrage, a well-thrown *pilum* could pierce armour or stick in an enemy's shield and drag it down, exposing the opponent to the oncoming crunch of the Roman front rank.

It was designed with a hard iron point and a softer, thin shank that bent on contact and rendered the weapon useless until beaten out straight again, so it could not be thrown back by the enemy. (Very early versions had a mixture of wooden and iron nails attaching the spearhead to the shaft so that it broke off on impact.) Each legionary was armed with two *pila*.

There were originally two versions of the *pilum*: a heavier one with a tanged and riveted head and a lighter one that used a socket attachment. Over time, they became more standardised and smaller, so to compensate extra weight was added to the reverse end knob. By the 3rd century AD, however, the *pilum* was being replaced, first with a shorter pointed thrusting javelin called the *spiculum*, then with a new version of the *hasta* that was more suited to the combat conditions of the period, being better able to cope with the

increase in enemy cavalry. (Its longer reach increased contact range and its heavier point and thicker shaft made it able to withstand impact.)

DART

Another missile weapon was the *plumbata* – a lead-weighted dart with a barbed arrow-like head used by infantrymen, cavalrymen and skirmishers alike from the 4th century AD. They were small enough for two or three to attach on the inside of a shield and were a relatively short-range weapon, to be used just as one was closing with the enemy.

▼ *A re-enactor of an end of 3rd century Roman soldier from the northern provinces, with long chain mail and undergarments, circular shield and a selection of* pila *javelins.*

OTHER WEAPONS

Though bows were known and used, there was no real tradition of war bows in the western Mediterranean. The Iberian, Italic and Greek peoples instead favoured the javelin as their ranged weapon. Slingers and archers were valued less highly than heavy infantry. Then the Romans met the Parthians and auxiliary mounted archers became an important component of Roman military power.

A CHANGE OF ATTITUDE

The *velites* (skirmishing troops) of the early Roman Army served at the front of a battle briefly to distract and disrupt the enemy using slingshots and light throwing spears until the phalanx could close and decide the outcome. Elsewhere, archers (*sagittarii*) were used in defence of city walls, to provide covering fire or else in surprise attacks and at various times they even saved the day. However, despite this, their value was never fully appreciated. Indeed, the Greeks saw archery as a barbaric, cowardly Eastern import, and while the Romans weren't quite as disdainful, they still did not consider it very 'manly'. The emphasis was firmly focused on heavy armoured infantry.

However, as the Romans campaigned in the East, where archery was a particularly prominent part of warfare, they came into contact with (and on the receiving end of) peoples who saw the bow and the sling as primary weapons, and so their attitude shifted. This was reflected by a change in tactics, to good effect: Parthian horse archers (famous for the ability to shoot at full gallop in any direction) and cataphracts (heavy cavalry) inflicted one of Rome's most severe defeats at the Battle of Carrhae (53BC).

Under Vespasian (r. AD70–79), archers became more proactive, even being used to take and hold ground, and by the later 4th and 5th centuries AD and after meeting the lethal bows and tactics employed by the Huns, Rome again adapted and adopted their style of archery and mounted bowmen became a prominent part of Roman armies.

COMBINED ARMS

The balance of heavy infantry against heavy mounted cavalry and archers/slingers was finer than first appears. At different times, each one defeated the other, which gradually led to the understanding and development of 'all arms' combat. Different kinds of unit could be used as supporting arms to attack in sequence one after the other or as combined arms attacking in unison. By combining the different elements of infantry, cavalry, artillery and missiles the inherent vulnerability of any particular formation to certain forms of attack can be countered. Also when attacking, by striking the enemy with two or more arms simultaneously his defending actions against one can leave him open to attack from the other. For this reason, after the Marian reforms to the structure of the

▼ *Roman recurved composite bows were made from horn, wood and sinew laminated together, with a draw weight of around 40kg (90lbs) and a maximum range of around 200m (218 yards). Their combination of smaller size and high power, made them also suitable for use on horseback. When facing heavily armoured troops, a narrower, more pointed, bodkin type arrow that could pierce through metal was favoured.*

▲◥▶ *A simple weapon but devastatingly effective and accurate in experienced hands – the ancient slingshot. Roman cast slingshots – from clay or lead – have been found, although the latter seems to have gone out of use in the 2nd century AD.*

army, Rome began to recruit auxiliaries in their own discrete units who were specialists in their fields, either as archers, slingers or cavalry.

REGIONAL SPECIALISTS

Slingers (*funditores*) and archers (*sagittarii*) were first recruited from the Greek islands. It seems that missile troops from islands or mountainous small states who didn't have the wealth to build hoplite phalanxes came to predominate, though almost all states had their own slingers and archers, too. Perhaps the dearth of other opportunities led them to concentrate on those particular weapons systems and the mercenary tradition.

Interestingly, slings could often outrange bows, depending on the size and type of ammunition used. This could include stones of varying size as well as lead slugs more like a bullet. Initially, the renowned slingers from Rhodes were recruited, who used small lead bullets that had a particularly long range. However, by about 200BC slinger recruits came almost exclusively from the Balearic Islands, where there was a long tradition and expertise with such weapons.

With archers it was the Cretans who first dominated. For instance, an auxiliary unit of mounted Cretan archers, Cohors I Cretum Sagittariorum Equitata, is recorded as having served in the Dacian Wars of AD101–106. Later, by the mid-2nd century AD, those from Thrace, Anatolia and especially Syria are attested.

The standard auxiliary archer bow was a compact recurved composite, made from horn, wood and sinew laminated together using glue made from hide, or fish bladders. With a draw weight of around 40kg (90lb) they had a maximum range of 165–230m (540–755ft), though they were most effective at 50–150m (165–500ft). The main advantage of composite bows over bows made from a single piece of wood is their smaller size with higher power, which also made them more suitable for use on horseback.

EQUIPMENT AND TACTICS

Archers and slingers both used small buckler-type shields, carrying them suspended from their shoulders on baldrics to leave their arms free for their weapons. They wore mail shirts and reinforced conical helmets, with their quivers carried high on their backs so they could draw a fresh arrow swiftly from over their shoulder. They usually carried a light axe as a secondary weapon. By the 5th century AD the chain mail of earlier periods had been replaced by leather jerkins or long-sleeved tunics, mainly for economy.

Different arrowheads were used depending on what sort of enemy was being faced. Against unarmoured opponents, broad-headed arrows that maximised flesh damage were employed; when facing heavily armoured troops, a narrower, more pointed bodkin arrow that could pierce through metal was favoured. A favourite tactic was to place them behind the legions where they could launch indirect arrow storms and barrages against the enemy. As bows became more powerful and armour-piercing, however, the use of slingers declined.

▼ *Beautiful intricacy. Bird feathers were used for the stabilisation of arrows, carefully bound and glued into slits on the shaft to ensure even flight and rotation.*

ROMAN METALWORK

The Bronze and Iron Ages are named for the increased understanding, production and use of those metals. With its vast size, the Roman Empire was at the forefront of these developments, expanding on the metalworking traditions of the Etruscans and Greeks although still constrained by the technological limitations of the time.

Roman techniques – from open-surface to deep-vein mining – were increasingly sophisticated in the search for iron, copper, tin, lead, silver and gold. Often, water was used, brought by aqueducts if necessary, to reveal and flush subsurface mineral veins but also to power stamp mills and trip hammers to crush the extracted ores.

IRON

Iron was used by the Romans to make tools, equipment, nails and weapons. Iron ore of varying quality was mined and collected from different parts of Europe (one of the biggest was at Noricum in modern Austria/Slovenia) but they also imported fine-quality seric steel cakes from India via Parthian merchants. The iron was then refined and produced in furnaces known as bloomeries, burning charcoal using foot bellows to intensify the heat, though this method rarely achieved the temperature required to fully melt the iron. Instead, lumps called blooms were produced and hammered into bars of wrought iron to undergo further heating and hammering treatment to remove impurities, according to its intended use.

The best-quality iron was used in the production of weapons and armour, being mixed with charcoal in a process called carburisation that produced steel. Being made with a high-carbon outside edge and a low-carbon body allowed swords to cut through harder objects and retain their sharpness, while a low-carbon body gave flexibility, allowing them to bend without breaking. Constructed using the forge-welding method (where cold and hot metals are combined in a mould allowing them to merge without actually melting), pieces of wrought iron could be built up to the required size. These were heated and hammered before being quenched to cool rapidly, with the edges then sharpened using further heating and hammering or a whetstone.

▼ *The Romans knew about mining and ores. At Charterhouse in the Mendips, dateable by pottery to the 1st century AD there were lead mines, from which stamped ingots have been found.*

WEAPON PRODUCTION

Armour and weapon production required the most skilled smiths, and each legion would possess either legionaries suitably trained or non-combatant blacksmiths on permanent attachment to maintain and repair the legion's equipment. Famous for standardising their production techniques, by the time of the Empire, weapons were produced in state factories and supplied to the army. However, a sword is a very personal affair and there would have certainly been a great deal of variation: there was army issue but also a sword that you might have acquired from a private source.

▼ *A 2nd-century blacksmith. The Romans would not have thrown away broken items of metalwork but, as with the Corbridge hoard of metal bits and pieces, kept them for melting down and reworking.*

THE WEAPONS OF THE *AUXILIA*

The equipment and attire of the auxiliary infantry, originally drawn from other Italic allies and peoples (the *socii*) was initially similar to that of the legions, receiving almost identical weaponry, armour and training. Later, beginning with Caesar's adoption of Gallic cavalry, foreign units (*peregrini*) kept various unique weapons and items of their national dress.

REGIONAL AND FUNCTIONAL VARIATIONS

The cavalry arm of the *auxilia* was considerably different from the legionary infantry, with its lighter equipment and with many specialist variations reflecting their particular country of origin in dress and weapons. For example, the legionary *scutum* was obviously impractical on horseback, as was the *lorica segmentata*, and the *auxilia* tended to favour round or oval shields. They commonly wore chain or scale mail, and their helmets were generally simpler than those of the legions, but there was a lot of individual unit helmet variation as a prime way of differentiation. They also used longer spears more like a lance, sometimes had a quiver of light javelins or darts attached to the saddle, and had a longer sword than the *gladius*, called a *spatha*, adopted from the Celtic cavalry auxiliaries.

At this point in time, stirrups had not been invented and although special saddles prevented a man from being unhorsed it still required much skill to fight on horseback. For

▼ *The* auxilia *outnumbered the legions by AD100. Much of it was cavalry or archers. Note the chain mail and oval shields.*

this reason, certain tribes who were renowned for their horsemanship were eagerly recruited. Other important units recruited for their specialist weapons and skills were archers and slingers.

NUMERI

As time went on, the differences between the legions and the *auxilia* blurred (citizenship having been granted to all within the limes of the Empire) and later – with the growth of the cavalry arm and the smaller, more mobile field armies (*comitatenses*) – the two arms combined to make a single entity. As a result, the 2nd century AD saw the growth of *numeri* – paid units that were not part of the Roman Army – raised exclusively from non-Roman peoples who kept entirely their own traditional dress and weapons and were attached to legions or battlegroups as required.

Various distinctive auxiliary units and their weapons are attested throughout the empire's existence – Gallic cavalry, Batavian infantry and cavalry, Rhodian slingers, Cretan and Syrian archers, Gallic and Pannonian cataphracts, Numidian and other African light cavalry, even dromedary or camel troops.

227 CS DSC_0697

CHAPTER SIX

ROMAN LEGION ON CAMPAIGN

The greatest strength of the Roman military was its cohesiveness – that is, every stage of a campaign was thoroughly thought out and planned, effectively forming a giant machine. This stretched from the provision of basic food and forage supplies through to the formation of incredibly advanced engineering feats, such as the construction of roads, bridges and siege engines. The consequence was that as armies advanced they established secure positions supported by excellent supply systems. While this is not necessarily the fastest way to wage war, it is one of the most remorseless, and few enemies were able to withstand a Roman onslaught for long.

◄ *The Roman Army lay siege to the Jewish fortress of Masada for nine months, during which time they built a two-mile long wall, and a garrison, and reinforced a natural ramp that can still be seen today.*

CAMPAIGN LOGISTICS

Roman campaigns were launched on the basis of political expediency. Usually, this began with diplomatic manoeuvrings but military force often followed. Whatever the reason for the campaign, the Roman Army became adept at organising large troop movements and sustaining them in the field.

POLITICAL STRATEGIES

Campaigns often involved the formation of alliances that in many instances later led to the target region becoming part of the Empire. As time went on, however, the Roman position with regard to the military evolved. In the early era, armies were raised each year to deal with specific issues. While this was efficient because there was no need to finance them during the winter, it was a piecemeal answer that could only work while the Empire was relatively small. As it grew bigger, professional standing armies became necessary to ensure peace and stability across their increasingly large and not always calmly settled territories.

THE ROLE OF CONSULS

Each year, two consuls were elected by the Senate and these would each be given a geographical area of responsibility together with an army and the necessary funding to run it. Sometimes, they would be allowed to expand this by raising further forces in specific areas. It would be their responsibility to deal with threats, such as to invade new territories, to fight off attacks on existing borders or to suppress insurrections. Some consuls led the campaigns themselves, while others appointed generals to do the work for them. Some undertook to implement the political aspirations of the Senate, while others had their own agendas. On occasion – such as with Julius Caesar – this was simply to cover themselves in enough glory to usurp power in Rome.

WANING AGGRESSION

While confrontation on the battlefield was the usual outcome in the early part of Empire, it changed towards the final years when political subtlety was usually preferred over direct military action. To a certain extent this was because Roman attitudes had altered with time. Early on, prowess in conflict was seen as a measure of societal standing, and it was considered the duty of every citizen to fight for his personal glories. It was impossible, for example, to gain high office without a history of glowing military achievements. Later on, however, Roman citizens often went to extraordinary lengths to avoid military service.

PROVISIONS AND MEN

The famous Chinese philosopher Sun Tzu once said that: 'The line between disorder and order lies in logistics', and the Roman military system certainly adhered to this maxim, for it treated the matter of its supplies of food, weapons and men with great care.

The Roman system's capacity to ensure that sufficient provisions were delivered to large armies at extended distances was one of its main strengths. It was not just food that was transported, however, for replacement troops often formed a large part of the consignments. This meant that even when they lost several battles in succession, the Romans usually won the overall war simply because they could keep fighting long after the enemy had run out of men and materiel. This was noted at the time by the classical Greek historian, Polybius, who stated that, 'the advantages of the Romans lay in inexhaustible supplies of provisions and men'. Caesar's own policy extended this philosophy further – it was to conquer his enemy 'by hunger rather than by steel'.

THE SUPPLY CHAIN

The supplies were delivered by a variety of means. Where possible, it was done by boat as this was usually the fastest method, since roads of that period were often close to non-existent. Seaborne provisioning was vulnerable to attack by enemy ships, though, so this factor had to be taken into consideration at the planning stage. There are numerous examples of naval ambush, such as the time the Macedonian king, Perseus, attacked and sank an entire Roman supply fleet at anchorage near Oreus. Likewise, Mithridates – one of Rome's most formidable and persistent enemies – was able to use his naval forces to prevent any seaborne supplies from reaching Sulla's army in Greece in 87–85BC. Consequently, whenever possible, the Romans took great care to protect their supply ships. Sometimes, however, the threat of enemy action caused them to have to take unsafe routes and many ships were lost to storms through using unsuitable anchorages.

When a Roman army was on the move, the supplies it had with it were usually kept well inside the body of the troops. When they had to be brought forwards overland to supply an army that was already in position, it was typically by wagon train. This

COMMENCEMENT AND DURATION

Campaigns usually began with the onset of spring – typically this was considered to be 1 March. This was in order that there would be sufficient forage to keep the cavalry's horses and the pack animals fed – without the supply of constant extra feed, any movement would be extremely limited. The duration of each campaign was dictated by two main factors: the scale of the operation and its distance from home.

STAYING CLOSE TO WATER

The Romans liked to exploit the presence of suitable rivers for the movement of supplies whenever possible, as goods could usually be delivered much faster and with less danger of attack. Many of the major campaigns were therefore planned so as to follow the course of the larger waterways. These included the likes of the Tigris and Euphrates (Mesopotamia), the Rhône (Gaul), the Rhine

▲ *Full scale replica in Mainz Museum für Antike Schifffahrt of a transport ship (*navis actuaria*) used by the Roman Navy on the Rhine and Danube. Fast and manoeuvrable, they were important for logistics in the Dacian campaigns.*

(Germany), the Nile (Ethiopia) and especially the Danube (Pannonia, Dacia and Noricum).

---

inherently necessitated good protection due to the risk of attack by the enemy or bandits. The convoy escorts were usually provided by the army, and were often commanded by senior figures. For example, the convoy that provisioned the forces of Pompeius Aulus in Spain in 141BC was led by a tribune. Although the exact numbers involved are not known, this fact suggests that the escort was comprised of a large body of men – several centuries or even a cohort or more.

The Roman method of operation was to subdue all opposition between the operational base and the area of action before actually taking on the enemy. In this way there would be fewer problems in keeping the troops supplied at the vital time. When Vespasian approached Jerusalem in AD67, for instance, he spent an entire season clearing hostile forts in the region. He then established a series of fortified supply depots in order to provide a secure supply line before he was actually prepared to attack the city.

SOURCING FOOD EN ROUTE

In addition to the supplies that were brought with them, the Romans also foraged. This was typically undertaken on a daily basis for two main purposes. The first, and most obvious, was to provide locally sourced supplies, but the second, and often

less considered aspect, was to intimidate the local population in order to put political pressure on their leaders. However, despite its advantages, foraging was by nature a dangerous occupation since it was hard to provide protection for parties of men spread over a wide area while they looked for food, water and firewood, and they were especially vulnerable to attack by fast-moving detachments of enemy cavalry.

WATER

Although having sufficient fodder was vital to the smooth running of a campaign, it was actually the supply of clean water that was the most immediate requirement. An adequate water supply was vital for the health of the soldiers and it was the primary task for the camp engineers to find a source when setting up a new camp. Where this was likely to be difficult, such as when Roman armies campaigned in desert regions, they often used pack animals to carry all their water supplies with them. Even today this is not easy to achieve, so it is all credit to the organisational skills of the Romans that they managed to do it so efficiently so long ago.

MILITARY RATIONS

Nourishing, regular rations are a vital requirement for any army – something the Romans understood well, with the result that they made every effort to ensure their men (and animals) were well fed. Indeed, Roman historians unanimously conclude that Roman soldiers were provided with an excellent diet in both quality and quantity.

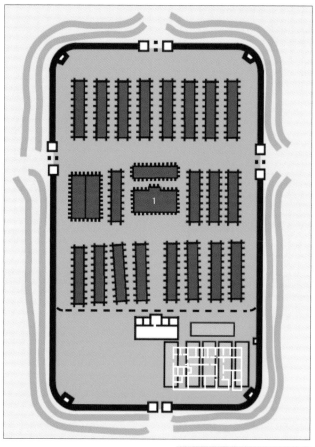

▲ *Arbeia in South Shields became a major supply base for Septimius Severus' campaigns in Scotland from 208, with many of the original buildings becoming granaries.*

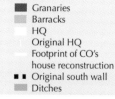

■ Granaries
  Barracks
  HQ
  Original HQ
  Footprint of CO's
  house reconstruction
■ ■ Original south wall
  Ditches

◄ *The West Gate of Arbeia was reconstructed in the 1980s. Plastered and whitewashed, they were probably taller.*

Proof that this usually worked, was that when legionaries were mutinously complaining about their conditions and grievances in AD14, none of them concerned bad or inadequate food and drink rations. Where possible, food was sourced locally, but in many parts of the Empire vital items such as olive oil would have to have been imported from the Mediterranean. The sheer quantities of food needed for people and horses placed huge logistical demands on the army and considerable effort must have gone into sourcing, buying/requisitioning, transporting, storing and distributing stores to fortresses and camps across the Roman Empire. This is borne out by the evidence, which includes the large granaries that are found at ports around the Empire, especially near navigable rivers that facilitated water transportation inland.

THE GRAIN RATION

Vegetius states that the staples of a Roman soldier's diet were grains, vinegar and salt, but judging by remarks and requests for special foodstuffs in a number of surviving Roman correspondence, it was routine for soldiers to supplement their issued rations with privately purchased or acquired foods. Nevertheless, we know that the Roman militia lived on a grain-based diet, overwhelmingly made up of wheat. It has been estimated that each soldier ate one-third of a ton of grain a year – *in extremis* this could also include barley (for soldiers on punishment duty), oats (for porridge), rye and spelt. This amounts to up to 75 per cent of his diet.

The grain was ground in hand mills that turned it into flour and made it more versatile for cooking into soups, porridge and maybe even a kind of pasta. The men cooked in their individual *contubernium* using ovens built into the barrack blocks or into the fortress walls.

THE NON-GRAIN RATION

Meat was eaten whenever possible, but depending on the season and posting, was not always available. Pigs were easy to keep and were eaten young and fresh but their meat was also salted into sausages (*farcimina*), ham (*perna*) and bacon (*lardum*). Cows tended to be eaten in the west, while goat was the commonest meat in the east. Sheep (*oves*) meat was a rare commodity.

In fixed encampments there were facilities to roast and boil meat, but with the exception of pig, the other animals were only

▲ *The Roman soldier on campaign subsisted on bread or hard tack, bacon fat and sour wine.*

slaughtered when their prime usefulness was over (providing the likes of eggs, wool and milk). When available, soldiers had mutton and goat meat and domestic fowl like duck and geese, plus wild meats such as venison, wild boar, rabbits, hare, freshwater fish and wild birds. Those billeted near the sea could also enjoy oysters, mussels, cockles and saltwater fish.

Archaeological evidence has suggested that chickens were kept at some units for fresh eggs. However, a unit in Valkenburg is known to have eaten duck, cormorants, petrels, spoonbills, herons, mallards, teals, geese, cranes and crows.

Depending on the territory and time of year, other rations included olive oil (*oleum*), beans (*faba*) of various kinds, peas (*pisa*), carrots, garlic, lentils, (*lentes*), which were often made into soup, salt (each legionary had a ration), cheese (*caseus,* from cows, goats and sheep), fruits and nuts in season, plus wine for drinking.

EATING ON CAMPAIGN

When soldiers went on campaign, each man carried rations for three days. This often comprised hardtack biscuits, a chunk of bacon, salt, and a flask of *acetum* (sour wine). Centurions were entitled to more generous rations than foot soldiers and probably had separate baggage trains to convoy their food.

An army also often took a herd of cattle with them – fresh food that transported itself – and would also forage from the surrounding countryside and requisition food from defeated enemies. Legionaries on Trajan's Column carry a stout stick from which hangs a bag for forage, a mess tin and a metal cooking pot.

CAMP MEALS

In camp, Romans soldiers ate two meals a day, the *prandium* (breakfast at around midday) and then *cena* (the main meal of the day) in the late afternoon. Food was issued individually and soldiers would gather with their *contubernium* (tent mates) to cook in a purpose-built oven and then eat together.

LIFE'S ESSENTIALS

WATER (*AQUA*)
No army can survive without a fresh water supply (*hudreia*). A marching soldier needed a minimum of 2 litres (3.5 gallons) of water a day, and it was one of the jobs of the officer known as a *metatores* to find and measure out that fresh water. Such was its import, Caesar, when he was campaigning, planned his camps where he could be sure of a good water supply. Romans clearly also knew about the dangers of stagnant water; Appian claims that during the siege of Carthage (149–146BC) the stagnant water the soldiers were forced to use caused disease throughout the army.

SALT (*SALIS*)
Appian believed that meat eaten without salt gave Roman soldiers dysentery and soldiers felt they were being deprived of an absolute necessity if their salt ration was missing for any length of time – something that could lead to unrest in the ranks.

BREAD (*PANIS MILITARIS*)
This was made from ground grain, usually wheat. From evidence of a bread stamp labelled 'Caerleon', it seems likely that a baker plus a couple of assistants made the bread ration for a century in the fortress oven. It is likely that a better quality of bread was baked for the officers.

WINE (*VINUM*)
Strong sour wine (*oxos*) and vinegar – always drunk mixed with water – became part of a soldier's ration from the Republican period onwards. Sour wine was mixed with water to make a drink called *posca*, which was also the drink of common Romans. It was regarded as an essential as its high calorific content added to the intake of the Roman soldier. They also recognised that it helped to prevent scurvy. On occasion, vintage wine (*oinos*) was issued.

BEER (*CERVISIA*)
Non-Roman ethnic soldiers, particularly those from northern Europe, preferred beer to sour wine. However, although they certainly drank it, no evidence that it was issued as part of the rations has ever been found.

TRANSPORT AND SUPPLY TRAIN

There are numerous accounts of Roman armies depending on good roads, the primary reason for their existence was not to move men and pack animals but to support wheeled transport. While horses could usually move easily on unsurfaced ground, wagons carried so much more in the way of provisions and equipment that they permitted far better logistics.

SHOULDERING A HEAVY LOAD

When soldiers were undertaking mobile warfare, they slept in groups of eight in a tent. Called a *papilio*, this structure would be made from either leather or goatskin and, it is estimated, weighed around 40kg (90lb). It was not the only communal piece of equipment they had between them, however, as standard issue also included a hand-mill (*mola*), 16 spiked defensive stakes (*pila muralia*), various tools and baskets, a cooking pot, and a pack saddle (*stramentum*). When added together, the total weighed about 145kg (320lb), but this did not include their rations, which would typically be sufficient for three days at a time. Little wonder, then, that legionaries usually had very little in the way of personal possessions.

Usually, all this would be carried between the men and at least one mule. When more provisions were needed, a second mule would be used – this could take about 15 days' worth of food, weighing around 150kg (330lb). When times were hard – such as on Antony's Parthian campaign of 36BC – and a lack of forage or disease brought about a lack of

▼ *Roman leather tents (with a useful amphora outside). There is some debate about the sleeping arrangements of the* contubernium, *with eight men and a servant.*

pack animals, much of this equipment would be abandoned as it was too heavy to be carried by the men.

THE OFFICER'S TRAIN

The restraint imposed upon the legionaries by the already considerable load they had to bear did not apply to senior officers, who took more or less whatever they wanted with them. Many were accompanied by their own servants, while others even took complete households on campaign. Indeed,

THE IMPORTANCE OF MULES

In *Logistics of the Roman Army at War* by Jonathan P. Roth (1998) he estimates:

'Assuming two mules per *contubernium* . . . this would mean twenty mules per century, a total of 1,200 for the legion. Adding 60 extra mules for the cavalry and the same number for the centurions, and 70 spare mules (5 per cent), adds up to around 1,400 mules. For a legion of 4,800, this works out to one animal for each 3.4 men.'

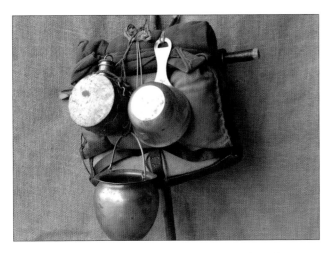

▲ *Gaius Marius reduced the size of the Roman Army baggage train by ensuring his men carried their own equipment and rations. They became known as Marius' mules.*

▲ *Note the depiction on Trajan's Column of personal equipment and the way it is carried: wooden poles from which are suspended cooking pot,* loculus, patera *and provisions; the helmets and shields were also hung on.*

TAKING THE SLOW TRAIN

This army train lagged behind the main force and could on occasion delay action. At best, it limited the speed at which the army could move and frequent attempts were therefore made to reduce the amount it carried. Furthermore, there could be a second, slow, train, the siege train, bearing heavy equipment and siege weapons.

Polybius said that behind the tribune's tents, a space of 50 Roman feet was allotted for all the extra tents, horses and pack animals. In stark contrast, Plutarch noted that Cato the Elder was an example of frugality because he only took five servants with him when he was commander-in-chief in Spain (195BC). Cato the Younger, meanwhile, had more servants than this, including a baker and a cook. He also took two freedmen and four friends with him.

Nevertheless, the mainstay of the officers' train – which usually had its own place in the marching order – would be composed of their tents and associated military equipment. The extent of who had what varied with rank, with younger officers, for example, sharing a tent, while more senior ones would have their own personal set-ups comprising one or more tents. In some instances, abuse of position was clearly rife. For instance, Plutarch described how when Caesar's army was crossing from Sicily to Africa in 47BC, a Tenth Legion tribune commandeered an entire ship to transport his own possessions, slaves and pack animals without allowing a single soldier on board.

THE ROAD SYSTEM

The Roman road network was already well established across the Italian peninsula by the end of the 3rd century BC. At this stage, they were generally unsurfaced except in built-up areas, but nevertheless, they provided fast military access when needed.

Throughout the period, the Roman Army built large numbers of roads – especially near frontiers – but did not have any dedicated road construction units since much of the work was simply manual labour. All that was needed was a few proficient engineers. Nevertheless, the Imperial Roman state spent huge amounts of money on building and upgrading roads right across the Empire. By the end of the 2nd century AD there were more than 90,000km (56,000 miles) of them, and they formed a vital part of all military planning.

There are many records pertaining to roads and their uses. For instance, Emperor Vespasian constructed and improved roads in Syria, Cappadocia and Asia Minor during his campaigns in the region in the mid-70s AD, and the leading Roman general Germanicus – who undertook successful campaigns against the Germanic Chatti tribe – appointed the commander Lucius Apronius (who later became a senator) to remain behind and oversee the construction of an efficient network of roads and bridges in the region. This was partly so that the local tribes would know that Roman forces would be able to respond very quickly, should they decide to cause any further trouble.

ADDITIONAL BENEFITS OF THE ROAD SYSTEM

During his tenure in the early stages of the Empire, Augustus exploited the existence of the road network by establishing an efficient commercial postal system with special houses spaced a day's journey apart. This was later taken over by the military and used as the basis for their logistical supply system.

Having permanent roads also improved communications, which in turn considerably boosted trade and brought in much-needed money to help fund their construction.

FUNDING THE ROAD SYSTEM

As the Roman Republic pushed its borders ever outwards, the road system was expanded too. Exactly who paid for them varied – during the Republic, the construction and upkeep was often designated as the duty of the local communities, but in other instances they were funded by the state. This changed quite early on in the period of Empire when such matters became the responsibility of the provincial governors, except during times of war when the military sometimes took over.

KEEPING THE ROADS ON TRACK

Before any road building took place, the area would be thoroughly examined by specialist surveyors. Once they were satisfied that a given course was to be followed, they would use instruments called *groma* – upright sticks with crosspieces near the top. These had plumb weights suspended from the ends that were visually aligned with other *groma* sited on adjacent beacons. Trial and error would eventually result in them all lining up, at which point their positions would be fixed. Although this was a relatively crude method, it led to the construction of roads that ran straight for mile after mile.

BRIDGES

From hard-won experience, the Romans knew that their armies were at their most vulnerable when attempting to cross large rivers. This was because the forces would not only be distracted and split between two banks, but those in the water would be unable to fight, too. Consequently, building bridges was seen as a vital component in the mechanism of their warfare.

Bridges needed for short-term tactical use would either be constructed from timber or out of pontoons since these were the quickest methods. Longer-term requirements were provided by substantial constructions made out of stone, large numbers of which still stand today, some 2,000 years later. Bridge building was therefore regularly practised in

▲ *The Column of Marcus Aurelius depicts a pontoon bridge over the Danube built by the army around AD172–175.*

peacetime, ensuring the highest degree of skill was available whenever needed.

A SHOW OF MIGHT

The construction of one of the first major bridges was undertaken by Julius Caesar's army during the Gallic War in 55BC and 53BC. This came about after several Germanic tribes had undertaken raids on territories under his command along the eastern border. Each time, they attacked across the River Rhine and then retreated back across it where they felt safe from any retaliation Caesar might choose to make. Although he was offered boats by allies, he decided that the creation of a large bridge would be a clear political statement of intent to his enemies. The bridge – over water that was up to 9m (30ft) deep in places – was completed in 10 days by his military engineers. Founded on large pile-driven posts, it had guard towers at each end and protective barriers upstream. When the enemy saw what was being done, they retreated into the forests, so Caesar decided to return to his own territory, dismantling the bridge as he did so. The point had been made – Rome could cross the river at will.

In a similar manner, Trajan built a large bridge across the Danube as part of his campaign into Dacia. This was written about by the statesman and historian Cassius Dio, and also recorded pictorially on Trajan's Column. Sometimes referred to as the 'Bridge of Apollodorus', it was in the form of a segmental arch bridge, and was the first ever structure to cross the lower Danube. Many consider it to have been one of the Romans' greatest architectural achievements

◄ *For his second campaign, Trajan had built a substantial bridge over the Danube – probably the longest arch bridge for a millennium. The architect was Apollodorus of Damascus and this is a replica.*

ON THE MARCH

Up until the end of the First Punic War, military operations were contained within the Italian peninsula, and as a result they did not need a very sophisticated logistical supply system. As they undertook more distant campaigns, however – such as the Second and Third Punic Wars, where they fought and defeated the Carthaginians – this changed dramatically.

Due to experiences where a lack of provisions impacted their fighting abilities, the Romans gradually improved matters until they were consistently and reliably able to move huge amounts of supplies over large distances, both over land and sea. A key part of this was the utilisation of the marching camp as a tactical supply depot.

Whenever the Roman Army was on campaign, it built a fortified marching camp every day that it moved forwards. This was used as secure accommodation and as a strongpoint from which to launch operations, making it a fundamental part of their modus operandi. Since this was such an important component in their military success, whenever there were periods of peace, soldiers of the standing armies (formed in the early part of the Imperial period) would undertake regular training in the building and strengthening of marching camps.

BUILDING CAMPS

The various tasks involved in establishing camps were standardised and organised so well that the construction of them was done extremely rapidly; it would take between two and five hours to build a camp. Some of the troops would be used as labour while others would be stationed as guards.

Each *contubernium* of eight legionaries, for instance, had as part of their standard equipment 16 spiked defensive stakes (*pila muralia*). These were incorporated into the palisades that formed part of the day's defences and then reclaimed on striking camp. Alongside the fenced structure

the troops would also dig a deep ditch. Around 60m (200ft) would be left between the palisade and the tents. This was for two reasons: first, to provide sufficient room for the troops to assemble and manoeuvre; and second, to keep the troops out of the range of enemy projectiles.

The basic format of the camp – which was usually rectangular – was always laid out on the same principle so that if attacked everyone would know where everything was. When the terrain forced changes, these would be incorporated as necessary. Whatever the situation, however, there would be four gates that linked two criss-crossed roads. The command tents as well as a religious area would be located at the point where they met. Particular units of men were always put in the same place, as were the baggage,

A SECURE LOCATION

The marching camp was not just a place for the troops to eat and sleep. It also acted as a tactical supply depot so that provisions and equipment were close to hand when needed. A key part of this was for it to act as a secure site for the baggage train during any hostilities, as supplies were particularly targeted by the enemy.

▼ *The Romans surrounded Masada with walls and camps as they built the ramp that eventually led to the stronghold's fall. This is one of the small camps in the desert nearby.*

◄ *Roman marching camps were intended to be secure but the army did not intend to fight battles from within them.*

equipment and supplies. For the same reasons, every officer had the same duties, as did the sentries.

The establishment of well-ordered camps by the Romans was noted by their enemies. Philip V, of Macedonia, for example, was full of admiration for the disciplined way that Sulpicius Galba's camp had been laid out near Athacus, during the Second Macedonian War.

STRIKING CAMP

When it was time to move on, the soldiers would be given an allotted time for breakfast and then buglers would give the signal for the camp to be struck. At this, all the tents and other structures would be taken down and readied for transportation. Buglers would give a signal to tell everyone to get ready for march, and any remains of the camp would be burned to prevent them from being used by the enemy. When the commander was satisfied that all was well, he would ask the troops three times whether they were also prepared; each time they would chant in unison 'Ready'. The buglers would then give the final signal and the march would begin.

MOVEMENT TO BATTLE

When a Roman legion was nearing battle, it advanced in a series of columns ahead of which was a strong vanguard made up of scouts, cavalry and light troops. These were often accompanied by a tribune, whose job was to look for potential locations for overnight camps. Travelling on both flanks would be other units, who had the role of reconnaissance and maintaining covering security. The heavy infantry would be positioned behind the vanguard with the rest of the formation behind them. If there were more than one legion involved, each one would be entirely distinct from the others, travelling with its own baggage train, servants, etc. A strong defensive force would also be deployed at the rear to minimise the risk of attack from that quarter.

When the reconnaissance troops found that the enemy were near, the whole column would usually slow down, and often stay in one position for several days while the terrain and opposition were studied in detail. While this was being done, the troops would be given rousing talks to keep their spirits up and sacrifices would be made to the gods. Good omens were sought, and when these were found, announced to the men. Before full battle was undertaken, dummy attacks would often be made to test the enemy's reactions. When the responses were frail, full use was made of such signs to boost morale.

PRE-COMBAT DEPLOYMENT

Before full combat was joined on the battlefield, there would commonly be a series of small skirmishes. These were often undertaken by both sides to determine the strengths of certain positions. Sometimes, however, these small-scale raids would develop into full-blown battle.

A BREAK FROM DISCIPLINE

Although the Roman Army was famous for the rigorous nature of its discipline, there are contemporary accounts of how certain elements completely lost all sense of direction. Plutarch stated that the tents of Pompey's army at Pharsalus (48BC) in central Greece were: 'decked out with flowered couches and tables loaded with beakers; bowls of wine were also laid out, and preparation and adornment were those of men who had sacrificed and were holding festival rather than of men who were arming themselves for battle'.

WINTER QUARTERS

When the army was far from home, winter quarters (*hibernacula*) had to be established as the campaigning season drew to a close. Sometimes this was achieved through the construction of dedicated sites (*castra hiberna*) on other occasions it was through imposition on the local population by billeting men in towns and villages. At other times, however, the men had to spend the winter under canvas (*sub pellibus*). This occurred during the Pyrrhic Wars when the armies of Consul Publius Valerius were defeated at the Battle of the Silarius River – as a penalty, the Senate told them they had to spend the winter of 280–279BC in tents. It is thought that the soldiers of Tiberius' German campaign of AD4 overwintered in a similar manner near the source of the River Lippe, and so did the men of the Roman general Domitius Corbulo, whose army lived in tents through winter during the war in Armenia (AD55–57), although in these latter two instances it was because of a lack of towns, and not as a punishment.

▶ *One of the Mainz pedestals shows soldiers on the march, a standard-bearer and a legionary with shield, helmet and* pilum. *The main army followed the standards in the order of march.*

One of the many features of the Marian reforms was that the Roman troops were ordered to remain silent before they attacked the enemy. This was unique in the era because it was otherwise typical for soldiers to make as much noise as possible in an effort to intimidate the enemy and boost their own confidence. The pre-battle silence was implemented for various good reasons: first, it was much easier to convey battle orders when it was quiet; second, despite opposite beliefs, it was considered to be more menacing to the opponents; and third, it is much easier to confuse and frighten the enemy if they can't hear where or how many enemy troops they are facing.

▼ *Although* lorica segmentata *is featured on the columns of Trajan and Marcus Aurelius. It's likely that it was not quite as widespread as these portray.*

ROMAN ARMY ORDER OF MARCH

Yosef ben Matityahu – better known in the West as Titus Flavius Josephus – led Jewish forces against Rome during the First Jewish War before being captured in AD67 by Vespasian's forces. Initially kept on by Vespasian as a slave – and probably an interpreter – he was freed when Vespasian became emperor and went on to assist the emperor's son and successor, Titus. Josephus has provided us with a record of the period and, in *The Jewish War* Book III Chapter 5, this description of the Roman Army's order of march:[1]

- The auxiliary lightly armed troops and archers were sent in advance, to repel any sudden incursions of the enemy, and to explore suspected woodland suited for the concealment of ambuscades.
- Next came a contingent of heavy-armed Roman soldiers, infantry and cavalry.
- They were followed by a detachment composed of ten men from each century, carrying their own kit, and the necessary instruments for marking out the camp.
- After these came the pioneers, to make the road level and straight, and to cut down the woods that hindered their march, that the army might not be in distress or tired with their march.
- Behind these Vespasian posted his personal equipage and that of his lieutenants with a strong mounted escort to protect them.
- He himself rode behind with the pick of the infantry and cavalry and his guards of lancers.
- Then came the cavalry units of the legions; each legion had 120 attached.
- These were followed by the mules, carrying the siege towers [which carried battering rams], and the other machines.
- After these came the legates, the prefects of the cohorts and the tribunes, with an escort of picked troops.
- Next the ensigns surrounding the eagle, which in the Roman Army preceded every legion, because it is the king and the bravest of all the birds … these sacred emblems were followed by the trumpeters.
- Then came the main army six abreast, [each legion] followed by a centurion, to superintend the order of the ranks.
- Behind the infantry the servants attached to each legion followed in a body, leading the mules and other beasts of burden which carried soldiers' kit.
- At the end of the column came the crowd of mercenaries [Goldsworthy says allies and auxiliaries].
- Last of all for the security of the whole army, a rearguard composed of light and heavy infantry and a considerable body of cavalry.

BATTLEFIELD TACTICS

Over a thousand years the way that the Romans fought changed appreciably. Initially adopting the phalanx formation used by the Etruscans, the dramatic attack of Brennus's Gauls led to changes that saw the maniple formation take over. This, in turn, was superseded after Marius' reforms and led to the cohort system. Strategic demands of the 3rd century saw further developments as the army split into static border forces and mobile *vexillatio*, cavalry units that were used as a mobile reaction force.

BATTLEFIELD COMMANDS

'*Repellere equites*'
When this command was issued, the men would adopt the formation used to defend against cavalry attacks. They would assume a tight square with their shields held robustly before them. Their *pila* (spears) were then positioned in the gaps between the shields.

'*Lacite pila*'
At this command, the legionaries would hurl their *pila* at the enemy.

'*Cuneum formate*'
The signal for the infantry to form a wedge in order to charge and break through enemy lines. It was very much a shock tactic.

'*Contendite vestra sponte*'
This command effectively told the legionaries to fight any opponent they could.

'*Orbem formate*'
This command was used to get the legionaries to assume a circle-like formation. The archers would then be placed in the middle to provide them with firepower support.

'*Ciringite frontem*'
The order to hold position.

'*Frontem allargate*'
The command to open up the position.

'*Testudinem formate*'
The order for the formation of the *testudo*.

'*Tecombre*'
The order to break the *testudo* and revert to the previous formation.

'*Agmen formate*'
The command to assume a square formation.

Whichever method of attack was employed, the main theme was that the soldiers who were in direct contact with the enemy would stand close together behind their shields, minimising any risk of injury. Meanwhile, they would use either a spear or a short *gladius* (sword) that was deployed through the narrow gap between adjacent shields in short, upward, stabbing motions. Through a combination of training, discipline, heavy armour and physical fitness, this would usually give them a distinct advantage over their foes.

THE PHALANX

One of the first battlefield developments was the extensive use of the phalanx – essentially a closely packed block of heavy infantry with files several ranks deep. The formation

▼ *The classic Roman soldier, protected by helmet and shield, with his short stabbing sword in hand.*

BATTLE OF LAKE REGILLUS (499 OR 496BC)

Sources: Dionysius of Halicarnassus; Livy
Opponents: Roman Republic against the Tarquinii and Veientes Etruscans
Location: Close to Tusculum, south-east of Rome
Result: Decisive Roman victory and the end of Tarquinian attempts to retake Rome
Romans: Infantry in centre, cavalry on wings
Etruscans: Cavalry on wings but also in centre
The cavalry first joined battle, then the infantry followed, the result being in doubt for some time in this ferocious battle in which almost all senior officers on both sides were wounded. The right wing of each army was victorious, the army of Tarquinii forcing back the Romans, while the Veientes were routed. The Roman cavalry then dismounted to join the infantry and decide the battle, with the Etruscans fleeing.

was directly borrowed from the Greeks, who – along with others such as the Sumerians – had used it extensively for at least 2,000 years.

The formation in which the core of the army fought was the phalanx, made up exclusively of infantry and was of Greek origin. A Greek phalanx was a group of tightly packed spear or pikemen who moved and fought as a single unit, but the Romans, with their penchant for adaption and standardisation, significantly refined how the phalanx was employed. For instance, it was structured with less depth and more width. As the enemy closed, the front rank of soldiers would move in towards each other and lock shields. In doing so, each man protected the man on his left. The rows behind were closer together, too, with only about 1m (3ft) between them. If a soldier were killed, the man immediately behind him would step forwards and take his place. A further principle was that because the shields formed a relatively solid wall, they could be used as a means of physically pushing the enemy back.

Troops used the thrusting spear (*hasta*) as the primary

weapon since these would work well in conjunction with closely arrayed shields. Regular tough training meant that the Roman soldiers became very efficient at the use of the phalanx, a matter that was improved by the use of specific one-word commands. This meant that when they were on the battlefield the men acted as a single entity, which made them even more effective and fearsome. On flat ground in a straight-on clash or against unorganised tribal armies who charged head first into their opponents, the phalanx was almost invariably successful. However, it was also a slow, single, dense mass that was extremely vulnerable to flanking manoeuvres or to losing its cohesion in broken terrain and its back ranks were really just reduced to pushing. This meant that as Rome expanded into mountainous central Italy, tricky terrain made the phalanx much less effective.

THE MANIPLE

Although the phalanx was used for several hundred years, it became obvious over time that it did not fare well when faced with well-disciplined fast cavalry or on the wrong terrain. It was therefore replaced by the maniple, which was sometimes described as a 'phalanx with joints'.

The composition of the maniple

In their wars with various hill tribes, especially the warlike Samnites (343–290BC), the shortcomings of the phalanx were revealed and after suffering various costly defeats, the Romans adapted and changed their fighting formation to the maniple (from *manus* = a hand) – a formation made up of multiple smaller, standalone units or companies: *velites*, *hastati*, *principes* and *triarii*.

It typically consisted of 120 soldiers arrayed in three ranks of 40 men when engaged in battle. Maniples were further subdivided into two centuries (*centuriae*), each of 60 *hastati*, 60 *principes* and 30 *triarii*. Each century had six squads – *contubernium* – with each squad sharing a tent when the legion was on campaign.

▼ *The manipular formation consisted of four lines of men, with lighter troops positioned to the front.*

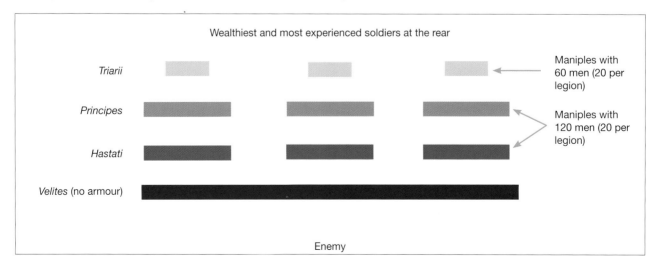

Wealthiest and most experienced soldiers at the rear

Triarii — Maniples with 60 men (20 per legion)

Principes — Maniples with 120 men (20 per legion)

Hastati

Velites (no armour)

Enemy

Alternative formations and variations in deployment

Wedge formation – lines thinned to provide concentration in centre to smash through enemy lines.

Single line defence/extended line – maniples all deployed in a single line to overlap enemy flanks or meet wider enemy formation and protect own flanks.

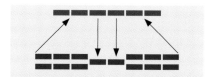

Cannae tactic (weak centre) – centre left weak to invite enemy centre attack and envelopment. Required tactical reserve behind vulnerable centre.

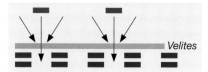

Maniple channels/Zama tactic – channels left between maniples for specific purpose of harassing and directing enemy war elephants away from heavy infantry. Tactically very dangerous since heavy infantry flanks vulnerable.

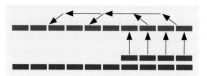

Strong right flank/rolling up the line – strength would be concentrated on the right flank, which would attempt to break the enemy left flank, and then 'roll up the line' attacking the enemy from the rear.

Protected flank – one flank protected by a natural barrier such as hillside, lake, etc. Light infantry and cavalry all concentrated on the opposite flank.

■ Romans   ■ Enemy

▲ *The maniple formation proved a flexible system, achieving considerable success.*

The *triplex acies* or three lines of the manipular legion contained its core of armoured infantry. It consisted of five *manipuli* of the youngest warriors in the front, the *hastati*, who were equipped with swords, shields and javelins. The second line, the *principes,* consisted of five *manipuli* of older and more experienced men in their prime, equipped with swords and shields. The final line at the back had two *manipuli* of *triarii* – the most experienced and elite veteran troops, equipped with spears. In fact, in addition to *the triplex acies* there was also a fourth line right at the front – the *velites* – made up of the poorest Roman soldiers, who acted as unarmoured skirmishers. Armed with a variety of missile weapons, they could harass the enemy and screen the main army before the battle proper.

Maniple formations
The favourite manipular legion formation was known as the quincunx, with the maniples arranged in a checkerboard pattern, having sufficient space to manoeuvre separately yet mix and flow with other neighbouring units. Set in three lines, this looser fighting space was much more fluid and reactive than the locked frontal approach of the phalanx. The front rank could form a temporary solid line to engage the enemy in close-quarters combat, but in the quincunx the *velites* could retreat back through the gaps and other maniples could also drop back and rest while being replaced immediately with fresh units when in combat, and when moving over rough terrain, they could maintain their shape and cohesion.

The first and second lines of *hastati* and *principes* bore the brunt of the fighting, rotating regularly in order to rest forward *manipuli*, who would soon tire in full armour. In this way, renewed impetus could be brought to the attack without losing momentum. The *triarii* (often hidden by kneeling until the last moment) could act as a defensive wall in the event of disaster or provide the final push to tip the balance of a battle. Individual *manipuli* could respond to attacks from any direction and support others in trouble.

This early manipular legion formation became the blueprint for the army from the 4th century BC until the Marian reforms of 107–101BC. At this time, the Roman Army consisted of four legions, each with the strength of roughly 4,500 infantrymen, and were supported by ten 30-man squadrons (*turmae*) of light cavalry (*equites*), and around 1,000 *velites*, skirmishing troops.

FIRST BATTLE OF PYDNA (168BC)

Sources: Polybius; Livy
Opponents: Roman Republic against the Macedonians
Location: Near Pydna in ancient Macedon
Result: Decisive Roman victory
Romans: 38,600, including two legions (2,600 cavalry and 22 war elephants)
Macedonians: 43,000, including 4,000 cavalry
In this battle of phalanx versus legion, the Romans were initially pushed back until the Macedonian phalanx lost cohesion in pursuit over rough ground and, having been penetrated through central and side attacks, was routed with devastating casualties.

Waves of attack

The *velites* were made up of young soldiers who lacked experience – their role was to make the first strikes against the enemy ranks, causing them to expend their weaponry and tire themselves out. Once this had been accomplished, the *velites* were recalled, whereupon they would pass through the troops behind them and then reassemble at the back. The next stage was when the *hastati* went into battle – their main armament at this stage was the javelin, which they would throw when they were about 35m (115ft) from their opponents. Having done so, they would then draw swords and charge. At the same time, the soldiers behind them would throw their spears over the heads of the *hastati*.

If the enemy managed to withstand this onslaught, the *hastati* would retire back through the ranks in the same way as the *velites*, and regroup behind the rest of the army. Now it was the turn of the *principes* to advance. Composed of the best Roman troops, this formation of fresh soldiers would exploit the tired state of the enemy and charge in and wreak what mayhem they could. In most situations, the enemy would give up at this point and attempt to leave the battlefield, but if they instead held their ground, the *principes* would give way to the *triarii*.

The *triarii* were the elite soldiers of the legion – made up of the oldest and thus the most experienced of the troops, they formed the heavy infantry. Armed with long spears and protected by high-quality metal armour that was further combined with large shields (*scuta*), they would advance robustly into the enemy. The battle was usually over before they were sent in, however, and if not, few survived their deployment.

Once the enemy had started retreating, the cavalry would take over since they were fast enough to overtake those fleeing the area. Until then, the main role of the mounted troops was to prevent any outflanking manoeuvres by the enemy.

▼ *Primarily an infantry army, it was mainly to the* auxilia *that the Romans turned for cavalry. Note the draco standard.*

Tactical formations used by the cohortal legion included:

Triplex acies – using four cohorts in the front rank and three each in the two behind
Duplex acies – consisting of two lines each of five cohorts
Simplex acies – consisting of one line of 10 cohorts
Agmen quadratum – a hollow square consisting of troops protecting a centre of baggage, supplies or prisoners
Orbis – a circular formation assumed when surrounded for 360-degree protection
Testudo – a turtle-like protective formation assumed using all-round raised shields
Cuneus – a wedge shape used to break through at a particular point of the enemy line

THE COHORT

Rome stuck with the manipular system for a long time, during which it rose from a regional power to become the dominant force in the Mediterranean. However, as it expanded, it began to face the bigger and more organised armies of bigger states and the manipular system that had been created to fight against other tribes or small federations was found to be insufficient to cope with the larger-scale conflicts that were being fought from 200BC onwards. Thus, following the Marian reforms of 107–101BC that enabled the creation of a larger professional standing army, a new, larger, basic tactical formation was created to replace the maniple: the cohort (*cohors*).

With the advent of the cohort, the three or four main distinctions of troops (*hastati*, *principes*, *triarii* and *velites*) were done away with, and all infantry was instead based on the *principes*. A legion's heavy armoured infantry was also now organised into 10 cohorts each of 480 soldiers, but with

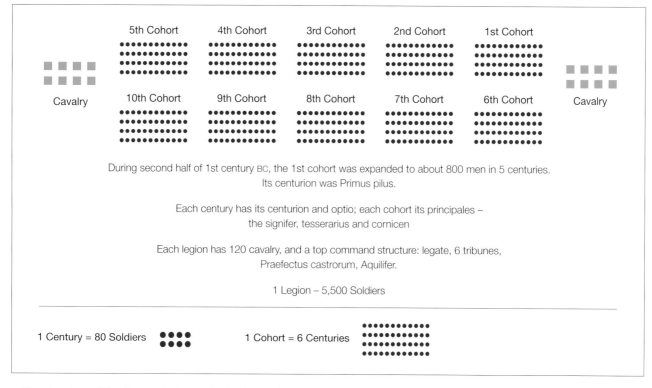

During second half of 1st century BC, the 1st cohort was expanded to about 800 men in 5 centuries. Its centurion was Primus pilus.

Each century has its centurion and optio; each cohort its principales – the signifer, tesserarius and cornicen

Each legion has 120 cavalry, and a top command structure: legate, 6 tribunes, Praefectus castrorum, Aquilifer.

1 Legion – 5,500 Soldiers

1 Century = 80 Soldiers

1 Cohort = 6 Centuries

▲ *The structure of the Roman legion, as it developed from Gaius Marius' reforms.*

the first cohort being double the size of the other nine and containing the best and most experienced fighting men.

The command structure of the cohort

A cohort was made up of six *centuriae* (centuries) of 80 men, each commanded by a senior centurion with an *optio* serving as his second-in-command. A *centuria* was made up of 10 *contubernia* (tent/mess units) and was commanded by a junior centurion. A *contubernium*, the smallest sub-unit of a legion, was made up of eight men, led by a *decanus*. Additionally, each legion had a 120-man cavalry unit called the *eques legionis*, who were used as scouts for reconnaissance and as messengers for fast communication. (It also had some non-combatants – an administrative staff of clerks, along with orderlies for the doctor and the quartermaster, plus mules and carters to transport equipment and supplies.)

In this new system, all cohort legionaries were equally multi-skilled, carried their own weapons and equipment and thus made the formation entirely self-sufficient. The cohortal legion became the quintessential Roman formation and with this standardisation of men and equipment the Roman Army outpaced all other armies of its time, going on to achieve famous victories in its relentless expansion across the ancient world.

The wedge

One of the battlefield formations that replaced the maniple was the wedge. This was, as its name would suggest, very thin at the front and relatively thick at the rear. Practised regularly during peacetime, when the commander issued the

order '*cuneum formate*', the men would follow their drills and fall into position before charging the enemy. Unlike the maniple, the wedge utilised several rows of its best men at the front instead of at the rear. They would penetrate the oppositions' lines, then the ever-swelling mass of troops behind them would surge forwards and push the defenceless enemy aside.

BATTLE OF WATLING STREET (AD60 or 61)

Sources: Tacitus; Cassius Dio
Opponents: Roman Empire against a confederation of British tribes
Location: English Midlands
Result: Decisive Roman victory with some 80,000 British casualties
Romans: 10,000 (one full legion and part of another in the centre and some auxiliary cavalry on the wings)
British: 230,000 (Iceni, Trinovantes and other tribes)
The final battle of Boudicca's rebellion is a clinical example of the Roman Army's professional expertise. Massively outnumbered, the Roman commander Gaius Suetonius Paulinus chose the time and place of battle (a narrow gorge with a forest behind him, opening out into a wide plain) so that when the Britons attacked they were channelled into a narrow front that rendered their numbers ineffective. Smashed back against their own wagons and non-combatants by the Roman killing machine of missile barrage and an infantry wedge attack (*cuneus*) followed by a cavalry charge, they were then massacred in their thousands.

THE *COMITATUS*

The Roman Army of the 4th century AD was very different to that of the Principate. Diocletian started the changes, separating the civil and military functions of government, creating *duces* to control the borders and increasing the size of the army by conscription. His work was continued by Constantine I, who ruled 312–37.

At the start of the tumultuous 3rd century AD, the emperor made an important change in the face of mounting internal and external pressures. With the AD212 Antonine Decree of citizenship for all within the Empire, another important source of manpower was made available. The legions lost their specific home-nation identity as they merged with the *auxilia*. Cavalry became increasingly important and developed into light, medium and heavy types. Basic equipment was refined or replaced and mass-produced in state-run factories.

The sheer size of the Empire ensured its inevitable division, with large imperial escort armies (*comitatus praesentes*) composed of the best troops (*palatini*) usually concentrated near the capitals of nervous emperors wary of usurpers. Rather like today's mobile rapid-reaction forces, smaller and more specialised mobile field armies (*comitatus*) were rushed to troublespots to support the stationary frontier units (*limitanei*) guarding the *limes* and who were increasingly stretched as barbarian incursions grew more numerous. Constantine disbanded the Praetorian Guard and placed military control in the hands of the *magister peditum* (infantry) and *equitum* (horse).

Legions became generally smaller as resources continued to dwindle, but the actual quality of the military was not seriously impinged. When trouble made it necessary, a *vexillatio* could be detached from a legion to be sent on a particular mission. Usually consisting of a number of cohorts, a *vexillatio* was a task force assembled and sent off separately or to combine with elements from other different legions into a temporary ad hoc battlegroup. (The name comes from the *vexillatum* – a square flag born by such a unit which would feature its parent formation.) This custom was a natural result of the cohort's sophistication and by the 2nd century the separation of some detachments from their parent units had become permanent. By the 4th century a *vexillatio* was made up exclusively of cavalry.

In this way legions were broken up into smaller units that became more and more autonomous. The compact cohort remained the most important tactical formation but as time went on they, too, became smaller stand-alone units, often composed of soldiers of a particular tribe, ethnicity or area.

Despite the upgrading of many existing border forts and the development of *numeri* native units and *foederati* allies (from outside the Empire) in the 3rd and 4th centuries, in the end weakened by years of civil war and following economic collapse the army couldn't be provided with regular supplies by the state. Instead it slowly devolved into private armies paid for by their warlord generals. It remained a formidable fighting force until political disintegration and barbarian invasion in the mid-5th century finally brought about it and Rome's demise.

▲ *The aqueduct outside Tarragona provides a background for these re-enactors who bear the insignia of the* Septimani Seniores, *listed in the* Notitia Dignitatum *as a* comitatenses *legion with the field army of Hispania. The unit probably stemmed from the original Legio VII Gemina.*

BATTLE OF ARGENTORATUM ad357

Sources: Ammianus Marcellinus, Libanius, Zosimus
Opponents: Western Roman Empire against the Alamanni
Location: Near Strasbourg, France
Result: Decisive Roman victory
Romans: 13–15,000, including 3,000 cavalry
Alamanni: 25–35,000
Outnumbered, the high quality imperial escort army of Emperor Julian (ruled AD361–363) managed to overcome a determined assault by the Alamanni, who, having hidden lightly armed infantry among their cavalry that savaged the Roman cavalry and heavy cataphracts and put them to flight, then punctured the shield wall with a massed infantry charge that was only defeated by the sheer professionalism and tenacity of the Roman infantry. Hemmed in at the flanks and pushed back against the river, some 8,000 Alemanni then perished in the ensuing slaughter.

THE *TESTUDO*

The battlefield formation that became known as the *testudo* (Latin for tortoise) was directly derived from the Roman soldier's use of the shield, which over time had evolved into a form that allowed a number of adjoining shields to be locked together, creating a relatively impenetrable barrier.

The *testudo* was a distinctive kind of shield wall formation used by Roman infantry when under attack from a distance by missile weapons such as arrows, slingshots, javelins and light spears. It is unclear when it was first used in battle, but it is known that it was regularly called upon from the 1st century BC onwards. It is described in use by various classical writers (Cassius Dio, Polybius, Frontinus, Livy) and is also illustrated on Trajan's Column.

HOW THE *TESTUDO* WORKED

It was a mainly stationary formation, although it could move, albeit very slowly, as it required everyone to move in unison. First, the whole unit would huddle closer together to compact its footprint and be able to lock or join their shields together seamlessly. Next, the front row of men would hold their shields low – either down to their shins while still standing or right on the ground while they knelt behind them. The ranks behind them would then raise their shields above their heads and lock them together in such a way as to make a solid roof over the entire unit. The soldiers on the sides held theirs on the same side of the body as their position – either to the left or right – and if necessary those at the back could mimic those at the front. The whole unit then braced their shields with their body weight and in this manner could be well protected from missile attack.

It was so firm that men could walk upon them, and horses and chariots could even be driven over them (Cassius Dio). Both Livy and Polybius refer to its strength being illustrated by

◄ *A testudo as depicted on Trajan's Column.*

infantry making a *testudo* in the games of the circus and soldiers or gladiators staging a mock fight on top of it.

Sometimes, the roof part of the *testudo* was sloped to face the enemy – a variation that was known as a *fastigiata testudo*.

HOW THE *TESTUDO* WAS USED

Because of its density, the *testudo* was not a fighting formation, as the soldiers would neither have been able to manoeuvre freely nor use their weapons properly. However, it seems that it was used regularly in sieges to approach the walls while under fire – as it allowed troops to get close to the enemy positions with a degree of protection against falling projectiles – so it must have had a degree of shuffling mobility. Depending on the height of the walls being attacked, other legionaries could climb on top of a *testudo* to make use of the extra height. (Machines also called *testudos* moving on wheels that were roofed over were used in besieging cities as well, under which the soldiers worked in battering or undermining the walls.)

The *testudo* was especially effective against long-range archery, when the risk was that arrows would fall almost vertically, potentially killing or wounding anyone who wasn't appropriately defended, but they were generally effective against most falling projectiles. The historian Cassius Dio recorded how Mark Antony's troops used such shielded formations in Armenia:

'One day, when they fell into an ambush and were being struck by dense showers of arrows, [the legionaries] suddenly formed the *testudo* by joining their shields, and rested their left knees on the ground. The barbarians ... threw aside their bows, leaped from their horses, and drawing their daggers, came up close to put an end to them. At this the Romans sprang to their feet, extended their battle-line ... and confronting the foe face to face, fell upon them ... and cut down great numbers.'

However, it was not invincible. At the Battle of Carrhae in 53BC, Cassius Dio relates the destruction of the Roman *testudos* by the Parthians. Having forced the Romans to assume that formation by using their horse archers, they then assaulted them with their heavily armoured cataphracts – with devastating results: 'For if [the legionaries] decided to lock shields for the purpose of avoiding the arrows by the closeness of their array, the cataphracts were upon them with a rush, striking down some, and at least scattering the others; and if they extended their ranks to avoid this, they would be struck with the arrows.'

LOGISTICS OF SIEGE WARFARE

Undertaking sieges was a major part of warfare during the classical era, and despite technological advances in the methods used, they remained fundamentally the same until the end of the Roman period. In essence, when threatened by a hostile force, the locals would hole up in a fortified position and try to outwait the enemy.

▶ *As well as for siege warfare, in the later years of the Roman era it became increasingly common to use large artillery pieces on the battlefield. To this end, it was not unusual for onagers and ballistae to be used as preliminary attack weapons to intimidate and reduce the strength of the enemy front lines.*

Forcing their way into such emplacements became a Roman speciality. For once, this was a matter where excellent soldiery came behind the need for engineering ingenuity and a robust logistical system.

Since the primary focus was on breaking the will of those caught up in the besieged city, the first requirement was to prevent either supplies getting in or anyone escaping. To this end, many Roman commanders ordered walls known as *circumvallations* to be built right around the target position. When guarded properly, such structures not only prevented the passage of enemy supplies and messengers, but also acted as strong defences against the desperate sorties often launched by the besieged. A good example of these can still be seen at Masada, where massive stone walls were built by Roman engineers as part of the assault.

CUTTING OFF SUPPLIES

The success or failure of a siege of a strong position generally depended on which side was able to maintain its supplies. To this end, many cities that were under risk of attack kept enormous quantities of stores, and this was often sufficient to keep them going for extremely long periods. During the civil war between Caesar and Pompey, for instance, Plutarch states that Cato the Younger – who was commander of the city of Utica – had stored 'grain and requisite provisions for very many years'.

Sometimes those under siege had rivers flowing through their position, and so were still able to obtain supplies. Such a situation faced the Roman Consul Scipio Aemilianus (Scipio Africanus the Younger) when he was besieging Numantia in 134–133BC, where the River Douro allowed provisions to get through. In order to prevent this, he had a large structure built across it. His thoroughness eventually resulted in the defeat of the Numantines.

In other instances, the besieged city was located on the coast, and thus had access to provisioning by sea. This was the case when the Romans undertook the siege of Syracuse (213–211BC) on the east coast of Sicily. The historian Polybius stated that the attackers realised that because it had a large population, the simplest way to take the city would be to starve it out. A Roman fleet therefore cut the supply route at sea, while its army prevented anything getting through by land. When the city was finally stormed, it fell. At this time Archimedes – who was one of those responsible for the city's strong defences – was killed.

SIEGE WEAPONS

The Romans were masters of the mechanisation of siege warfare, having subsumed the best of what they had seen used elsewhere, especially in Greece. Torsion artillery learned from the ancient Greeks was further refined by Roman

▲ *The* ballista *could fire bolts or balls and came in a number of different sizes. Their power comes from coiled ropes.*

LAYING DOWN STORES OF WATER

As mentioned previously, water was often the key component to withstanding a siege – without it no quantity of food would suffice. Most fortresses were therefore built on the site of natural springs, but where these didn't exist, water storage tanks were installed. At Masada, for example, King Herod (who died many years before the siege) had ordered the construction of 12 large cisterns, which together held about 40,000cu m (1,412,600cu ft) of water. These were fed by floodwater via a series of complex aqueducts. It was considered that each was enough water to supply 1,000 people for 10 years. This did not help in the end though, since when the force of 15,000 Romans attacked, they built a massive ramp up to the fort's walls – an action that prompted almost all of the 960 inhabitants to commit mass suicide, ending the siege.

technical skill and their increasingly metal construction gave Roman artillery the greatest strength, range and accuracy of the ancient world. The torsion-carrying element was made from twisted sinew leather, hemp or human hair, especially women's.

A legion came equipped with some powerful missile weapon systems – Josephus and Vegetius say 55–60 *ballistae* – no doubt with their own specialist *immunes*' crews who operated and maintained them. They began as two-armed machines but a single-armed weapon evolved later in the 4th century AD. There is some confusion in the sources with the same weapon given different names. They originally all went under the name *tormenta,* and the *ballista* was a two-armed heavy stone thrower. Later, under the generic name *ballistae* there were two main types – the man-portable metal-bolt catapults (*manuballistae, cheiroballistrae*) and the stone-throwing *ballistae* mounted on a mule-drawn carriage (*carroballistae*). The heaviest were the later onagers (*onagri*) – large one-armed catapults firing the biggest of mainly stone ammunition and named after the wild ass because of their huge recoil.

Requiring a specially built firing base and a crew of eight to operate, Vegetius states that 10 such weapons were assigned to each legion, one for each cohort. All the larger *ballistae* were disassembled for transport.

Next came the smaller two-armed catapults. Crossbow-like in appearance and design, they were operated by winding

◄ *This is an onager, a catapult whose arm is ratcheted back for use, its power derived from coiled rope.*

▶ *The Ermine Street Guard load and fire a small* ballista. *The re-enactment version is surprising both for its accuracy and its range.*

back a windlass held by a rack and pin or cog, or else a block and pulley. There was also a smaller one- or two-man, single-arm weapon called a scorpion (*scorpio*), which fired armour-piercing bolts. *Manuballistae* and *cheiroballistrae* were sometimes mounted upon carts for mobility and used in siege towers and they had a considerable reputation for accuracy. A *ballistarius* (artilleryman) was concerned with the upkeep, transport and operation of the legion's heavy weaponry.

If the bombardment of a city failed to break the inhabitants' spirits sufficiently, then the next stage was to make a direct assault. The first stage was to send men to fill in any defensive ditches around the walls. To protect them while they were doing this mobile wooden huts called mantlets were pushed into place on wheels. At the same time, taller versions manned by archers were also pushed into position nearby.

Once direct access had been gained to the walls, battering rams would be brought into play. These were constructed from heavy wooden beams with an iron head, and were repeatedly hammered against the wall by teams of men.

Although it was slow, desperate work, such a device would usually result in a breach. As soon as this had occurred, it would be followed up by a similar device that featured a hook on the end. This would be pulled rather than pushed, with the purpose of making the hole bigger by snagging any adjacent stones and dragging them out. When this was achieved, a group of men would advance with their shields locked using the *testudo* formation and attempt to get close enough for those at the front to fight their way through.

There were also several other methods of getting inside the walls – these ranged from simple scaling ladders to assault towers and even cranes that would swing parties of men across the defences.

▶ *Small* ballista *can be seen positioned behind a wooden revetment in a scene from Trajan's Column.*

TWO GREAT SIEGES

Battle: Alesia (49BC)
Sources: Caesar; Plutarch; Strabo
Opponents: Roman Republic against a confederation of Gallic tribes
Location: Alesia, Gaul
Romans: 60,000–75,000 (10–11 legions and 10,000 auxiliaries)
Gauls: 80,000 besieged and 248,000 relief forces
Result: Decisive Roman victory and the final conquest of Gaul

▼ *Today a museum, the reconstructed Roman fortifications outside Alesia in central France show the Roman battle lines as they invested Vercingetorix.*

Progress: One of Caesar's greatest military achievements was the siege and Battle of Alesia, where he built an intricate bifacial 16km (10 mile) defence network with 24 towers to both contain Vercingetorix and prevent the massive relief forces from breaking through to join him. After a dogged defence with the adroit use of extra cohorts inserted into areas under pressure in the final stages of the battle, the relief force was defeated by a simultaneous attack led personally from the front with the Roman cavalry attacking its rear. Following the defeat at Alesia Gallic, resistance ended and the Gauls surrendered their weapons and delivered their chieftains. Vercingetorix adorned Caesar's Triumph in Rome.

Battle: Masada (AD73)
Sources: Josephus
Opponents: Roman Empire against Jewish liberation group Sicarii
Location: Masada, Judea
Romans: 10,000 (one legion and auxiliaries)
Jews: Almost 1,000
Result: Decisive Roman victory with the final mass suicide of the Sicarii
Progress: The Sicarii thought they were safe in Herod's impregnable mountaintop fortress, until the Romans pulled more extraordinary engineering out of their helmets and built firstly a *circumvallation* around the entire mountain and then a massive siege ramp up against its western face to reach the plateau on top. Knowing the inevitable end, the Sicarii chose mass suicide.

▼ *Masada, showing the steepness of the mountain. At right the slope of the ramp the Romans built to access the plateau where the defenders were sited.*

TRAJAN'S CAMPAIGNS IN DACIA

Trajan's Column is located in Trajan's Forum in Rome, Italy. It stands around 30m (98ft) high. Finished in AD113, it tells the story of the campaign against Dacia (which roughly equates to parts of modern Romania) from beginning to end in a series of magnificent bas-reliefs that spiral around the column (bottom to top).

◄ *Trajan's Column provides a narrative of Trajan's campaign and of the techniques used to fulfil it.*

It was a story worth telling because of the province it delivered, one rich with mines and fertile land, and the booty it brought to Rome – as well as the slaves – which is said to have been half a million pounds of gold and a million of silver.

THE PURPOSE OF THE COLUMN

As its name suggests, the column was erected to honour the deeds of Emperor Trajan – not just for the glorification of his campaigns: the emperor's ashes and those of his wife Plotina were interred at the base and his statue placed on top (it later disappeared and, in 1587, the statue of St Peter we see today was put there by Pope Sixtus V). The column contains a spiral staircase to a platform that affords views of Trajan's forum and the surrounding city.

THE CAMPAIGNS

The first of Trajan's Dacian Wars (AD101–102) was fought for a variety of reasons: to expunge the memory of the Dacian victories over Domitian's army; the fact that Dacian forces under the leadership of King Decebalus continued to threaten the security of Roman territory; and, as Dio says, 'resented the annual sums of money they were getting, and saw that their powers and their pride were on the increase'. After being beaten by a prolonged Roman campaign, Decebalus agreed to observe peace. However, he soon reneged on this, and as a result the second Dacian War (AD105–106) took place. After a long and often bloody war, the Dacian capital, Sarmizegetusa, was taken and Decebalus fled before committing suicide. Hostilities persisted for a while but eventually the whole region was subsumed as part of the Roman Empire. Dacia remained Roman until the end of the 3rd century AD, when – after devastation by the Goths and other tribes – Aurelian was forced to give up the bulk of the province beyond the Danube in AD274.

INTERPRETING THE COLUMN

The column is a primary source of information on Roman arms, equipment, methods of waging war – and those of their enemy. It has over 2,500 figures in 155 scenes, the most noticeable figure being the emperor, who appears 58 times. The column was meant to be read like a scroll and the fact that it was closely overlooked by Hadrian's library means that it may have been possible to view it from a raised vantage point. It is a wonderful source that has influenced our view of the Roman Army of the period and records many of the duties of the Roman soldier, but the viewer must also recognise the pitfalls associated with its information. First, it is Hadrian's tomb and its basic message is that Hadrian was a wise and glorious leader. The second propaganda message says to all viewers: Rome is an implacable and powerful state that will vanquish the barbarians it attacks. The student of arms and

▼ *The base of the column houses a crypt for Hadrian and his wife's ashes.*

armour also needs to be wary of drawing too many general messages from its specifics: for example, all the legionaries are dressed in *lorica segmentata*. This is almost certainly a visual shorthand to distinguish them from the auxiliaries, who universally wear *loricae hamatae*, the cavalry elements distinguished from the Sarmatian cataphracts who wear *lorica squamata*. Some of the Romans' allies are unarmoured, even bare-chested, shown wielding clubs, whereas Dacian soldiers are shown without helmets, shaggy with long hair. Bishop and Coulston, doyens of the study of Roman military equipment, certainly identify the limitations of drawing too much information on the detail from the column.

Finally, consider the javelins (*pila*): where are they? These would – as is often the case on such reliefs – have been added into the scene as metal attachments. These are long gone.

The following photographs and captions give a commentary on some of the column scenes to show aspects of the Roman Army on campaign – and not following the story to describe the war itself. This was a big army and the near 2,000 years separating us and Trajan's expeditionary force does not hide the remarkable level of organisational sophistication that this undertaking required: the careful planning, substantial logistic base and discipline. The column, however, also emphasises the cruelty involved. In one scene a soldier (specifically, an auxiliary not a Roman – an important distinction) fights with a severed head hanging from his teeth that grip the hair; others show heads on spikes or shown to the emperor. There are women torturing captives (although there is some debate whether this is grieving Roman widows torturing Dacians or vice versa). The defeated monarch, Dencebalus is shown committing suicide rather than surrender while his people were enslaved: it is said there were 500,000 prisoners, 10,000 of whom went to the arena. The booty helped pay for Trajan's forum, this column and its attendant libraries.[2]

▶ *Logistics*[3] *are emphasised from the start of the column. Here, a boat is loaded with stores – barrels that could contain water – on the banks of the River Danube (the personification of the river is seen at right). It seems likely that the Romans appointed a number of logistics officers for a campaign – an inscription found on a statue base in Corinth identifies Gaius Caelius Martialis, military tribune in Legio XIII Gemina during the first campaign, as a supply officer in the second; later, he would be made procurator of the province of Achaea and of the iron mines.*[4]

◀ *Trajan holds a war council with his officers. Note the* sella castrensis, *the camp stools used by Trajan and his entourage. Adrian Goldsworthy in his indispensible* The Complete Roman Army *sums up the pre-battle* consilium *as an order-issuing session that would be attended by legionary legates, military tribunes, auxiliary prefects and senior legionary centurions.*[5] *After the* consilium *the cavalry moves off: note the* vexilla *standards.*

▶ *Well-ordered marches were a fundamental part of how the Roman Army operated. Carrying their gear, they had to be able to march at both military pace and a faster pace – as Vegetius explains, 20 or 24 Roman miles in five hours. Without any other form of transport, and the need to build a marching camp at the end of the day, the legionaries would have marched across the country in sensible bounds, probably around 12–15 miles a day, all the time prepared to meet the enemy. Note the horsemen leading their horses over the pontoon bridge and, in the background, the cornicens with their cornu horns.*

▶ It's easy in the modern age to forget the importance of religion to the ancients. The Romans had many festivals dedicated to their pantheon and the surviving evidence (dedicatory altars, a 3rd-century AD legion calendar, etc) shows the importance of gods and cults to the military. Romans always sought to enlist the gods before any kind of conflict by undertaking sacrifices. Once across the Danube, this is a suovetaurilia which invoked the gods – usually Mars – to purify, protect and ensure the success of the army through the sacrifice of a pig (sus), a sheep (ovis) and a bull (taurus): the ritual establishing the army as 'an entity under the protection of a deity'.[6]

◀ On many parts of their journey, the Romans cleared the way for new roads to be constructed. Here, their troops can be seen felling a forest which could be for this purpose – something Josephus identifies in his analysis of the Roman Army order of march. By the end of the Principate, over 90,000km (56,000 miles) of road had been built. The army would have built a lot of this, particularly around the borders. However, the soldiers here could also be cutting the trees for firewood that would probably then be carried back to camp by calones – the 'servants' of the soldiers who could have been slaves and of whom there is no trace on the column.

▶ Moving large quantities of supplies needed beasts of burden – the Romans used mules and oxen as draft animals. How many animals is a matter of debate as it isn't recorded anywhere. Roth suggests around 1,400 mules per legion – a carrying capacity of 175 metric tons or some 350 wagons, although there's some thought that this shows the army train and that the legions would use pack animals rather than wagons.

◀ Horses and pack animals need food and Roth suggests that the soldiers cutting grain 'may well have been collecting it for fodder'. While many of the animals would have been able to graze, if other factors came into play emergency measures were necessary. Roth quotes Caesar about the siege of Dyrrachium (48BC) when Pompey's forces' access to fodder was cut off, 'There was a great scarcity of fodder (pabulum), so much so that the Pompeians fed their horses on leaves stripped from trees and on ground-up roots of reeds, for they had used up all the grain (frumentum) which had been sown inside the camp.'

AFTER THE BATTLE

Dulce et decorum est pro patria mori! (It is sweet and fitting to die for one's country!) Horace said it first, over 1,900 years before Wilfred Owen, as he exhorted his audience with his Roman Odes (Book III, 1–6). It shows – as if proof were needed – that patriotism was alive and well in the early years of the Principate.

◀ *As with Trajan's Column, the Column of Marcus Aurelius shows beheadings taking place; see details at right.*

Romans had strong feelings of patriotism towards their homeland – as we have seen, for many years its army was composed of citizens who accepted the obligations of military service. It had to cope with heavy losses in many of its wars, and there is no doubt that death on the battlefield was a common occurrence. Accidents, training wounds and disease would also have taken their toll, as they have always done to soldiers.

There are many triumphal arches and important state reminders of battles and campaigns in the Roman Empire, but – surprisingly – as Valerie Hope says, 'There were no war memorials that listed the names of the dead, no military war cemeteries that acted as places of pilgrimage, little battlefield tourism and no annual commemorative rituals.'[7]

Soldiers are concerned for their casualties and dead and the Romans were no different, as the many private, usually peacetime, memorials attest. They buried their war dead – Valerie Hope references Caesar (*Gallic Wars* 1.26) delaying the pursuit of the Helvetii after the Battle of Bibracte (58BC) as he tended the wounded and buried the dead. It was felt that the dead were dishonoured if they weren't buried – which may account for the lament by Lucan that, later, Julius Caesar didn't bury the dead of his civil war opponents after Pharsalus, something even Hannibal had not done. (Caesar, however, also seems to have afforded clemency to those who surrendered after the battle.) The fact that so few mass battle graves have been excavated makes it difficult to generalise about whether the bodies were cremated before burial. The Romans believed the soldiers went to a better place, but once buried there seems to have been no obvious official mechanism of remembrance.

One thing seems certain: the weapons were not interred with the dead. Swords and armour were far too valuable commodities to lose. The dead's military equipment was stripped and returned to use – there are a number of examples of this including a Coolus helmet from Köln as identified by Bishop and Coulston.[8]

AFTER A BATTLE

So, the battlefield was – if circumstances permitted – cleared up: weapons were collected, Roman bodies probably buried or cremated and buried (there is little archaeological evidence), captives rounded up and killed or sold to the slavers who followed the legions. Enemy dead were left to rot where they lay after having been looted. There may have been some markers – Germanicus was said to have erected a cairn on the mound that covered the dead he buried at the site of Varus's defeat in the Teutoberg Forest: 'And so, six years after the fatal field, a Roman army, present on the ground, buried the bones of the three legions; and no man knew whether he consigned to earth the remains of a stranger or a kinsman, but all thought of all as friends and members of one family, and, with anger rising against the enemy, mourned at once and hated. At the erection of the funeral-mound the Caesar laid the first sod, paying a dear tribute to the departed, and associating himself with the grief of those around him.'[9]

The world of antiquity was harsh and brutal and did not have the internationally agreed rules we have today. The bones of Varus's men had been found in 'heaps, as the men had fallen, fleeing or standing fast. Hard by lay splintered spears and limbs of horses, while human skulls were nailed prominently on the tree-trunks. In the neighbouring groves stood the savage altars at which they had slaughtered the tribunes and chief centurions.'[10] The retribution of the Romans would be equally harsh. Germanicus, Tacitus reports, said: 'Prisoners were needless: nothing but the extermination of the race would end the war. At last, in the decline of the day, he withdrew one legion from the front to begin work on the camp; while the others satiated themselves with the enemies' blood till night.'[11]

This was by no means unusual. Trajan's column shows *auxilia* taking enemy heads and what probably are Roman soldiers being tortured by Dacian women. To lose a battle against the Romans meant death or slavery. To lose a war meant slaughter of civilians and destruction of cities: rape and booty for the troops. The Jews at Masada preferred mass suicide to capture. 'In the Roman world,' Joanne Ball outlines, 'captured combatants, whether they had voluntarily surrendered or not, were judged to have surrendered their legal rights becoming reliant on the Roman state to decide their ultimate fate – *deditio in fidem populi Romani*.'[12]

As we have seen earlier (pages 24–5 box on Slave Taking), that usually meant slavery – although the toughest, best-looking prisoners and the enemy leaders were reserved to be shown-off at the successful general's triumph. Vercingetorix's fate after Alesia was to be paraded by Julius Caesar and then publicly executed; Caratacus escaped this fate after giving a rousing speech to the Senate. On the other hand, Josephus, who started off being enslaved after capture, was taken on to Vespasian's staff and served as an adviser to Titus. As enslavement was not an option in civil wars, as Roman prisoners were not usually enslaved, more often than not death ensued.

The Roman soldier would have been aware of this. He knew that capture meant death and was as likely to fight to the death or kill himself rather than face torture, mutilation or slavery. When the roles were reversed and Rome was victorious, as soldiers have always done, he reacted the same way, enjoyed the spoils of war and, no doubt, gave his thanks to his gods that he had survived to fight another day.

THE SACK OF JERUSALEM

This is graphically described in Josephus. After the Romans took the city following a long siege:

'They slew the aged and the infirm; but for those that were in their flourishing age, and who might be useful to them, they drove them together into the temple … [of these they] slew all those that had been seditious and robbers, who were impeached one by another; but of the young men he chose out the tallest and most beautiful, and reserved them for the triumph; and as for the rest of the multitude that were above 17 years old, he put them into bonds, and sent them to the Egyptian mines. Titus also sent a great number into the provinces, as a present to them, that they might be destroyed upon their theatres, by the sword and by the wild beasts; but those that were under 17 years of age were sold for slaves. …Now the number of those that were carried captive during this whole war was collected to be 97,000; as was the number of those that perished during the whole siege 110,000.'[13]

▼ *Details of beheadings from the columns of Trajan (below) and Marcus Aurelius (bottom).*

SOURCES

Historians who study the Roman world are remarkably well served by source material, in particular those who would examine the military history. Rome was built on battle and well over 1,000 years of military history left their mark on Rome and its empire and inform historians today.

ARCHAEOLOGY

First, and most visible, the archaeological record. As an example one need go no further than the substantial construction we call Hadrian's Wall, a interlinked complex of earth and stone walls, infantry and cavalry forts, fortlets and signal towers, ditches and ramparts. Add to the structures the mass of information derived from religious sites, altars and votive offerings, burials and the occasional hoard, and there is almost an embarrassment of riches. Archaeology on or near Hadrian's Wall has provided many revelations – from the Vindolanda letters to the Corbridge hoard.

There are numerous representations of Roman military subjects visible in museums and in situ: statues, friezes, tombstones, coins. There's much we can learn from these works of art – although one has to be careful how one interprets the images. As experts Bishop and Coulston identify in their analysis of Roman sources, propaganda played an important role in determining how events and participants are represented. A triumphal arch was constructed to show victory and its intent was more important than its visual accuracy. These pieces 'were largely the product of metropolitan sculptors, often men trained in a Hellenizing style, whose knowledge of military matters was restricted to the guard units in Rome.'[14]

Before Trajan's Column, there weren't many sculptures that show fully armed soldiers. After Trajan, other similar offerings – such as the Column of Marcus Aurelius – had less detail, but nevertheless are extremely useful for the military historian. There are also other important sculptures of Trajanic Roman military figures, such as those in Adamclisi at the *Tropaeum Traiani*, which show more military detail and less pomp and ceremony.

Tombstones and memorials to dead legionaries are another important source of visual information – not only for the visual representations but also as locators of people, military units or events. While some of the representations become formulaic – such as the cavalryman on horseback towering over a naked barbarian – many show fighting men in armour, bearing arms.

Finally, a word about living archaeology and re-enactment. Yes, occasionally one can accuse some re-enactors of being fat blokes who like dressing up, but at their best they are enthusiasts who live and breathe their period, providing a glimpse of what Roman life was like. We are lucky to be able to call on the professionalism and accuracy of the Ermine Street Guard for this book. With more than 50 years of experience, and time spent at prime locations on the Continent as well as in Britain, the Guard educates and enthuses onlookers. However, it is worth remembering that few re-enactment societies have built a marching camp, fought the Caledonii or made military use of their equipment. They and we may only glimpse a part of the reality of the Roman legionary from their displays.

WRITTEN SOURCES

The primary, and most visible, form of written source material available to military historians is epigraphy: the study of inscriptions. For example, inscriptions on altars help us locate military units, as do ones on graves or tombstones; triumphal arches or stelae may supply details of events. Inscriptions can also show boundaries: the most easterly inscription discovered so far is by a legionary detachment near Baku in Azerbaijan on the shore of the Caspian Sea.

Then there are the Roman military diplomas – military discharge certificates made of bronze and issued to retiring veteran *peregrini* (foreigners without Roman citizenship). These men were not, at that time, Roman legionaries because only Roman citizens could become legionaries. However, they had served with distinction and were honoured by being granted Roman citizenship by the emperor.

The complete diploma was made of two bronze rectangular plates around 10 x 12cm (4 x 4.7in) and 21 x 16cm (8.3 x 6.3in) depending on the period. There was text on both sides. They were bound together by bronze wire and sealed with witnesses' seals, the latter covered by three bronze strips to protect them from wear. (Unfortunately, the fact they were bronze meant that in later years they were worth salvaging; fewer than 1 per cent of the likely number issued have been found.)

The first of these diplomas we know about is dated AD52, during the reign of Claudius. After Caracalla opened citizenship to all in the Empire by the *Constitutio Antoniniana* of AD212, they ceased to be issued except for certain units that employed people from outside the Empire. Nevertheless, more than 1,000 have been discovered since and they supply significant information, each having:

- the date (day and month) of issuing, with the year defined by the names of the two consuls
- the unit in which the soldier had last served
- the unit commander
- the soldier's rank
- his name and that of his father; his origin
- the name of his wife and her father; her origin (if applicable)
- the names of their children (if applicable and diploma issued before c.AD14)
- confirmation that the original bronze plates were stored in Rome

The other main written sources were written on less durable material than bronze. The ancient world used a number of different types of media. First, there was papyrus, made from the pith of the plant. Then there was parchment and vellum: prepared from untanned animal skins (sheep, calves and goats). Parchment has an interesting side story. In later centuries, many ancient parchments were cleaned and reused. These palimpsests, as they are called, can reveal their original content under ultraviolet light. As parchment became difficult to acquire, libraries were raided for old material that could be reused for Christian texts: many ancient books were lost this way.

The pages produced by these methods were often joined together to make scrolls, but scrolls are unwieldy and other, smaller versions were produced. The Romans used wax-covered wooden tablets. Later, papyrus or parchment codexes looking more like modern books would take over.

Writing was important in the Roman world and literacy flourished. This is not to say that literacy levels reached anything like modern levels, but the ability to read was not limited to the better-off. There are many levels of literacy and the Roman Army was a good example of some of them.

Most, if not all, of the officers would have had to be literate to understand the things that keep armies moving: written orders, listings of supplies and stores, requests for provisions, manpower levels, rosters, work rotas, etc. There would also have been a number of scribes. However, the high number of inscriptions linked to the army, such as ones on altars, speak of a reasonable level of literacy – at least a functional literacy that was helped by using common forms and abbreviations such as VSLM – *v(otum) s(olvit) l(ibens) m(erito)* =
willingly and deservedly fulfilled his vow

Other forms of writing reinforce this idea of widespread literacy. First, the Vindolanda letters written in ink on thin wooden tablets. These are not just letters from the garrison commander's wife; instead, they were generated, 'not by a corps of scribes, nor even by an educated elite of Romans or Italians, but by the officers and lower ranks of non-Roman auxiliary units recruited from Gaul and Germany.'[15]

There are many other examples of letters from soldiers, such as this from an Egyptian soldier, Aurelius Polion, serving with Legio II Adiutrix in Pannonia, who was sent home in the 3rd century AD and reveals classic signs of homesickness:

'... I pray that you are in good health night and day, and I always make obeisance before all the gods on your behalf. I do not cease writing to you, but you do not have me in mind. But I do my part writing to you always and do not cease bearing you in mind and having you in my heart. But you never wrote to me concerning your health, how you are doing. I am worried about you because although you received letters from me often, you never wrote back to me...'[16]

Then there are requests for equipment. For example, one Claudius Terentianus asked his father Tiberianus in AD112–115 for:

'a battle sword (*gladius pugnatorius*), a javelin (*lancea*), a pickaxe (*dolabra*), a grapnel (*copla*), two lances (*lonchae*), a hooded cloak (*byrrum castalinum*) and girdled tunic (*tunica bracilis*) together with his trousers (*braccae*).'

Another soldier demanded of the letter's recipient that: 'You will send me an *abolla* [a thick woollen cloak] and a hooded cloak ... and a pair of *fasciae* and a pair of leather tunics, oil and a cuplet like you told me ... and a pair of pillows.'[17]

Lost stories

Up until the Punic Wars there are no surviving Roman histories. Unlike Greece, Rome did not have a strong oral tradition, but it did have myths and legends that formed an important part of the subject matter. On this basis, many historians have started their coverage of Roman history with a reworking of the founding of the city – *Ab Urbe Condita Libri*. The first Roman historian we know about, Quintus Fabius Pictor, provided the template for written histories after the Second Punic War. Many others followed him. Soon, a form of historiography emerged – annals – that supply year-by-year accounts. These followed the style of the *Annales maximi*, the annals kept by the chief high priest (*pontifex maximus*) of the Roman Republic, which were published in 80 books around 130BC. They have been lost, as has Quintus Fabius Pictor's original history and many others since antiquity. Tantalisingly, we know about many more sources that are not available to us today than those that survive. Fortunately, however, many of these 'lost' books live on with passages repeated verbatim, or used as sources for later works. Writers worth particular examination are (in date order):

Lucius Cincius Alimentus (c.208–116BC), Polybius (c.208–116BC), Diodorus Siculus (c.90–c.60BC), Julius Caesar (100–44BC), Sallust (86–c.35BC), Dionysius of Halicarnassus (c.60–after 7BC), Marcus Vitruvius Pollio (c.80–70BC–after c.15BC), Titus Livius Patavinus (65–59BC–AD12–17), Marcus Velleius Paterculus (c.19BC–after AD30), Plinius Secundus (AD23–79), Titus Flavius Josephus (AD37–c.110), Sextus Julius Frontinus (c.AD40–103), Publius Cornelius Tacitus (c.AD56–c.118), Gaius Suetonius Tranquillus (c.AD69–after 122), Appianus of Alexandria (c. AD95–165), Cassius Dio (c.AD155–c.235), Ammianus Marcellinus (c.AD330–400), Publius Flavius Vegetius Renatus (late 4th century AD), Zosimus (unknown: lived turn of the 5th century AD), Joannes Zonaras (12th century).

In addition there are the *Fasti Annales* (753BC–AD19) – a list of the magistrates (*Fasti Capitolini*: consuls, censors, tribunes etc) elected from 483BC to AD19 and a list of the triumphs awarded (*Fasti Triumphales*). There are significant gaps and doubts about accuracy, but the list helps provide a chronology. Finally, the *Notitia Dignitatum* (end of 4th/early 5th century AD) lists the offices of the Roman government and army of both Western and Eastern empires, the former from around AD420, the latter c.AD395.

BIBLIOGRAPHY

ARTICLES/THESES

Ball, Joanne: 'The Treatment of Captured Combatants in the Roman World'; paper presented at the International Ancient Warfare Conference 2017 (Aberystwyth), (www.academia.edu/33749240/The_treatment_of_captured_combatants_in_the_Roman_world).

Belfiglio, Valentine John: 'Sanitation in Roman Military Hospitals'; *International Journal of Community Medicine and Public Health*, 2015 Nov 2(4): pp462–465 (https://www.ijcmph.com/index.php/ijcmph/article/view/999).

Belfiglio, Valentine John: 'Control of epidemics in the Roman Army: 27BC–AD476', *International Journal of Community Medicine And Public Health,* vol 4, 2017, p1389 *(https://www.ijcmph.com/index.php/ijcmph/article/view/1389).*

Birley, Anthony R.: 'The "Cohors I Hamiorum" in Britain', *Acta Classica* Vol. 55, pp. 1-16; Classical Association of South Africa, 2012 (www.jstor.org/stable/24592565).

Bishop, M.C.: 'A catalogue of military weapons and fittings', Jahresbericht 2001; Gesellschaft Pro Vindonissa, 2001 (http://dx.doi.org/10.5169/seals-282467).

Bishop, M.C.: 'On parade: status, display, and morale in the Roman army', *Akten der 14. Internationalen Limeskongresses in Bad Deutsch-Altenburg/Carnuntum, 14.–21. September 1986*, Römische Limes in Österreich Sonderband, pp. 21–30; Vienna 1990.

Coulston, Jon: 'Courage and Cowardice in the Roman Imperial Army', *War in History*, Vol. 20, 1: pp. 7-31; Sage Journals, 2013 (https://doi.org/10.1177/0968344512454518).

Cupcea, George, and Marcu, Felix: 'The Size and Organization of the Roman Army and the Case of Dacia under Trajan', *Dacia*; cat.inist.fr, 2006.

Dzino, Danijel: *Illyrian Policy of Rome in the Late Republic and Early Principate*; DPhil Thesis, Adelaide University, 2005 (https://digital.library.adelaide.edu.au/dspace/bitstream/2440/37806/10/02whole.pdf).

Holder, Paul A.: 'Auxiliary Deployment in the Reign of Trajan', *Dacia* New Series vol. 50, 141-174; Editura Academieri Române, 2006 (www.academia.edu/9010983/Auxiliary_deployment_in_the_reign_of_Trajan).

Hope, Valerie Margaret: 'Dulce et decorum est pro patria mori': the practical and symbolic treatment of the Roman war dead. Mortality: Promoting the interdisciplinary study of death and dying, 23(1) pp. 35–49; The Open University, 2017 (http://oro.open.ac.uk/48585/3/Mortality4.pdf).

Maxfield, Valeria A.: *The Dona Militaria of the Roman Army*; DPhil thesis, Durham University, 1972 (http://etheses.dur.ac.uk/10339/).

Rocco, Marco: 'The Reasons Behind *Constitutio Antoniniana* and its Effects on the Roman Military', Acta classica Universitatis Scientiarum; dialnet.unirioja.es, 2010 (www.academia.edu/1775284/The_reasons_behind_Constitutio_Antoniniana_and_its_effects_on_the_Roman_military).

Rossi, Corinna, and Magli, Giulio: 'Wind, Sand and Water. The Orientation of the Late Roman Forts in the Kharga Oasis (Egyptian Western Desert)'; 2017 (https://www.researchgate.net/publication/317740010_Wind_Sand_and_Water_The_Orientation_of_the_Late_Roman_Forts_in_the_Kharga_Oasis_Egyptian_Western_Desert).

Salways, Benet: 'What's in a Name? A Survey of Roman Onomastic Practice from *c*.700 BC to AD 700'; *The Journal of Roman Studies*, Vol. 84; Society for the Promotion of Roman Studies Stable, 1994 (www.jstor.org/stable/300873).

Sasel Kos, Marjeta: 'The Role of the Navy in Octavian's Illyrian war', Histria Antiqua, 21/2012, pp. 93–104 (https://hrcak.srce.hr/file/148673).

Schuckelt, Sebastian: Evidence for horse armour in the Roman Army and the use of chamfrons by the Roman cavalry; Landesmuseum Bonn, online library, (www.scribd.com/document/296437969/Evidence-for-Horse-Armour-in-the-Roman-A).

Silver, Morris: 'Public Slaves in the Roman Army: An Exploratory Study', *Ancient Society* 46, pp. 203–40; Peeters Online Journals 2017 (www.academia.edu/29968292/Public_Slaves_in_the_Roman_Army_An_Exploratory_Study).

Simon, Bence: 'The (Grain) Supply System of the Early Imperial Roman Army', *Studia archaeologica Nicolae Szabó LXXV annos nato dedicate*; L'Harmattan, 2015.

Smith, R.E.: 'The Army Reforms of Septimius Severus', *Historia: Zeitschrift für Alte Geschichte; Franz Steiner Verlag, 1972 (*www.jstor.org/stable/4435278).

Speidel, M.A.: 'Roman Army Pay scales', *Heer und Herrschaft im Römischen Reich der Hohen Kaiserzeit*; Stuttgart, 2009, pp349–380.

Swidzinski, Andrew: 'Italian Aims in the First Civil War 87–82 BC', *Hirundo The McGill Journal of Classical Studies* Vol. 5 Pp. 118–146. ; McGill University, 2006–2007 (https://www.mcgill.ca/classics/files/classics/2006-7-08.pdf).

Tomczak, Juliusz: 'Roman military equipment in the 4th century BC: pilum, scutum and the introduction of manipular tactics', *Folia Archaeologica* 29; Acta Universitatis Lodziensis, 2012 (www.academia.edu/28024251/Roman_military_equipment_in_the_4th_Century_BC_pilum_scutum_and_the_introduction_of_manipular_tactics_Folia_Archeologica_29_2013_s._38-65).

Wheeler, Everett L.: 'Rome's Dacian Wars: Domitian, Trajan, and Strategy on the Danube, Part I', *The Journal of Military History* 74 (October 2010), pp. 1185–1227 (https://www.academia.edu/4104242/Romans_Dacian_Wars_Domitian_Trajan_and_Strategy_on_the_Danube_Part_I).

Wheeler, Everett L.: 'Rome's Dacian Wars: Domitian, Trajan, and Strategy on the Danube, Part II', *The Journal of Military History* 75 (October 2011), pp. 191–219 (https://www.academia.edu/4104248/Romes_Dacian_Wars_Domitian_Trajan_and_Strategy_on_the_Danube_Part_II).

Wilkes, J.: ' The pen behind the sword: power, literacy and the Roman Army'; *Archaeology International*, 5, pp32–35 (https://www.ai-journal.com/articles/abstract/10.5334/ai.0510/).

Zerbini, Andrea: 'Greetings from the Camp. Memories and Preoccupations in the Papyrus Correspondence of Roman Soldiers with their Families', p287. (www.academia.edu/7104192/Greetings_from_the_camp._Memories_and_preoccupations_in_the_papyrus_correspondence_of_Roman_soldiers_with_their_families).

BOOKS

Bingham, Sandra: *The Praetorian Guard: A History of Rome's Elite Special Forces*; Baylor University Press, 2013.

Bishop, M.C.: JRMES Monograph 1 *Lorica Segmentata Vol. I A Handbook of Articulated Roman Plate Armour*; The Armatura Press, 2002.

Bishop, M.C.: *Roman Legionary Fortresses*; Pen & Sword, 2012.

Bishop, M.C. and Coulston, J.C.N.: *Roman Military Equipment From the Punic Wars to the Fall of Rome*, second edition; Oxbow, 2006.

Bruun, Christer, and Edmondson, Jonathan: *The Oxford Handbook of Roman Epigraphy*; Oxford University Press, 2014.

Campbell, Duncan B., and Hook, Adam: *Elite 126 Siege Warfare in the Roman World*; Osprey, 2005.

Collins, Rob, and McIntosh, Frances: *Life in the Limes*; Oxbow Books, 2014.

Connolly, Peter: *Greece and Rome at War*; Greenhill Books, 2006.

Copeland, Tim: *Life in a Roman Legionary Fortress*; Amberley, 2014.

Cornell, Tim, and Matthews, John: *Atlas of the Roman World*; Phaidon Press Ltd, 1982.

Cowan, Ross, and Hook, Adam: *Elite 155 Roman Battle Tactics 109BC–AD313*; Osprey, 2007.

Cowan, Ross, and Ó'Brógáin, Seán: *Warrior 166 Roman Legionary 69–AD161*; Osprey, 2013.

D'Amarto, Raffaele, and Dennis, Peter: *Elite 221 Roman Standards & Standard-Bearers (1) 112BC–AD192*; Osprey, 2018.

D'Amarto, Raffaele, and Rava, Giuseppe: *Men at Arms 506 Roman Army Units in the Eastern Provinces 1 31BC–AD195*; Osprey, 2017.

D'Amarto, Raffaele, and Ruggeri, Raffaele: *Men at Arms 479 Centurions 31BC–AD500: The Classical and Late Empire*; Osprey, 2012.

D'Amarto, Raffaele, and Ruggeri, Raffaele: *Men at Arms 511 Roman Army Units in the Western Provinces 1 31BC–AD195*; Osprey, 2003.

D'Amarto, Raffaele, and Sumner, Graham: *Arms and Armour of the Imperial Roman Soldier*; Frontline Books, 2009.

D'Amarto, Raffaele, and Sumner, Graham: *Men at Arms 451 Imperial Roman Naval Forces 31BC– AD500*; Osprey, 2009.

Edwards H.J. (trans): The Loeb Classical Library *Caesar The Gallic War*; Heinemann, 1919.

Erdkamp, Paul (ed): *A Companion to the Roman Army*; Wiley-Blackwell, 2011.

Fields, Nic: *Battle Orders 27 The Roman Army of the Punic Wars 264–146BC*; Osprey, 2008.

Fields, Nic: *Battle Orders 34 The Roman Army; the Civil Wars 88–31BC*; Osprey, 2008.

Fields, Nic: *Battle Orders 37 The Roman Army of the Principate 27BC–AD117*; Osprey, 2009.

Fields, Nic, and Embleton, Gerry & Sam: *Elite 172 Roman Battle Tactics 390–10BC*; Osprey, 2010.

Gibbon, Edward: *History of the Decline and Fall of the Roman Empire* (revised 1845); Accessed from www.gutenberg.org/files/25717/25717-h/25717-h.htm

Goldsworthy, Adrian: *The Complete Roman Army*; Thames & Hudson, 2003.

Kocsis, László (ed): The Enemies of Rome, *Journal of Roman Military Equipment Studies Vol. 16*; Hungarian National Museum, 2008.

Le Bohec, Yann: *The Imperial Roman Army*; Routledge, 2000.

Macdowell, Simon, and Embleton, Gerry: *Warrior 9 Late Roman Infantryman 236–565AD*; Osprey, 1994.

Milner, N. P. (trans): *Translated Texts for Historians Vol 16 Vegetius*; Epitome of Military Science; Liverpool University Press, 1993.

Peterson, Daniel: *Europe Militaria Special No 2 The Roman Legions Recreated in Colour Photographs*; Crowood Press, 2003.

Peddie, John: *The Roman War Machine*; Sutton Publishing, 1994.

Pollard, Nigel, and Berry, Joanne: *The Complete Roman Legions*; Thames & Hudson, 2015.

Potter, David S. (ed): *A Companion to the Roman Empire*; Blackwell, 2006.

Rankov, Dr Boris, and Hook, Richard: *Elite 50 The Praetorian Guard*; Osprey, 1994.

Roth, Jonathan P.: *Columbia Studies in the Classical tradition Vol. XXIII The Logistics of the Roman Army at War 264BC–AD235*; Brill 1999 (http://www.legioxxirapax.com/zasoby/The_Logistics_of_the_Roman_Army_at_War_(264BC_-_235AD).pdf).

Scarre, Chris: *Chronicle of the Roman Emperors*; Thames & Hudson, 1995.

Sekunda, Nicholas V., Northwood, Simon, and Simkins, Michael: *Caesar's Legions The Roman Soldier 753BC to 117AD*; Osprey, 2000.

Sheppard, S.I., and Dennis, Peter: *Campaign 252 The Jewish Revolt AD66–74*; Osprey, 2013.

Southern, Patricia: *The Roman Army: A History 753BC–AD476*; Amberley Publishing, 2016.

Stephenson, I.P.: *Roman Infantry Equipment: The Later Empire*; Tempus, 2001.

Sumner, Graham: *Men at Arms 390 Roman Military Clothing 2 AD200–400*; Osprey, 2003.

Taylor, Don: *Roman Empire at War: A Compendium of Battles from 31BC to AD565*; Pen & Sword, 2016.

Watson, G.R.: *The Roman Soldier*; Thames and Hudson, 1969.

Wilcox, Peter, and McBride, Angus: *Men at Arms 175 Rome's Enemies (3) Parthians & Sassanid Persians*; Osprey, 1986.

Wiseman, Anne and Peter: *Julius Caesar: The Battle for Gaul*; Chatto & Windus, 1980.

WEBSITES

https://www.alisonensis.de/EN/A%20Teutoburg%20Forest%20Battle/A%20Teutoburg%20Forest%20Battle.html. An interesting analysis of the Battle of the Teutoburg Forest.

http://whc.unesco.org/en/tentativelists/6067/ Detail of the Egyptian WHT submission to UNESCO.

http://penelope.uchicago.edu/Thayer/E/home.html. Transcriptions of many of the classic authors of antiquity.

GLOSSARY

Roman mile = 1,620 yards; 140 yards short of a modern mile

Acceptum Amount received by soldier after deductions from his pay

Acies Battle line (*duplex* = double; *triplex* = triple).

Adcrescens Adolescent; soldier's offspring that would follow in the hereditary military service of the 4th century AD and received rations before taking up actual service

Adiutor Assistant; batman

Adiutrix 'Supporter'; title borne by two legions raised from naval soldiers

Aedes Sanctuary in the HQ where the standards were stored and a likeness of the emperor was kept

Aenator Military musician

Aerarium Treasury; pay chest

Aerarium militare Military pension fund

Agrimensor Surveyor

Ala 'Wing'; (1) unit of the allies; (2) unit of auxiliary cavalry

Ala milliaria Auxiliary cavalry unit with an establishment strength of some 1,000 men

Ala quingenaria Auxiliary cavalry unit with an establishment strength of some 500 troopers

Angusticlavius Thin purple stripe on tunic indicating membership of the equestrian order

Apollinaris Dedicated to Apollo

Aquila Eagle standard

Aquilae natalis 'Birthday of the eagle'; anniversary of the official founding of a *legio* (LA)

Aquilifer Eagle bearer; standard bearer carrying the legion's eagle

Arcuballista Crossbow siege weapon

Aries Battering ram

Armilla Armband used as military decoration

Ballista Siege weapon

Balteus Military belt

Batavus Batavian

Beneficiarius Soldier on special assignment; military policeman

Bucculla Helmet cheek piece

Bucina Musical instrument

Bucinator Trumpeter

Calceus Shoe; boot

Caliga Military boot

Campus Cavalry training area; exercise field

Campus Martius Field of Mars, where during the Republic troops were assembled prior to military campaigns

Carroballista Siege weapon

Castellum Fort

Castra Camp

Castra aestiva Summer campaigning camp

Castra hiberna Winter base

Castra movere To break camp

Cataphractus Heavily armoured cavalryman

Catapulta Siege weapon

Classis Fleet

Clavis lignea Wooden practice sword

Cohors alaria Allied or auxiliary unit

Cohors equitata Unit of auxiliary infantry with attached mounted squadrons

Cohors milliaria 'Thousand-strong unit'; military unit with an establishment strength of 1,000 soldiers

Cohors peditata Infantry unit

Cohors praetoria (1) Bodyguard of a general during the Republic; (2) unit of Imperial guard

Cohors quingenaria Military unit with an establishment strength of 500 men

Cohors vigilum Cohort of the watchmen; unit of the police force, annex fire brigade

Cohortes urbanae Urban cohort; military police unit

Constitutio Service regulation. Several sets of military *constitutiones* (LA) were formulated by emperors, among them Augustus and Hadrianus

Consul Consul; highest magistrate in Republican Rome commanding major military forces

Contubernium Tent party; group of soldiers sharing a tent

Crista Helmet crest

Crista transversa Transverse helmet crest used as recognition mark of centurion

Cristatus Crested

Cuneus 'Wedge'; (1) attack column or wedge formation; (2) cavalry unit

Cursus honorum The public career path of Roman nobles consisting of both civilian and military posts

Decanus Commander of *contubernium* (LA) or tent party

Decurio Cavalry officer; (1) officer commanding 10–30 horsemen in the legion of the early Republic; (2) officer commanding a *turma* (LA) in the *auxilia* (LA)

Defensores 'Defenders'; troops in close-order defensive formation

Dictator Senior magistrate granted emergency powers originally appointed for a period of six months

Diploma Discharge certificate

Eques alaris Cavalryman belonging to auxiliary *ala* (LA)

Eques Augustorum Praetorian cavalry trooper

Eques Batavus (1) Batavian horseman; (2) Imperial horse guard trooper, not necessarily recruited from that particular tribe

Eques cohortalis Trooper belonging to *cohors equitata* (LA)

Eques legionis Legionary horseman

Eques praetorianus Cavalryman attached to *cohors praetoria* (LA)

Eques sagittarius Horse archer

Equitatus Cavalry

Equus Horse; *publicus* horse provided at state expense to a select body of Roman knights and senators; *privatus* mount provided at own expense

Fabrica Workshop

Feriale Duranum Military calendar of festivals

Focale Scarf

Foederatus Ally. Outlying nations to which ancient Rome provided benefits in exchange for military assistance. The term was also used, especially under the Roman Empire, for groups of 'barbarian' mercenaries of various sizes, who were typically allowed to settle within the Roman Empire

Foedus Treaty

Frumentatio Collection of grain supplies; foraging

Frumentum menstruum gratuitum Free monthly grain allowance; privilege enjoyed by praetorian soldiers from Nero's reign

Furca Baggage-carrying pole

Galea Helmet

Gentilis Foreigner; barbarian

Gladius General term for sword, NOT necessarily a shortsword

Gladius Hispanicus 'Spanish sword'; double edged cut-and-thrust weapon with a tapering blade and a point suited for ripping open mail armour

Gregarius Private; ranker

Groma Surveying instrument

Hasta Spear

Hastatus 'Spearman'; legionary heavy infantryman

Hastile (1) Wooden practice spear; (2) staff of the *optio centuriae* (LA)

Horrea Granaries

Imaginifer Standard bearer carrying a likeness of the emperor

Imago Standard with the emperor's portrait

Imperator Commander-in-chief; emperor

Imperium (1) The right to command absolute obedience; (2) empire

Lectus (1) Draftee; conscript; (2) chosen man; elite soldier

Legatus Subordinate commander

Legatus Augusti pro praetore Imperial legate with authority of praetor; provincial governor

Legatus legionis Legate of the legion; senatorial legionary commander

Legio pseudo comitatensis Frontier legion serving in late-Roman field army

Legio urbana 'City legion'; legion raised for defence of the city of Rome itself

Lorica Body armour; *hamata* mail shirt; *plumata* 'feathered armour'; ribbed scale armour; *segmentata* modern term for laminated plate armour; *squamata* scale armour

Manica Arm protector

Manipularis Soldier serving in *manipulus* (LA); heavy infantry soldier

Manipularis classis Naval soldier

Manipulus 'Handful'; (1) unit consisting of two *centuriae* (LA); (2) late-Roman army squad

Manubiae Spoils; plunder

Mensor Surveyor

Miles Soldier

Miles classis Fleet soldier

Miles cohortis Soldier belonging to a cohort

Miles gregarius Private; common soldier

Milliaria 1,000 strong

Missio agraria Discharge with grant of land

Missio causaria Honourable discharge on medical grounds

Missio honesta Honourable discharge

Missio honesta ex causa Honourable discharge granted to wounded or sick soldiers

Missio ignominiosa Dishonourable discharge

Missio nummaria Discharge with grant of money

Missus Discharged veteran

Missus ante tempus Veteran discharged before his time

Natalis aquilae Birthday of the eagle; military holiday

Obelos (GR): 'Spit'; the long iron point of a *pilum* (LA) or *soliferrum* (LA) javelin

Obsidio Siege

Ocrea Greave

Optio 'Chosen one'; (1) NCO; (2) private with special responsibilities

Ordinatus Centurion

Paenula Cloak

Pedes Foot soldier

Peregrini Free provincial subject of the Empire who was not a Roman citizen

Phalanx Close formation of heavy armed infantry equipped with spears and round shields

▼ *The ruins of the Forum in Rome, administrative and political hub of the vast empire fought for and held by its soldiers.*

Phalera Decorative disc

Phalerae Set of discs used as military decorations

Pileus Pannonicus 'Pannonian cap'; late Roman military cap

Pilum Heavy javelin with long metal shank

Pilum praepilatum Training weapon tipped with a ball to prevent injury

Pilus posterior Deputy to *pilus prior* (LA)

Pilus prior Centurion commanding a *manipulus* (LA) of *pili* (LA)

Pomerium Sacred boundary of the city of Rome within which the wearing of war gear was prohibited

Praefectus 'Someone put at the front'; senior officer

Praefectus alae Commander of a cavalry regiment

Praefectus castrorum Camp commandant

Praefectus cohortis Commander of a *cohors* (LA)

Praefectus classis Fleet commander

Praefectus equitatus Cavalry commander

Praefectus equitum Cavalry commander

Praefectus fabrum Officer in charge of artisans

Praefectus legionis Equestrian legionary commander

Praefectus legionis agens vice legati 'Prefect of the legion acting in place of the legate'; equestrian acting legionary commander

Praefectus urbanus City prefect

Praefectus vigilum Commander of the *vigiles* (LA)

Praemia militiae Discharge benefits

Praetor 'Someone who walks at the front'; (1) senior Roman magistrate; during Republic commander of minor military forces; (2) commander of allied contingent

Praetorianus Soldier belonging to a *cohors praetoria* (LA)

Praetorium Commander's living quarters; HQ

Primus ordo 'First officer'; centurion of the first cohort, whose officers outranked the other *centuriones* of the legion

Primus pilus 'First spearman'; highest-ranking legionary *centurio* (LA)

Princeps castrorum Centurion in charge of a camp's administrative staff

Princeps ordinarius vexillationis Centurion in command of a detachment

Principalis NCO

Principia HQ building

Proconsul Former consul (LA) exercising similar *imperium* (LA) after his term of office; provincial governor

Procurator Official of the emperor's administration

Pugio Dagger

Quadrata Rectangular shield

Quaestor (1) State official with financial responsibilities; (2) soldier of financial administrative department

Quingenaria 500 strong

Quinquatria Religious festival that opened campaigning season

Quinqueremis 'Fiver'; *quinquereme*; ship with five rowers on either two or three levels

Sagitta Arrow

Sagitta ballistaria Catapult bolt

Sagittarius (1) Archer; (2) arrow maker

Sagma Pack saddle

Sagum (sagulum) Cloak

Sagularis Camp road running along the inside of the rampart

Sarcina Marching pack

Sarissa Macedonian pike

Scorpio 'Scorpion'; (1) torsion gun; (2) artilleryman

Scorpionarius Artilleryman

Scutum Shield

Senator (1) Senator; member of Roman Senate; (2) late Roman senior officer in the centurionate

Signifer Standard bearer

Signum (1) Standard; (2) identification tattoo worn by soldiers

SPQR Acronym for *S(enatus) P(opulus) Q(ue) R(omanus)*; the Senate and people of Rome

Stipendium (1) Regular soldier's pay; (2) year of military service

Taverna Bar

Testamentum militare Military will; soldiers were granted the right to make a will that did not have to conform to all formal legal requirements

Testudo Tortoise formation

Torques Neck ornament awarded as military decoration

Tres militiae The three postings of a full equestrian military career: (1) *praefectus cohortis* (LA) (2) *tribunus angusticlavius/tribunus cohortis* (LA) (3) *praefectus alae* (LA)

Triarius 'Third liner'; heavy legionary infantry soldier

Tribunal Raised platform in front of the HQ used for addressing the troops or administring justice

Tribunus Senior officer

Tribunus angusticlavius 'Narrow-striped officer'; equestrian legionary officer

Tribunus laticlavius 'Broad-striped officer'; senatorial legionary officer

Triremis Trireme; galley with single rowers on three levels

Tubicen Trumpeter

Tunica Tunic

Turma Cavalry unit

Valetudinarium Hospital

Vallum Wall

Vexillatio Detachment; provisional unit

Vexillifer Standard bearer

Vexillum Standard with a flag on a crossbar

Via Road

Via decumana Camp road leading to rear gate

Via praetoria Camp road leading to *porta praetoria* (LA)

Via quintana Camp road passing the encampment of the fifth *manipuli* (LA); road dividing *praetentura* (LA) in half

Via sagularis Road running along the inside of a wall

Victrix Victorious

Vicus Civilian settlement attached to military base

Vigilia Watch

Vigilis Watchman; member of the Roman fire brigade or police force

Vitis Vine stick used as centurion's badge of office

Vocale Verbal command

Volones Freed slave volunteers

NOTES AND REFERENCES

INTRODUCTION

[1] Salways, 'What's in a Name? A Survey of Roman Onomastic Practice from c.700 B.C. to A.D. 700' (www.jstor.org/stable/300873).

CHAPTER 1

[1] Translation accessed from http://penelope.uchicago.edu/Thayer/E/Roman/Texts/Polybius/1*.html.

CHAPTER 2

[1] Sekunda, Nicholas V., *Caesar's Legions*, p. 23.

[2] Hopkins K.: *Conquerors and Slaves*; Cambridge University Press, 1978, quoted in *Battle Orders* 27 p. 27.

[3] *Battle Orders 27* p. 28.

[4] Polybius 3, 6:5.

[5] Livy 27:9; Everyman Library; translation by Rev. Canon Roberts, Dent & Sons, 1905 (http://mcadams.posc.mu.edu/txt/ah/livy/).

[6] ibid 21:1.

[7] Herodian 4.4.7 (www.livius.org/sources/content/herodian-s-roman-history/herodian-4.4/).

[8] Gibbon: *History of the Decline and Fall of the Roman Empire*, Chap. V (www.gutenberg.org/files/25717/25717-h/25717-h.htm).

CHAPTER 3

[1] Belfiglio, V.J. 'Control of epidemics in the Roman Army: 27bc–ad476', p1389.

[2] Vegetius, *De re militari*, 1.6 from Milner, *Translated Texts for Historians Vol 16 Vegetius*.

[3] Belfiglio, V.J. (2017) op cit.

[4] Vegetius, 2.5 from Milner, op cit.

[5] Belfiglio, V.J. (2017) op cit.

[6] Josephus, *The Wars of the Jews*, III.5 (www.gutenberg.org/files/2850/2850-h/2850-h.htm).

[7] Source: Speidel, M.A.: *Heer und Herrschaft im Römischen Reich der Hohen Kaiserzeit*; Stuttgart, 2009, pp349–380. Bold numbers are based on literary evidence.

[8] Belfiglio, V.J. (2017) op cit.

[9] Ibid, p463.

[10] Ibid.

[11] Tacitus, I.3. Loeb Classical Library, Translation by J. Jackson: Tacitus *Annales*, Harvard University Press, 1925–1937 (http://penelope.uchicago.edu/Thayer/E/Roman/Texts/Tacitus/home.html).

[12] Ward, Graeme A.: 'From Stick to Scepter: How the Centurion's Switch Became a Symbol of Roman Power'; Paper presented to the SCS, Toronto, January 2017 and accessed through Academia.edu.

CHAPTER 6

[1] Loeb Classical Library, Translation by H. St J. Thackeray: *Josephus II*; William Heinemann Ltd, 1956.

[2] German historian Conrad Cichorius (1863–1932) produced a survey of Trajan's Column along with photographs of all panels. His numbering system tends to be used as standard to reference the images and is included here.

[3] Much of the information about logistics in this section comes from Jonathan P. Roth's encyclopaedic *The Logistics of the Roman Army at War (264BC–AD235)*. Volume XXIII of Columbia Studies in the Classical Tradition (Brill, 1998).

[4] Kent, John Harvey: *Corinth Vol VIII Pt III The Inscriptions; American School of Classical Studies at Athens*, 1966, p53. [4]

[5] Bennett, Julian: *Trajan Optimus Princeps*; Taylor & Francis, 2004, p90 identifies a number of Trajan's generals: 'one of the Praetorian Prefects, Ti. Claudius Livianus, and his friend and confidant L. Licinius Sura, recently returned from the administration of Germania Inferior. Among his entourage were some of the most skilled generals in the empire, of whom the most notable was Q. Sosius Senecio, son-in-law of the great strategist Frontinus: now given the honorific rank of legatus pro praetore'. He goes on to list others of consular rank – C. Julius Quadratus Bassus, Cn. Pinarius Pompeius Longinus, L. Julius Ursus Servianus – ending with 'Lusius Quietus, commander of the irregular Moorish cavalry; the equestrian C. Manlius Felix, quartermaster for the campaign; and Trajan's cousin and the husband of his great-niece, the 25-year-old P. Aelius Hadrianus [later emperor]'.

[6] Bendlin, Andreas: *'Suovetaurilia', The Encyclopedia of Ancient History;* Wiley-Blackwell, 2012.

[7] Hope,'Dulce et decorum est pro patria mori', (http://oro.open.ac.uk/48585/3/Mortality4.pdf). This section borrows heavily from this paper).

[8] Bishop and Coulston, *Roman Military Equipment*, pp. 43–5.

[9] Tacitus, op cit I.61.

[10] Tacitus, op cit I.62.

[11] Tacitus, op cit II.21.

[12] Ball, 'The Treatment of Captured Combatants in the Roman World' (www.academia.edu/33749240/The_treatment_of_captured_combatants_in_the_Roman_world).

[13] Josephus, op cit V.8–9.

[14] Bishop and Coulston, *Roman Military Equipment*, p2.

[15] Wilkes, J., 'The pen behind the sword: power, literacy and the Roman Army'. *Archaeology International*, 5, pp32–35 (www.ai-journal.com/articles/abstract/10.5334/ai.0510/).

[16] As translated in 2012 by Grant Adamson and published in *The Bulletin of the American Society of Papyrologists* Vol. 49 (2012), pp79–94.

[17] Zerbini, 'Greetings from the Camp. Memories and Preoccupations in the Papyrus Correspondence of Roman Soldiers with their Families', p287 (www.academia.edu/7104192/Greetings_from_the_camp._Memories_and_preoccupations_in_the_papyrus_correspondence_of_Roman_soldiers_with_their_families).

INDEX